ISLAND HOME

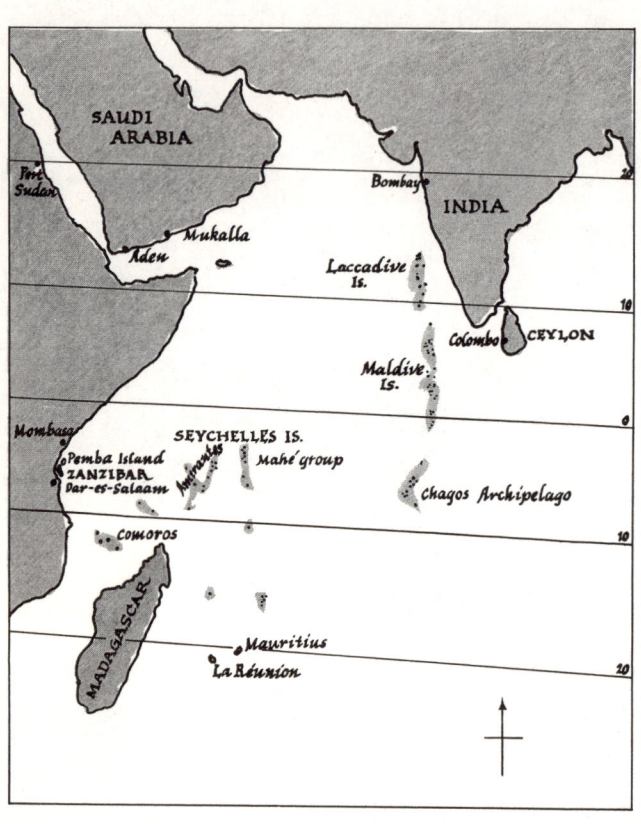

Island Home

by WENDY VEEVERS-CARTER

Random House
NEW YORK

To Mark and the children,
for their patience
And to my mother,
in part-payment of a debt

Island Home

Copyright © 1970 by Wendy Veevers-Carter

The right of Wendy Veevers-Carter to be identified as the author of this work has been asserted by her in accordance with the Copyright, Designs and Patents Act, 1988.

This book is sold subject to the condition that it shall not, by way of trade or otherwise, be lent, resold, hired out, or otherwise circulated without the publisher's prior consent in any form of binding or cover other than that in which it is published and without a similar condition including this condition being imposed on the subsequent purchaser.

Printed and bound in Great Britain by
CPI Bath

Typography and binding design by Mary M. Ahern

9 8 7 6 5 4 3 2

Contents

ONE
On the Way to the Island   1

TWO
Gappy, the "Great Disorder," Marcel   53

THREE
Liliane and Léonie—Feline Disturbance   195

FOUR
Our Third Christmas: Reflecting   287

APPENDIX A
From Pirates to the Present   323

APPENDIX B
The Wreck of H.M.S. *Fire* on African Banks   341

FORWARD

When Wendy and Mark Veevers-Carter decided to set up home on Remire with their young family, most of the outer islands of Seychelles had changed little since they were first discovered, uninhabited, by French mariners over 200 years previously. This family's adventure starts in 1963, when even the main island of Seychelles was relatively isolated, without an airport and connected to the outside world solely by shipping lines, whose steamers called infrequently. Seychelles was still a British colony, with an economy dependent mainly on copra, cinnamon and the export of essential oils. It had a composite population of French, English and African origin - with some Indians and Chinese - whom Britain seemed reluctant to propel into the modern world. Wendy's tale of life on Remire reflects the perceptions and attitudes of these past times. Much has changed since, both as regards the physical environment of Seychelles and the status and aspirations of its people. Indeed, the lives of Seychellois have changed so markedly that a visitor to the main island of Mahé, would find the style of their living much like his own.

In hindsight Wendy and Mark were making their new life on the cusp of change . The signs were already there, as evidenced in the epilogue that Wendy has written for this edition. Wendy eventually faced difficulties imposed by the loss of Mark and financial constraints, but in truth the substance of what they experienced on Remire was about to disappear for ever.

One of the principle aims of republishing 'Island Home' is to give visitors to Seychelles an idea of what life used to be like on these remote islands, as well as provide the younger generations of Seychellois with a glimpse of the Nation's past.

Readers wanting information on current day Seychelles and the islands can view the following sites:

www.nature.org.sc
www.sif.sc
www.aspureasitgets.com
www.atlas.net

ONE

On the Way to the Island

I

WE HAD COME to our island at last. Since dawn we had been standing on the deck of the schooner, watching the small clump of feather-duster palms and casuarina trees grow on the horizon; now the beach and trees rose and fell in the background as the island's pirogue approached us. Soon it bumped alongside. I climbed over the schooner's gunwale and dropped into the pirogue's wet bottom, bracing myself while our two small children were handed me on the upsurges of the swell; then my husband Mark got in, and our two black Labradors were passed, all legs and waving tails, heavily down to him. They stood poised uneasily in the bottom of the boat while we were rowed ashore, and stayed there until they were sure we were really disembarking. The landing was accomplished with the usual shouts and confusion and wetness even though the sea was fairly calm; we were all tired.

The sand of the beach was blindingly white after the blue of the sea, and it seemed a long climb up to the boathouse and on, thankfully in the dark shade of the coconut palms, down a wide sandy avenue to the house. It was an old bungalow covered with shaggy thatch, and it looked cool and peaceful in spite of the disorder our baggage was fast making, and in spite of the delegation of women waiting on the veranda.

As I climbed the steps the oldest one came forward, taking it upon herself to ask me a string of questions about where shall she make the beds, and what with, and where is my teapot, she will bring tea right away, give her my cups and saucers now. I thought: Busybody, to be kept out of the way. But I thanked her and the others scrupulously for—cleaning the house, I supposed, and wished they would clear out. Being English, Mark said yes to the tea, however, so the cups were unearthed and a teapot borrowed from somewhere. An hour later the tea appeared, but by then Mark had given it up and gone to see to

Our House, Remire, November 1963

the unloading, while I was trying to put some order in the mess of boxes and canvasless deck chairs; it was placed on one of the crates and forgotten. Meanwhile, the other schooner with the rest of our possessions had turned up, and both the captains came ashore for lunch, as is customary. Hurriedly I had some of the island's scrawny chickens caught and cooked, and they did well enough; the captains were not particular, and after a day and night of curried food and seasick children in an airless cabin, we were as hungry as we were tired.

The children recovered immediately with food in their bellies and new places to explore, but there was no respite for us. Even here in the Seychelles, schooner masters like a quick turnaround; while the unloading was completed and checked, the island's produce had in its turn to be weighed and listed and loaded; letters of instructions to be written; the accounts of laborers

On the Way to the Island / 5

returning to Mahé to be verified; last-minute orders to be placed for the next boat down. In something of a daze, all these things were accomplished. From one moment to the next, our life had changed completely; we had become island planters. Now it was we who watched the boats in the anchorage preparing to leave; for the first time, we were the left and not the leavers. But when the schooners were ready to go, we had no qualm about staying behind; rather, we only wanted to have the extraneous people clear of the place as fast as possible. Our island, keep off.

I suppose that most people dream of abandoning the world to its weary way, of giving up everything and retiring to some far-off island, preferably in the warm latitudes of the southern seas. But to live there forever—well, it would hardly be practical. The things one would have to give up numb the mind, and the things one would have to take numb it even more. Then too there is the nasty problem of earning a living in such a place. And schools for the children, and this, and that. Once you begin to think about it, it becomes more and more impossible. How many people could pick up and go, leaving home, relations, jobs behind them, and settle happily on a coral island? It's a fine dream, but if the person is honest, I think he would confess himself happier keeping the idea in the vague limbo of dream world, where the details and problems do not intrude.

But for us, there has been no real mental difficulty in translating this dream into reality. Reflecting on our years of life together in the various backwaters which are (or were) the remnants of Britain's empire, we see it as almost inevitable that we should have fetched up somewhere like Remire, one of the Seychelles Islands in the Indian Ocean. For we have been slowly weaned of cities and their pleasures, of the immediacy of art and the theater and music, or the comfort of having our family and old friends nearby; weaned even of expecting the stimulus of seasonal change, and of too longingly remembering the beauty of autumn and winter. They are all things we miss, but not sorely. We are used, now, to life in the tropics, and while we recognize that no one can be self-sufficient (we are in the best possible position to know this), we can perhaps better adapt to a near-self-sufficient (when necessary) attitude of mind than some, and more easily find other mental pastures in which to graze; nor are we not too tied to the physical comforts and conveniences of modern life, peace and space being such ample substitutes.

Indeed, in being free of commitment to any single way of life, we have had a lot of training, since we are both by inclination travelers, and it is to a certain adventurous predilection for out-of-the-way places that Mark and I owe our having met at all.

Mark likes to think his travels were forced on him by a father determined to have his son see the world and see it on a shoestring (£100) because giving a boy the money to do it with only spoiled him, but I don't think he would have kept on traveling if he hadn't come to enjoy it, or at the very least come to think of every place as offering a potential way of life. His childhood, however, was all spent in the environs of Poole on the south coast of England—he was born there, went to a convent school there, then a preparatory school, and finally to public school in the same part of the same county; his vacations he passed fishing or exploring or shooting over the empty miles of creeks and marshes that make up Poole's great harbor, and when he left school, he promptly joined in with a local fisherman. This time of his life he now recalls with great peace and nostalgia, claiming that if he had been left alone he would probably have spent the rest of his days as a Poole man, pure and simple. But Mark was his father's only boy (there were two girls from a previous marriage) and leaving him alone to become a Poole fisherman was not part of his father's plan. So just after the war, when Mark had finished serving in the Royal Air Force, his father arranged for him to obtain a working passage on a yacht to the West Indies.

"That will do for a start," said his father. "And be sure to see as many of the islands as possible—you can look out for a plantation that might suit us. Ever since old Lee sailed over and bought that place of his in St. Lucia, I've been thinking of pulling up roots myself."

Pennington Lee had been a good friend of the elder Veevers-Carter, and the two men had done a lot of sailing together.

So Mark set out with this goal in mind. From his point of view it was a lot better than going all that way without a reason, and he island-hopped assiduously. Thus the news that buying an estate in the Caribbean had only been one of his father's temporary enthusiasms took a long time to reach him, and when it did, he found himself in Trinidad, with the hundred pounds an ancient memory. He had one marketable asset, however: a West Indian schooner master's ticket he had picked up along the way. He had noticed among the islands that there were always small boat owners looking for masters, and his training in seamanship and as a fisherman enabled him to pass the examination without difficulty.

In Trinidad, he hoped to find a yacht bound for England and needing a hand; a walk along the waterfront told him he was out of luck, but he did hear that the owners of Admiral Perry's old codbanker, *Northern Light,* were looking for a master and hadn't found one. Small wonder. There can't have been many qualified masters willing to take the *Northern Light* to Tahiti through the Strait of Magellan (the owners refused to consider the cost of a Canal passage) for the magnificent sum of two hundred fifty pounds, out of which the crew was supposed to be paid; the captain was allowed a further hundred twenty pounds for provisions, but even in 1948 this didn't go very far.

Still, Mark had to do something, so he accepted, and wrote immediately to Pennington Lee, begging him to send down Palumon, a West Indian and great bear of a sailor who had been Lee's first mate on his yacht in Poole. Palumon came, and took the twenty-year-old Mark in hand. He knew his way around Trinidad, how to "impress" a crew, where to get what cheap, and taught Mark. And in learning to handle this crew, which Palumon picked up dead drunk with a wheelbarrow outside the waterfront bars and replaced the same way in every port, Mark was learning a great deal, in a tough school. Nor was the elderly schooner easy to sail; as they approached Tierra del Fuego, crew difficulties faded by comparison with the worsening weather, the contrary winds, and the currents of that notorious passage. When nearly through the Strait, the schooner was dismasted in a storm, and they had to limp jury-rigged to Tahiti. No sailing we will ever do in the Indian Ocean can compare with that first voyage of Mark's.

Once in Tahiti, he and Palumon could find no suitable tree for a new mast and so had to send back to the owners for another pine. Knowing they would have a long wait and no extra pay for waiting, Mark took a passage to the Marquesas Islands, where things were cheaper, leaving Palumon working as a laborer in Tahiti, ready to send him word when the mast arrived. In the Marquesas he managed to live entirely on what he could hunt or exchange, and when the message came from Palumon he was almost reluctant to go back; the momentum of that initial hundred pounds had pushed him, already, halfway around the world. But the return voyage was uneventful by comparison; Mark, no longer so anxious to get home, had told the owners that unless the money was forthcoming for a Canal passage, he would abandon the *Northern Light* where she was (and pay Palumon's trip back by other means). They returned in safety via Panama.

After leaving the schooner in Trinidad, Mark went to St. Lucia and stayed for a while on nearby Pigeon Island as tutor to Lee's sister's grandchildren. It was a peaceful life, for which nine months in the Marquesas had trained him well. The grandchildren, he admits, learned woefully little Latin, but they became experts at catching crayfish, and at ambushing the canny wild goats when everyone tired of the diet offered by the sea.

A few months passed, and Mark decided to move on, knowing that if he was to earn some real money with his ticket, he would have to be on an island more central to Caribbean traffic, such as Jamaica or Trinidad. Jamaica had proved very expensive, so he returned to Trinidad, and to the waterfront. There he met up with a young Australian, and together they found a strong old sailing lifeboat going so cheaply that Mark's small savings just managed to meet the cost of his half. In this boat the two boys sailed slowly up through the West Indies, taking passengers when they could. Eventually they reached Nassau; from Nassau they went to Bermuda, and from Bermuda it seemed possible to them to sail her over to England, which, half pursued by the bad weather and half helped by the strong winds, they did, making the Inverness Canal in twenty-eight days. In Inverness they sold the boat, and Mark—the seat of his only suit so badly chewed by cockroaches that it was only just wearable—took the train for London, Poole, and home.

Once there, he decided to leave the sea alone for a while and took a job with a friend as an apprentice farm hand in return for his keep. Again, his father talked of "finding something," and Mark was to keep his eyes open while he trained. But times were difficult then for small farmers, which discouraged father and friend alike, and when the friend finally moved to Australia, Mark, at a loose end, decided to go abroad again himself. His uncle had spent many years as a tea planter in Burma; perhaps Mark too could find a job with one of the plantation houses. So he went up to London, walked down Threadneedle Street, and entered the door of the first company he came to. Yes, he could certainly have a job, as an assistant manager on a rubber estate in Malaya. No, they had no special requirements, except a basic knowledge of agriculture—nor, as Mark discovered, could they afford to be too fussy, since the Communists were accounting for so many of the men the company sent out from England to run their estates. When Mark arrived in Kuala Lumpur, he soon learned he was replacing a dead man, as had that dead man replaced another before him; and even for someone of Mark's sanguine humor this was discouraging news. He decided to do out his eighteen-month contract to the day, if he lived, and leave promptly. To this end, he took certain sensible precautions that his predecessors had neglected; not for Mark the ethic of the usual innocent: "they won't shoot me, for what harm have I done them?" Nor did he necessarily trust those supposed to be on his side. In daylight he went everywhere well armed, while at night he would slip out of his laxly guarded compound unseen, to help the army in its ambush work, using information he or other planters had gathered in the daytime. For Mark has never been one to stay aloof or uninvolved, and as he points out, so many planters had been killed in their lighted houses at night that it was almost safer in the jungle.

While he was in Malaya, he heard, through friends in the government fisheries department, that the post of Red Sea Fisheries Inspector in the Sudan was vacant. To try his luck, he applied, stating his experience and qualifications, and somewhat to his surprise, was accepted. So on the expiry of his Malayan contract, he left for the Sudan.

This post was Mark's first in the British civil service, but considering the mésalliance that was to follow, it was a painless enough introduction. He had the whole of the Sudan's Red Sea coast as his province, and much autonomy in a department that was run from Khartoum, nine hundred miles away by road and track. He enjoyed his time there, and not least the fact that as the fisheries officer it was to him that all the underwater photographic expeditions were referred for help in finding photogenic sites, reasonable anchorages along the coast, or local labor when needed.

At the time we met, he had established his fishing camp on the small island of Um Sharifa, three miles off the northern Sudan coast, and it was to this flat barren sand cay only a hundred yards long, with its collection of tattered tents, nets, coils of rope and drying shark, that he brought us. The tops of the tents were the only things on that island (besides the people) that stood more than four feet above the level of the Red Sea.

The expedition I was a member of was the third to arrive in Mark's tenancy and certainly must have been the least organized, taking its character from the personality of its leader, a genius in many ways, but not one to pay much attention to the tiresome details of moving his equipment and "girls" through official red tape, and over difficult terrain. In fact, I'm sure there has never been a film expedition with such ancient equipment, erratic leadership, and odd personnel. I am only glad that we fell into Mark's hands and not into the clutches of one of the many unscrupulous Sudanese businessmen who volunteered to "help," "knew of a boat," "would supply all goods," "had a car to hire," and so on, all at exorbitant prices. As an expedition we had weathered a good deal of this sort of thing in Kenya and Tanganyika, which taught us that if there is a willing official of the game or fisheries departments handy, reach for him fast; his financially disinterested help will be invaluable.

We were working on a film which had been many years in the making; this session in the limpid waters of the Red Sea was supposed to put the finishing touches on a masterpice in which, by that time, only its creator believed. But we girls—there were two of us—were hardly professional actresses or even beautiful; we had come for the trip. We well knew that anyone not trying to make a film on so impossibly low a budget as Anstruther's would have hired voluptuous budding starlets in Hollywood, or found something similar closer to home, rather than allowing himself to be persuaded (by me) to take on two dubiously photogenic, argumentative college graduates, whose measurements, to say nothing of whose talents, wouldn't have got them as far as an agent's office. Poor Anstruther. I fear I used him disgracefully.

Anstruther being one of my mother's oldest friends, his expeditions had formed a part of my childhood; I used to think idly how nice it would be when I was older to be on one of them. But I was a well-protected only child, living in a household full of women, and not given to being very adventurous except in the safety of my imagination. Nor does a city childhood offer much scope for developing an instinct for exploring. I was not often allowed out alone, and out was mostly grimy and dirty anyway, except for Central Park, which, rightly, was not considered much of a place for a young girl alone either. Besides, my grandmother, who lived with her early-widowed daughter and me, regarded the whole of New York as an evil godless place where hardly a soul spoke English any more and nothing good could be expected of such surroundings as that.

Our income, however, was derived mostly from a play based on one of my father's books, *Life with Father,* and the work this entailed for my mother as technical adviser (to keep things tastefully done; there was some feeling, as it was, between Mother and my father's two remaining brothers about "putting the Family on the stage"). So in New York we had to live. Still, compared to many people, I suppose, we really managed to move around quite a lot. There was a trip to England when I was five, after my father's death and just before World War II; there was a springtime trip to Puerto Rico when I was ten. Then for the making of *Life with Father* into a movie, we spent a whole year in Los Angeles, which my mother loathed because there were hardly any civilized people there and all the film people called her "darling" or "baby," and I loathed because I had to go to boarding school. Boarding school is a nasty shock after the private ways an only child gets used to in a house of busy adults. Nor was the experience made any better by the open friendly manner in which the Californians teased us for our mincing Eastern refinements. But a sense of humor as applied to oneself has to be acquired, and I hadn't any then. I was just thirteen, with my teeth firmly in braces, a flat chest, long feet, and tall for my age, in a school full of "cute" curvy blonde or dramatic raven beauties; statistically we were the same age, but I might have come from another world—I did. The best thing about California, from my point of view, was how normal it made me feel when I got home.

And even though New York was officially home, we never stayed at home in the summers. Mercifully the theatrical and school vacations more or less coincided, and during them my mother with admirable energy would haul us all out to the country: the various governesses, the seamstress with asthma, my aging grandmother, a series of violent cooks; and John, really Giovanni, who had helped to look after my arthritis-stricken father before his death, and stayed on as our one embattled male handyman. At first she used to establish her household in the old Day house in Harrison, New York, but finally she made a

On the Way to the Island / 13

giant break with New York and bought a small sea captain's house in Truro, at the far end of Cape Cod.

So many people go to the Cape now that I hesitate even to speak of it, but it was very deserted then, during the Second World War, especially far out on its lower end. To get there, we used to drive the two hundred miles from New York to the Canal, then another hundred miles out to sea over beautiful but endlessly twisting, hilly, narrow roads; or when we came by train during the war (with our many bags, and the dog and the cat and John at the very minimum), there was the change at Providence or Boston, then another change at Hyannis into a bus, which stopped everywhere (for friends as well as in the line of duty) between Hyannis and Truro, where the house was. And once in Truro, there was an even longer trial of endurance which recommenced every summer: that of becoming accepted as a resident with rights.

In those days, the only people who actually lived down at that end of the Cape were either Artists or Natives, supplemented in season by a sprinkling of "Summer People" (who had houses) and "Tourists" (who didn't). The artists despised both the summer people and the tourists, who were such weaklings or so undevoted to the Cape that they went somewhere else half the year, and the natives despised all three groups. Never mind that the natives themselves were a warring mixture of second- or third-generation Portuguese and old New England. They stuck together when it came to the rest of us. Poor Mother. Being a naturally friendly and gregarious sort of person, and at the same time a bit nervous and shy, she likes people and will go to any length doing things for them, but wants reassurance of some loyal feeling in return. Who wouldn't? On the Cape, however, it was hard. The mere fact that my mother was making her living in the artistic world didn't help her very much with the artists, who were dog-in-the-mangerish about being old residents; nor did the fact that she had actually been born a New Englander (though on the mainland) help her with the natives. To them mainland, New York—it was all the same. Even now, after nearly thirty years, she's still "summer people," no matter how much of the winter she spends there, and "summer" she will remain.

I'm rather grateful to this attitude, as a matter of fact. Since living in Truro, I've never really worried about being accepted by the natives of the places we've lived in. Respect is as much as one can hope for—and that is a great deal.

And as far as being a native of any place myself, I am, I suppose, a native of New York City, where I was born, but there is no cozy comfort in the thought of belonging there. Besides, in New York we were only "winter people."

Mark, who spent all his childhood in the same area where he was born, and where the surroundings were more amenable to being loved, is homesick for Poole in a way I can never be, even for Truro. I loved the Cape, but I could not grow roots there, when every fall I was returned like an ungainly Persephone to the dark underworld of the city. But what the many summers on the Cape did do for me was to make me love the sea, and to love leading a simple life, with no dressing up or hated formal dances, near it or, preferably, in it. And to this, life on our island is close indeed. The training in fortitude inculcated by the Cape's vigorous insects hasn't gone wasted either.

But meanwhile, there was still the wall of education to be got over, and I know I never saw what I wanted out of life until I began to get glimpses of its possibilities in college.

As I have said, I was not very adventurous. Timid would be a more positive way of describing my relations with almost everyone except my small mongrel dog, and at least half my timidity came from worrying about how different I was. My trip to California toughened me somewhat, but the thought of leaving the shelter of home to go away to college—well, everyone in my New York day school was leaving home and trying to get into the best (or most preferred) college that would take her; so must I. I wanted to. I even half realized how lucky I was. But I was thoroughly frightened just the same. This was all the sillier (as my mother pointed out) because I had already traveled to so many places, including, by now, a summer spent (at sixteen) in England, Scotland, France, Italy, and Switzerland, albeit close at my mother's heels. But at this time, I only thought of these places as backdrops to all my private agonies, sophisticated settings against which my gaucheries showed up in startling bas-relief.

Still, a Career and Making a Living loomed ahead too. There was no nonsense in my home about a woman not having to support herself, my mother having supported so many people besides herself for so many years. That I secretly hoped some man I could love would want me for a wife before that awful day dawned might have been treated as normal enough, if I had dared to admit it, but I was not expected to sit around on the off chance of its happening soon. Besides, there were things that prevented me from being even hopeful. It was not so much my big feet, or my sad lack of self-confidence, but rather the noticeable fact that the only males who had ever shown any interest in me were far closer to my mother's age than mine. I was determined not to repeat what I thought of as my mother's tactical error in marrying a man so much her senior that he became old (fifty-six is very old to seventeen) and died while she was still quite young (thirty-five). No amount of love, I said to myself, would make up to me for possibly having to be a self-sufficient independent widow the rest of a lonely life.

So I entered Radcliffe (Radcliffe was almost familiar territory, not far from the Cape), and though no young male appeared immediately to want me, the scholastic side turned out to be very absorbing. That one could audit courses as well as take them made my schedule heavy, but being interested in so many things brought me no closer to deciding on my "major." The time came when this decision had to be made, and still I had no idea, except perhaps, like too many others, English.

Rather despondently, I turned up at the Tea at which Important Seniors made themselves available to Freshmen choosing their majors. So many people seemed to have decided already. I took a cup of tea and started to wander around. One of the seniors I knew by sight; she lived in the same dormitory. She was in anthropology, whatever that was. I had read the list of courses offered to Harvard-Radcliffe students many times and from cover to cover, and anthropology was right at the beginning. I moved closer.

"But what *is* anthropology?" the senior was being asked, over and over again.

"The study of man," she would say, rather grandly.

"But what sort of thing? Biology?" Everyone at Radcliffe seemed to think first about the body.

"Yes," the senior answered, "but not all biology—only human and simian biology."

"But isn't most of anthropology just what you study in sociology? What's the distinction?"

"Well yes, in a way, but we don't study the same sort of societies they do. I mean, they go in for more sophisticated societies or our own culture more than we do, at least at Harvard." Her voice trailed off. She knew very well that anthropology, not then offered as a departmental discipline by very many universities, was divided differently in each one. "But we do have archaeology," she added, brightening. "No other department has archaeology, unless you count fine arts, who don't go in for much pre-Classical stuff or digs outside the Mediterranean area. And besides, you can specialize, and certain courses in other departments which apply can count toward your major in anthropology, if you want them to."

All around us, seniors were talking about their particular subjects with a sort of missionary fervor, and the more anxious this one got about her dwindling audience, the more I warmed. By this time I was in the front row. Considering the diffuseness of my interests, this grab bag of potsherds, ape measurements, and studies of "simple" peoples sounded all right. I had a feeling that if I could fit in anywhere it would be in this unnichelike niche. "Put my name down, please," I said quietly.

My mother's comment: "Anthropology provides too many people with an excuse to imitate primitive people because they can't discipline themselves enough to behave properly in their own society." She knew, it transpired, several anthropologists who were always popping off to odd places and behaving oddly when they got back, and she was not at all impressed by my choice. I, however, was very impressed by her vehemence (and by her having heard of it) and stuck by my decision.

Once I had become a convert to anthropology, no other field of study seemed so perfect or so complete, and the atmosphere of a small department where young graduates I knew personally were always going out on field trips and actually doing something gave one's studies a visible goal; though I hesitated at the thought of taking on a whole tribe of strangers in some far-off place, presumably I could be weak in some things and still pull my weight enough to be expedition-worthy.

"You'll never get on an expedition if you don't become an expert in one thing," said my mother, eying me severely.

"But someone must be needed to take notes, or to draw all the ornaments and utensils, or portraits," I answered (I could draw quite well).

"Hmmmm," she said sadly. She was ambitious for me to be more ambitious. "You've never even wanted to go to art school."

I suppose, what with my mediocre involvement in anthropology and lack of ambition, she decided she had better remind me forcibly of broader vistas—or else (more likely) the trip was simply planned without my knowing anything about it because I was away—but at the end of my sophomore year Mother suddenly called up from New York and said we were going to Europe. That I was on the verge, I then told her, of signing on for a summer with the Friends, teaching art to Mexican children (all female personnel must wear two petticoats because of the strong sun), she regarded as no sort of impediment.

"Just tell them you're not coming. They won't mind. Besides —the Friends? You wouldn't like it, you know." She was very firm.

They might not have minded, but I did. It was my first independent decision that counted, because it was so far away, as really Doing Something. And instead of being respectfully thrilled at the thought of Europe, I remember being most ungratefully annoyed at the interruption of my plans. I fear that by this time, my mind was turned in opposite directions, toward Mexico, or the Andes, or Polynesia, or Bali, or Darkest Africa—anywhere but Europe. Besides, I thought I had already "been" to Europe—twice. And Mexico held a particular interest: an archaeologist I liked very much was going to be there himself that season.

On the telephone, none of these reasons could be stated in so many words; I merely hesitated, while my mother, at the other end, expressed astonishment.

I went to Europe, I am sorry to say, with bad grace. But the trip undoubtedly did me far more good than wearing two petticoats somewhere in Mexico. If nothing else, traveling through Europe when I was old enough to have to take responsibility for myself did a great deal to make the mechanics of travel familiar. One suspects, in fact, that the parental reasons for providing the Young Gentleman with a World Tour were concerned as much with making him the master of the way to get about as of his cultural heritage, and now I am properly grateful to my mother for acquainting me with both.

But at the time I returned to anthropology wholeheartedly, and when I heard, early in my senior year, that Anstruther was planning another expedition to Africa, I was determined that now there was not only nothing to stop me but that the opportunity was heaven-sent as well. With complete single-mindedness, I set about getting myself on it. When Anstruther, beleaguered, finally said yes, my mother, knowing him well, was more alarmed than amused. But she could see that I was really determined, so her only stipulation was that I could not go alone.

This presented more of a stumbling block than had Anstruther himself. I might know Anstruther well too, but could I explain him to anyone else? And the trip would most probably involve long hot uncomfortable visits to remote places no one had ever heard of, which would offer me endless opportunities of being half artist, half anthropologically trained observer, but what could it offer someone else? After a lot of searching, I finally found the perfect companion, but at the last minute she got married and went to Japan. And the girl who did come with me proved just as conservative as I had feared—which, however, is another story.

And so we set off in June of 1953 to Africa. Anstruther had gone on ahead to collect the jeep station wagon he had left in the Congo (still peaceful then) the year before on his reconnaissance trip. Joining him in Nairobi, we spent most of the next nine months in the driest and bushiest parts of Tanganyika, completing his jungle film, after which we moved north to the Red Sea's quiet water and magnificent coral to finish an underwater movie he had started in the Pacific in the 1930s. The jungle film starred the animals, with girls in the background, but in underwater photography, Anstruther reasoned, girls were important. He'd had one in 1930, and now, for better or worse, he had two, but never mind—continuity was appeased by our wearing white bathing suits, same as the other girl had; Oliver wasn't one to worry about differences in appearance or style, as long as we did the same sort of thing.

The things he wanted us to do, on the other hand, were not so easy to arrange. Mark found himself trying to tie a dead shark's mouth up with sacking that didn't show, so that one girl or the other could be carried off by it as it was (inconspicuously) towed through the water, or having to manhandle a huge manta ray so that it would hover over the innocent white-bathing-suited figure down on the bottom, trying in its turn to balance its top-heavy helmet and violent air hose (the aqualungs never worked). Then just when things had been got right at last, the camera would pack up. After three months of this, the expedition succumbed to its difficulties. But Mark and I had already decided that we would like to go on, together.

On receiving this news, my mother flew out and took me on an educational tour of the Holy Land, during all of which I mistook a lengthy bout of bacillary dysentery for the deep-seated derangements of thwarted love. There followed a rather hectic period of traveling for everyone. I went back briefly to the States, then my mother did; Mark came back to England, I went back to England, then my mother did, and so on; Mark got an extension of leave from the Sudan, and finally we were married, on the last day of it, and flew off to Khartoum, and then Port Sudan. There we climbed into the fisheries inspector's lorry for the last lap—a hundred and twenty miles—up the Sudan coast to Mohammed Qol; into the launch, from launch to canoe, and from the canoe onto the sand of Um Sharifa to set up once more the tents of the fisheries camp—this time as our first home.

II

NOT THE LEAST of Mark's attractiveness as a marital prospect was the life he was leading when we met, and the likelihood that such a well-traveled person would keep on living in strange places. For by this time, I was all set to go anywhere and do anything. I fear no more thoughts of a Career, or getting a Ph.D. in anthropology, or Settling Down got their toes in the door. Though, even then, Mark used to talk nostalgically of the wonders of duck hunting in the far reaches of Poole harbor, he was just as happy talking over all the other places he'd seen. I listened with envy. And if he said, seriously, that it was only a lack of money that prevented him from settling in England, he talked equally seriously of living on board a yacht he couldn't afford, never to settle anywhere. Or of returning to the Marquesas Islands, where we could really give up the dreary necessity of having a job, shed cares and responsibility, and abandon the world forever.

The yacht was, of course, impossible to realize on our finances, but the Marquesas? Sitting in the evenings in front of our tent, watching the moonlit water or listening idly to the chatter of the fishermen around their fire, we talked about it a lot. I think the discussions finally bogged down, though, on my rather American insistence on being within reach of a doctor. We agreed that if I died, Mark would be able to find companionship, brokenhearted though he might be. But if *he* died, there I'd be, possibly with children, all my writing paper used up, no money to buy any, and certainly no money to go away. What would my fate be? A fat Polynesian husband, if he would have me along with the rest of his wives, and out to the taro patch with the lot of us. Besides, I had so much of the world left to see before I gave it all up! No, I'm afraid life on one of the small Marquesas Islands entailed sacrifices I wasn't ready to make—yet.

So in the end, we began Mark's ten years of government service, an association Mark has found as dissatisfying professionally as we have both found satisfying in other ways. For even if frustrated by the endless paper work and cumbersome slowness with which governments bury Ideas and Initiative, Mark has always matched interest in his work with what I would call a true traveler's fascination with strange surroundings. Government service has at least meant ten years of paid traveling in little-frequented parts of the world. Backwaters, as I said. And in them we have been doing what most travelers to out-of-the-way places do: collect. I fear it is an impulse irresistible to all but the purest of them.

When I said we are not particularly tied to the physical comforts or conveniences of modern life, I had in mind things like electricity and plumbing, and did not mean to imply such a liking for the abstractions of peace and space that material possessions are of no importance to us. Quite the contrary: like a snail, we carry our real home on our backs, and derive much pleasure from its smooth fit and the fine polish its inner surfaces and chambers have acquired through use. Possessions are a great comfort.

But the heavy portage of material possessions from place to place can be a nightmare. Bad enough to me were my mother's biennial hejiras from city to country and back again, transporting great carloads of furniture, food, people, and other might-be-usefuls between the two households three hundred miles apart. Yet we have chosen to do this over long distances in the Middle East, where, as everyone knows, everything is much slower, more difficult, more complicated, infinitely less efficient, and vastly hampered by the climate.

It seems a long time ago now that we started out, newly married, with one small case of wedding presents, two suitcases, a typewriter, and, because of being married in England, our umbrellas. Our dubious relatives had been told about the tent, so all our presents had a down-to-earth air of utility, and I had been able to keep my trousseau very simple—I bought five bathing suits. But once back on Um Sharifa and properly unpacked, I found that Mark had numerous homey possessions I'd known nothing about: rice bowls and figurines from Malaya, a ceremonial sword, Beja knives that were the gifts of his fishermen's tribe, sets of boar tusks, small carved wooden boxes and rough-woven head cloths from Khartoum, all mixed in with the spear guns, fishing rods, shotguns, and other equipment of his trade and sports. Even so, in those carefree days, everything we had, everything the fishermen had, as well as the nets, the tents, fuel, drinking-water supply, used to fit into the back of one Bedford pickup, with the fishermen on top. And we moved many times during that year.

Yet each time we set up the tent we congratulated ourselves, saying complacently that few had ever made a tent seem so like a home. We had no comforts as such—we sat on the floor, slept on a string bed, bathed in a small bowl of rationed water—but looking at a polished wooden carving on a red cloth or eating from Mark's pretty chinaware made us feel that we lacked nothing. We could have gone on forever.

On the other hand, "Sudanization" was approaching, and the head department in Khartoum became harder and harder to work for; the rigid, domineering attitudes of those suddenly elevated to positions of power affected even Mark, so far away in his tent. Also a series of well-bred young dandies were being foisted on us—relatives of this person and that—to whom Mark was supposed to teach the art of being a fisheries inspector. Mark had no patience with youths who were never willing to get their feet wet or their hands fouled with fish, while the trainees were appalled by the standards this rough Englishman expected them to abandon—in front of the lowly fishermen too. There was no meeting of the minds.

In spite of these difficulties, Mark was asked to stay on, but we both realized that for this kind of self-effacing diplomatic work he was not suited. He resigned, and the Colonial Office then offered him a fisheries officer's post in Mukalla, in the then Eastern Aden Protectorate. But by this time (1955) we did have some savings, and I had an inheritance from my grandmother in the bank. The Sudan government owed Mark a gratuity and our passages back to England. We had come to the point when we had to decide one way or the other: should we Leave or Go On?

Bravely we decided to leave; we might never be so well-off again. Taking the leave passages and the gratuity, we'd emigrate, we thought, to New Zealand, where Mark could earn his living deer-culling. On the way there we would pay what would probably be the last visits we would ever be able to afford to our families in England and in the States, going on to New Zealand by freighter. So we thought. But once we reached New York, a friend of my mother's talked us into what turned out to be an unlucky adventure financially (I am ashamed to admit it was a treasure hunt in the Bahamas), and this effectively bounced us straight back with our tails between our legs to the Colonial Office and the little pile of possessions we had left behind in London.

Because we had both been to our homes and scavenged, however, we were now arriving in Aden with twenty-five separate items. Fortunately the Aden government is generous with its paid-baggage allowance for its married servants—three-hundred-odd cubic feet—and the extra treasures cost us nothing but the mental wear and tear of organizing them. From Aden we proceeded to Mukalla, Mark's station. Here we lived, in three successive houses, but more or less settled in the same area, for four years, with golden opportunities for collecting. The combination, anyone will recognize, was fatal. Also, we had a six months' leave that we spent in Kenya—which sounds innocent enough. But Mark is very fond of shooting, and naturally every shooting man likes to keep his trophies. We returned to Arabia with two more packing cases full of antelope heads and, I might add, the plaques to mount them. This last was really an economy; in Arabia wood is scarce and expensive.

These wooden plaques were the first small breaks in the dam holding back wooden possessions. Because even if you have only small or at least portable things, like most people who work abroad and leave their homes at Home, and even if you faithfully forswear carrying any actual furniture around, when you get the opportunity to buy a beautifully decorated Arab chest, do you think of it as furniture? Nor are these chests very expensive. They are made in India, of ben-teak, which is plentiful there, then shipped to Arabia, where local craftsmen decorate them with brass. They then become sea chests of Arab sailors, dowry containers for young girls, and the common receptacle for pillows, clothes, and household linen in a land where people sit on the floor and do not go in, the way we do, for furniture. They also represent a cash investment which the owner is occasionally forced to realize, in which case the chest goes into the back of some merchant's dark shop, to lie around gathering dust until someone with a keen eye comes along and sees what it must have been like in its glory. Once discovered, it is bought; where would one ever get such a chance again? Mark has a very keen eye. We ended up with eleven, and when it came time to leave Arabia, of course, we could simply pack in them and move off.

That this turned out to be a foolish dream will surprise no one who has had anything to do with antiques. Instead of being the answer to our problems of storage *in situ* and *en voyage,* they turned out to be just eleven more bulky items to be packed separately and carefully. But they were (and are) beautiful.

And in refurbishing these lovely chests, in collecting Bedouin jewelry (which is sold in Arabia for the weight of its silver), in making each of our Arab houses into a work of art (we thought) by painting all the faded old carved doors and windows black to stand out against the whitewashed walls and hanging on them the well-mounted trophies, Mark salved some of the soreness of his job. For in southern Arabia, he found himself tied to a desk (paper is cheap), given no boat, no nets, no equipment, no transport of any sort, and no money to get any; thus hampered, he was asked to survey the coastal fishing. But when he had (we borrowed an ancient lorry from the Residency), he was told that none of his recommendations was possible. He was, however, to submit a monthly report of his activities.

Mark's reaction to all this was explosive, and he set to work to circumvent the red tape and lack of funds. After a year, some driblets of equipment and an old boat, an ex-Scottish herring drifter, arrived for him; it wasn't what he had asked for, but by then he was glad to see anything. At least the boat gave him some "face" in front of the Arabs, who had been quick to notice that the British did not particularly back any of the schemes he put forward, or set much value on him (in terms of money spent), and so had felt able to ignore him themselves.

The boat helped Mark to try another tack: since his requests got nowhere, he would get the "mayors" of the villages and the head fishermen to "demand" instead. This he goaded them into by consistently catching more fish than they did on the same banks, then inviting them on board to look at his equipment. While they were on board, drinking coffee, he'd say casually that he believed Sultan Alawi of Bir Ali was getting one of those (indicating a net), or that Naib Muhammed had been promised that (indicating the long lines with their special hooks which had by this time arrived). Jealously, the local officials would rush back on shore to pour Arabic script onto paper, addressing the letter firmly to The Resident, Mukalla. But though the Arabs vyed with each other to put in demands for loans or grants for the equipment Mark suggested, the British were not about to spend any money—however popular the demand—on a "quiet" place, and a protectorate at that (not a colony).

So Mark went back to Mukalla and tried yet another method: the Qu'aiti Sultanate, of which Mukalla was the capital, was the richest in the protectorate and the seat of the Resident Adviser. With the Residency, the Sultan's Council formed a sort of condominium. Perhaps he could get money from the council. It was a novel idea, and Mark had to do a great deal of "promoting," but the Council—several of whose members "owned" fishermen, boats, and crews body and soul—began to see ways of getting richer still, and Mark thought this should be condoned if the end result was a practical demonstration of the efficacy of improved methods of fishing. Soon a fleet of motorized local boats left Mukalla harbor each dawn and were back each afternoon with better-than-ever catches. But the price of fish did not drop. The merchant council members had no intention of its doing so, either. Other political elements in the town, playing on this, began to be restive and cleverly accused the Residency of letting its fisheries adviser practice gross favoritism toward Shaikh A and Shaikh B, and so on, just because they were on the Council. Why couldn't they get loans for putting engines in their boats?

Even though this was just the sort of spirit that Mark wanted to foster, it put the Residency on the spot; if the Qu'aiti Sultanate was willing to grant "loans" for engines, why not the British government? Ponderously, government machinery was put in motion, and the giant civil-service computer came out with one of its favorite answers: all the nasty merchants on both sides were to be quietly dropped, and the fishermen formed into a cooperative. Cooperatives solve everything; the government can never be accused of being unfair if all the benefits it can confer are placed in the common ground of a cooperative—never mind who benefits then, it's not the government's fault.

"Behind his back," as Mark said, the cooperative officer was brought up from Aden and "given" "his" fishermen. Four years of frustration exploded in a giant rage, and Mark resigned. He was not polite about it.

I suppose Mark should have just written the "reports," distilling them out of the hot tropical air for the delectation of his betters, and bottled odd specimens in formaldehyde, for this is what nice well-behaved fisheries officers do. But not Mark. Nor could he sit cynically on his hands, knowing that he had only to hold on long enough, making no serious mistakes, and wait for a pension, or for "compers" (compensation for loss of career) in the case of a country's attaining independence while he was still in office: for Mark, impossible. Yet no matter how rude he was or how irregular, nothing ever seemed to make a dent in the government attitude. A fisheries officer should, we understood, do only small surveys and scaled-down experiments, to reassure the local populace with science enacted for their benefit. *By no means* should any fisheries scheme attempt to have a commercial basis. Native business interests will be alienated, and besides, no government undertaking should ever be run for a profit.

No, clearly there were plenty of grounds for divorce. But the Colonial Office can also make a very clinging spouse. When you have finally made it clear that you will really leave her, she comes around with all sorts of concessions and tempting pay raises, and turns so reasonable and sweet a face, promising to do better by you. The hope is forever there, quiescent, awaiting fair words to make it spring up: hope that this time things will be different. Far from being easy to lose, hope is with Mark a most persistent sort of foolishness. So much so that even after the four years of frustration in southern Arabia, when the Colonial Office offered him another job in the Seychelles Islands he not only accepted it, but built castles again.

After all, how many times had Mark gazed at the charts of the Indian Ocean and seen in the islands of the Seychelles, sitting in the middle of it, the ideal center for a fishing industry? And hadn't he talked with interested businessmen in Mombasa, the Japanese consul in Nairobi, and Arab merchants from Kuwait, Aden, and Zanzibar on this very subject? Was the British government at last realizing that while in Mark they may not have had a perfect civil servant, they did have someone with the imagination to see and the knowledge to bring about the development of a commercial industry in this one of the few remaining outposts of the Empire? Mark was nothing if not sanguine. And think of the benefits it would bring the Seychelles! Islands subsisting on a coconut economy bolstered by grant-in-aid funds from England, when they lie in the middle of some of the finest fishing in the world!

Buoyed by this vision, we set off from southern Arabia early in 1960. We needed to be buoyed; we now had seventy articles of baggage, not counting suitcases. This numerical explosion was partly because of the Arab chests, and partly because we embarked from Mukalla itself and no one box could be any bigger or heavier than one man could carry on his back. This time we well filled the government baggage allowance, with nothing to spare. Then in Mombasa we learned that although the Aden government is a three-hundred-cubic-foot-allowance government, the Seychelles government is only a measly one-hundred-and-sixty-cubic-foot government, and we had blithely accepted the arrangement that the Aden government would get us to Mombasa, paying all, and there the Seychelles government would take over. It does not require any brilliant arithmetic to figure out that in Mombasa we suddenly had one hundred and forty cubic feet of possessions too many, and there was nothing in the world that we could do about it.

And if that wasn't enough, by this time we had acquired several live appurtenances as well. First came the two Labrador puppies we hadn't meant to accept, from Kenya. Then our son Rory was born in Arabia. Then we decided to bring our Arab servant, Ahmed, almost like another child, to the Seychelles. Then in Mahé (the main Seychelles island) our daughter, Ming

Our old Sorry

Felicity, was born. The accumulations had suddenly seemed to snowball to terrifying proportions; were they too huge to think of moving again?

For needless to say, the Colonial Office's attitude in Mahé was no more ambitious than in Mukalla—less so, if anything. Because the Seychelles are difficult to rule, the budget allocated them can be low, thus releasing valuable funds for soldiers to police trouble spots or for expensive gifts to keep the more riotous ex-colonies within the Commonwealth. In spite of the fact that Mark had been sent directly from Mukalla because the government was "in a hurry to submit its development estimates" and wanted him "to make out the program," the only thing he found ready was, as usual, one small office and a pile of file covers. Mark spent fully a year in Mahé before wrangling permission to purchase a local schooner and getting a special grant to buy an engine and some fishing gear. He also soon discovered that everything he did was seen in the gloomy shadow of two magnificent failures in the fisheries, on a scale of expense Mark's most extravagant estimates had never pretended to, which meant that his every move was watched with wariness by the government and, at first anyway, with scornful cynicism on the part of the Seychellois. But we personally had to face the fact that we had got ourselves and all our baggage out onto some islands in the middle of the Indian Ocean at considerable expense, and that if we did leave, the Seychelles government was only bound to pay for moving half of it. So while we thought about things, Mark spent two years making many friends (he always does) but just as unhappy and rebellious in his job as he was becoming difficult to get along with at home. More and more the scales became weighted in favor of leaving government service before we became too old. There comes a point when even people as casual as we are realize that it will soon be too late.

But how to go? Didn't going anywhere really mean we would have to sell every treasure we had collected? What about our cases of books? We could never build up our precious library again. And my mother, thinking we would be in the Seychelles for a long time, had sent me a complete dining-room set from our old house in New York, heavily carved in Victorian Jacobean style: a huge sideboard, a serving table, twelve chairs, two mirror-backed glass cabinets, the table capable of seating twenty—it was part of my childhood, and I loved every piece of it, but it had more than doubled the cubic footage we'd take up on our next move.

Even granted that we could be tough enough to wrench ourselves out of the tenacious grip of our possessions, where should we go? If only, I used to think, I could persuade Mark to be more hypocritical in his job—then we could take a leave to travel to our old love, New Zealand, see if we liked it, come back, do another three years, then settle there for good. But Mark was even more upset about the Seychelles than about Arabia. The opportunities were so obvious to him—and, by then, to the Japanese, who to their great advantage were operating tuna long-liners around the islands. "All the way from Japan!" Mark would rage. "While the Seychelles does nothing!" No, he couldn't compromise himself to that extent, and I wouldn't really have wanted him to.

Besides, letters we had written to the New Zealand government fisheries department about our chances of starting up some small specialized fisheries (such as eeling) in which the initial outlay in equipment would be within our means left us in no doubt about the pall of socialized government over everything, and of its generally negative attitude. And Mark was getting on in age for deer-culling. Wonderful countryside, of course, but we had a living to earn. Then there was England. There is always England, a place which binds to itself the hearts of its citizens with gossamer threads of quite magical strength and endurance. There can't be an Englishman in the world, no matter how expatriated, who doesn't dream of—Home. But a further few months of letter writing put us straight on that score: an unskilled, thirty-three-year-old ex-fisheries officer, married, with two children, seeks rewarding employment out of doors—no, this was clearly impossible.

So we looked around us, and the conclusion was inescapable

that we had better make up our minds to stay more or less where we were. With what money we had (not spent on moving) and some we could borrow, we must be able to find something to do in what was, after all, a fairly easygoing place with no overt signs of political unrest, strife, or violent hatreds, and a place where the British are well enough established as residents to make a fellow-Britisher feel safe in settling too.

III

SAFE, yes we were safe enough—politically; but on our island, with a labor force to manage single-handed, I was not to make such statements so lightly.

We did not start out by determining to lease one of the far coralline islands, thus choosing for ourselves a bedrock existence remote from the center of activity, in Mahé. Nor did we think of using an island as a base for a private, as opposed to a government, fishing venture. The approach was much more gradual. Mark was, if anything, sick of struggling to make do in fishing, where failure shows up so starkly; his idea was to settle down on land and become a planter—a planter of coconuts if necessary, but hopefully of something more interesting and less land-consuming for a given financial return. So we started to look for smallish properties in Mahé or nearby Praslin, properties off the roads, whose purchase price would take only a minor proportion of our capital so that we could invest whatever remained in developing the land.

Our first idea was to grow tea on the heights on La Misère, near where we had been living in a government house. But the area was too expensive. Then we found two small estates on the western side of Mahé, but one owner was advised by her witch-doctor not to sell and the other estate was too inaccessible. We then went to Praslin, the next-largest island, and though we considered many places there, either the titles were not clear or they did not suit us: too swampy in the lowlands, or too bare (Praslin has had bad fires and consequently bad erosion) in the hills. Finally our eyes turned to the many small islands dotting the sea near Mahé and Praslin. What about one of those?

But when we first came to the Seychelles it was hard enough to find out about properties for sale on the mainland, much less offshore. There were—and are—no estate agents as such. Sales depended on a microscopic *avis* (notice) in one of the papers, or on the goodness of one of the two notaries who always handle transfers and who are therefore reservoirs of information. But to make things additionally complicated, according to the Napoleonic Code,* a man must divide his property equally between his children. His wife may get a share as well but more often gets the *jouissance,* the enjoyment of the property in every way, until her death. Legally the owners are the children, which means, of course, endless subdivision of land unless the children can agree among themselves to reamalgamate by selling all to one, or to an outsider.

For this they must each agree absolutely and on paper, and since the heirs are hardly ever in one place, finding out what they might think can be very time-consuming. Also, for any given piece of property, one child may own the house, one the source of water, another the coconut plantation, or to make things more equal between them, their progenitor may have arranged for each of them to have a piece of mountain land plus a piece of *plateau* (the flat rich land near the sea). To attempt to buy property can therefore be imagined.

Finally, a small island did come up for sale, and we eagerly started to negotiate even though there were more than the usual number of complexities. A widow had the *jouissance,* and of her (legal) children, one was in England, one in France, and two in Mahé. That two were in Mahé was a hopeful sign, but not for long. One, the girl, had had two black babies, so no one

---

* Still retained by the British for civil legal procedure. The criminal code follows English jurisprudence.

could take her word seriously, while the other, a boy, went mad in phase with the moon and was overfond of cows. We persisted. Letters to the children abroad revealed them to be, most satisfactorily, intertested ony in the money—that was simple. We then started to haggle in a notary's office, with the mother and the two children on Mahé, when they could all be collected—according to the phase of the moon. But in the end, it was the widow herself who withheld consent; it transpired that while she never lived on the island, she had living there as manager a man who had once had the privilege of living with her, and the whole idea of selling the place had been nothing more than an ex-lovers' tiff over how much copra he was producing. Returns improved under a threat of sale: therefore, no sale. But everyone had had a splendid time with all these trips to town to Discuss Important Business—something to break the dull routine.

It was after this that we began to consider seriously leasing one of the "outer" islands from the government—we did not have enough money to buy any that were privately owned. It would—it must be—so much simpler.

These outer islands, *les îles éloignées,* (*éloignée,* or far, from Mahé, that is), consist of many groups of coral islands, sand cays or raised reefs, solid blobs or lagoon-filled atolls scattered over the southwestern Indian Ocean through six degrees of latitude. Unlike the mountainous granitic islands of the Mahé group, they are quite flat, except for the occasional sand dune; they have no rivers or streams, no towns or villages, less rainfall, little soil. Nearly all of their acreage is put down to, bow low, the coconut palm. Their plantations, which cumulatively produce more copra (dried coconut) than the main islands, are run from Mahé with transient labor and a manager in residence to keep order and the accounts. Manager and labor both being employed by the owner or lessee of the island, they leave when he sells out, and each new owner (or lessee) has to start afresh.

The only impediment to our leasing one of these islands was that there didn't seem to be any vacant at the time. But after talking patiently to many people, Mark found a Seychellois businessman whose partner was willing to sell his share in the lease of the four government-owned islands in the Amirante archipelago. Something in the Amirantes sounded reasonable to us. These islands lie scattered at roughly twenty-mile intervals along a north-south bank over one hundred and ten miles long by five to twenty-five miles wide, and the bank is only one hundred and twenty miles west-southwest of Mahé at its northern end. This was not so far that we would immediately become involved in ruinous transportation costs, and though the islands in question were among the smallest and poorest of the archipelago, bankfishing for shark, Mark reasoned, could sufficently supplement the income from the island's coconuts.

And an outer-island property had, we thought, a big advantage over properties on the large islands of the Mahé group: no stealing! For all our investigations had indicated that the most costly plague of a property owner in the Seychelles was the incessant pilfering of anything and everything remotely portable. One hundred twenty miles of sea should certainly fix that.

Meanwhile, the business discussions continued. In the end it was agreed that the lease, which included four widely separated islands, should be divided so that Mark would be able to lease the two northernmost islands, of Remire and African Banks, directly from the government, while the original lessee retained the two southern islands, larger but more distant and difficult to land on. This division was fair in that each partner was left one "living on" and coconut-producing island and one sea-bird-nesting island, from which eggs could be collected in season—the other traditional source of income on the coralline islands. Our sea bird island, African Banks (actually two small sand cays), would in itself be a good fishing base, while Remire with its palms would be our home.

Nor were we complete strangers to Remire. We had visited the island two years before and had been struck by its attractive air—not too large, tidy, with neat thatched houses and a whitewashed reservoir, manager's house, shop, and hospital. This last was nothing grand, just a partitioned-off part of the storeroom with space enough for two beds required by law, but carefully

53°E

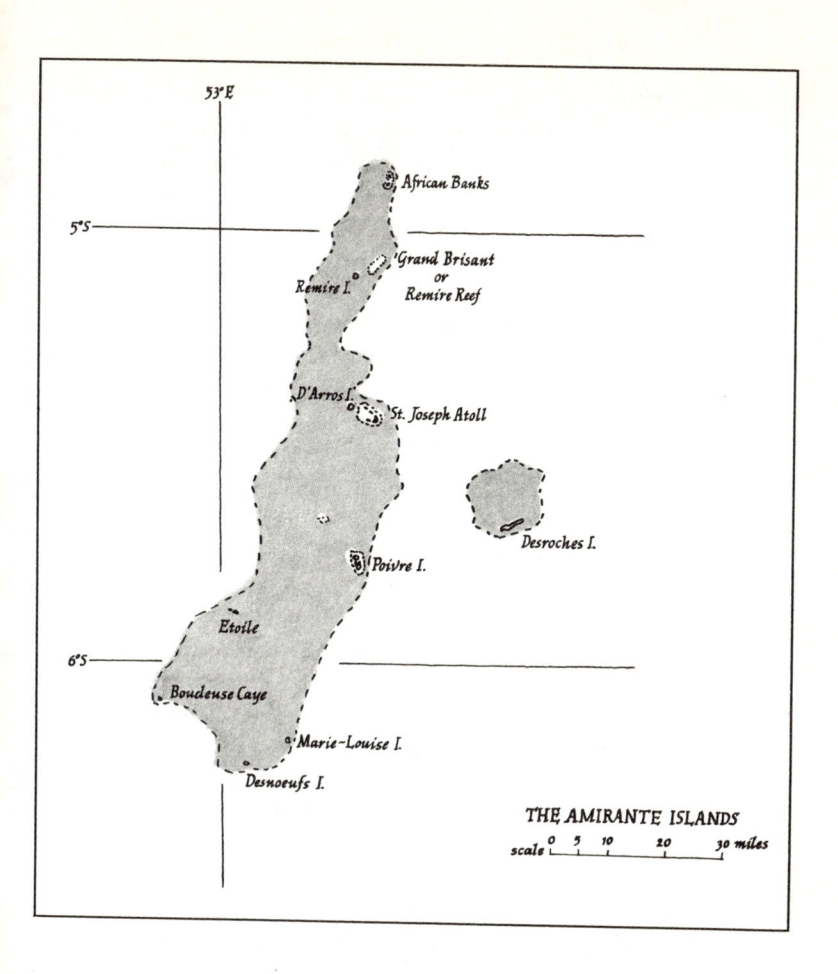

5°S

African Banks

Remire I.
Grand Brisant
or
Remire Reef

D'Arros I.
St. Joseph Atoll

Desroches I.

Poivre I.

Etoile

6°S

Boudeuse Caye

Marie-Louise I.

Desnoeufs I.

THE AMIRANTE ISLANDS

scale 0 5 10 20 30 miles

labeled HOSPITAL on a white placard in a wavery hand. The compound area was swept clean, down to bare earth, so that the brush strokes showed in arclike patterns. It was January, very hot and still, and we sat on the manager's tiny sun-baked veranda, drinking strong tea and sweating, while the customary politenesses were gone through. A pretty place, but we were glad to get back on board the schooner.

Yet now the island was ours, at least ours for eighty years. We had actually and finally torn ourselves away from our last port of call and moved ourselves, our children, our dogs, nine Muscovy ducks and drakes, six white turkeys, three half-breed Rhode Island cockerels, the set of Victorian-Jacobean dining-room furniture, seven (real) Persian carpets, the eleven Arab chests, the antelope heads, beds, prints, paintings, sheets, towels, kitchen utensils, silver, a stove, our Pepsi Cola bottle-cooler freezer (which runs on kerosene like the refrigerator), lamps, plates, glasses, books, books, and books, our Gramophone, records, tape recorder, sewing machine, fishing rods, lines, hooks, flippers, masks, snorkels, nails, files, saws, hammers, shovels, spades, paper, pens, ink, pencils, paint, and certain staple foodstuffs like rice, flour, tea, coffee, and powdered milk in two boats over the one hundred twenty miles of sea. It had been a nightmarish effort of packing and planning, and included months of hanging around in Mahé, living on crates and out of suitcases, waiting for one large or two small schooners to be available to sail us to Remire; the vagaries of what cannot, in Mahé, justify the name of "the schooner trade" have to be experienced to be believed. During those last three months, friends who had said good-bye to us so often and with such good will ended up, like us, in a state of apathetic disbelief in the whole idea.

Then, suddenly, we had twelve hours' notice. Mark shot off to arrange the loading—taking, to my honor, our faithful Ahmed as guard. I have, during the course of our travels, been subject to recurrent packing nightmares, the kind where you pack and pack and the transport is meanwhile slowly moving off. But this was reality. I have rarely come so close to despair. At the last minute everything seemed to be out instead of in, and I knew that since I did not plan on returning, if anything was left out it was lost forever.

I was still shaking from superhuman physical effort—and Mark was, if anything, more frayed by the embarkation of all of us—when we landed on the beach of Remire at the other end. We watched with feelings of some ambivalence the terrible size and number of our possessions that poured steadily out of the boats, onto the sand, crept into the boat shed, past the shop, along the path to our house, up its steps, and onto the entire forty-five-foot length of veranda. Hastily, I made a dam out of a trunk and installed two deck chairs and a lamp stand behind it in the one small seaward corner left; the main flow, diverted, swept on into the two bedrooms. It was then that we swore that never again would we move our home, and come what may, we had made our final decision. All we had to do now was to make the decision work.

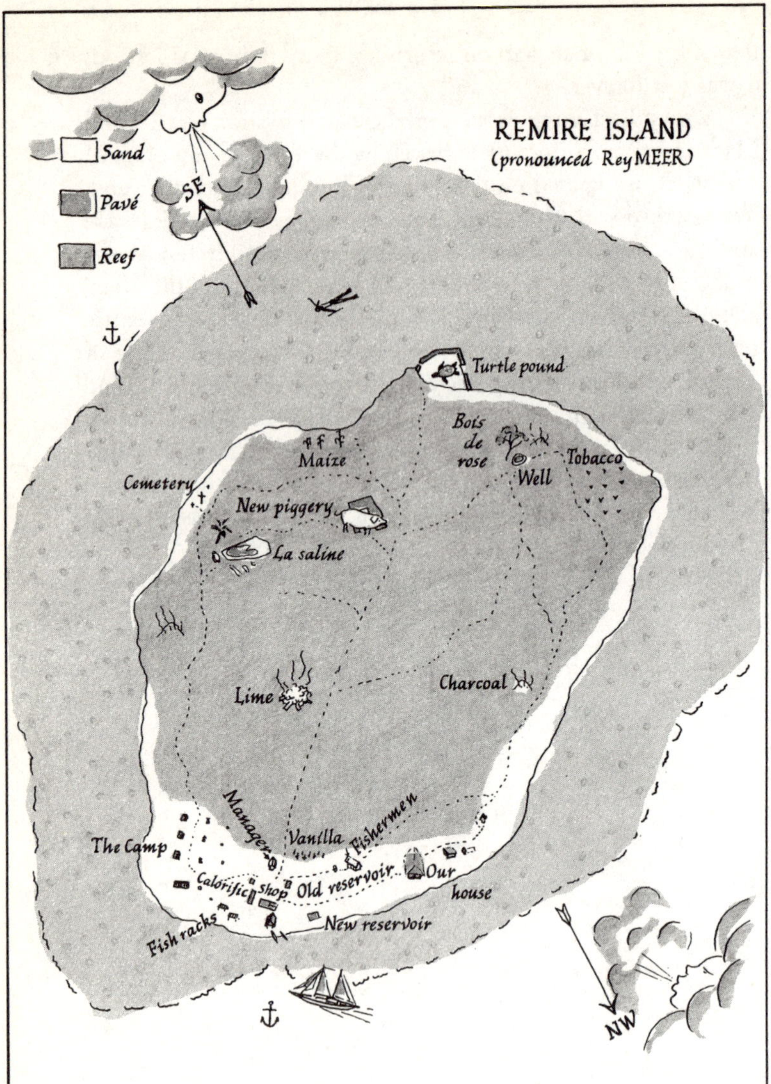
REMIRE ISLAND
(pronounced ReyMEER)
Sand
Pavé
Reef
SE
Turtle pound
Bois de rose
Well
Tobacco
Maize
Cemetery
New piggery
La saline
Lime
Charcoal
Manager
Vanilla
Fishermen
The Camp
Calorific
Shop
Old reservoir
Our house
New reservoir
Fish racks
NW

IV

WE BEGAN by exploring our new kingdom. Remire, the dot in the western Indian Ocean at the junction of 5°6'30" south and 53°8'30" east, a bit of land nine hundred miles from the east coast of Africa and five hundred from the northern tip of Madagascar; Remire, marked on the charts as Eagle Island (a puzzle to wonder about when we had time); Remire as a base on which to build, at last, something permanent for our children; Remire till death do us part. We looked carefully around us to see what we had.

The island was certainly small. Not small by Um Sharifa standards perhaps, but still small. Everywhere we turned we could see the sea, long vistas of it reflecting the clouds on calm days, miles of small whitecaps on the windy ones, sea shining blue through the stems of the palms from one side of the island to the other. But there was no feeling of impingement in being so ringed by water; rather, we felt a dominion over land and sea as far as we cared to go: the extension of Remire under the waters was a part of our acreage, to swim over the way we walked the lands; and northwards stretched the long line of breakers of Grand Brisant, while farther away on the northern edge of the Amirante bank lay the African Islets, ours too. The confines of Remire were only the walls of a castle, for to us the only boundary was the liquid far horizon.

In shape Remire is a roundish island, sixty-two acres in area. It takes about ten minutes to walk across it slowly, and an hour to do the circuit if you are looking for shells at the same time. The beach alternates between broad gentle slopes of sand and piles of broken coral heads tumbled one on top of the other by the waves, or, in places, great flags of beach sandstone worn full of scooplike holes by the sea. Just offshore on every side except that of the anchorage, there is the reef on which the island sits. Toward the southeast it extends for more than a mile, the waves

sketch map—Remire Island

breaking continually on its outer edge. During the low tides of the new and full moons, the reef flats dry out, revealing acres of turtle-grass beds whose roots and blades provide nurseries for so many varieties of shells that walking through them in tennis shoes festoons the laces with baby cowries, winkles, augers, and tritons, while there is always the chance of finding their parents sheltering under the stray slabs of sandstone or lumps of stony coral thrown there by the sea. The turtle grass is also the home of millions of small shrimp, mussels, and crabs, and thus is pasture land for fish and sea turtles, which are in their turn preyed upon, while they graze, by the sharks. (But the big sharks come close inshore only at night.)

Between the beach and the interior is a continuous belt of shrubbery, a low barrier broken only by the paths currently in use and punctuated occasionally by the feathery sweep of the casuarina pines. The shrub, called *veloutier** locally, grows wild on all the coral islands of the Seychelles, left along the beaches to act as a windbreak—ocean islands exposed to the full force of the trade winds badly need windbreaks—but it is a straggly plant, a thickety harbor for mosquitoes, and will turn into a scrawny tangle of bare bent elbows, producing leaves only on the youngest shoots, if it is not pruned. It survives, however, on nothing at all: pure sand, and air full of salt spray. And for this we are grateful. Remire has so little soil—almost none—and it does stop the wind, salt-laden, from blowing straight across the island.

The single place where the *veloutier* is kept permanently cleared away is on the shore opposite the anchorage. It is here, about one hundred feet from the sea's edge, that all island business is transacted; here is *la cour,* the yard. As a gateway to Remire, the yard with its conglomeration of buildings was not, we decided, particularly attractive. Our first impression had been one of neatness, yes. But it was not born out by familiarity. The buildings were all old, for one thing, and a curious hodgepodge of materials had been used in their construction that a coat of whitewash hid from our casual glance. They were dilapidated,

* *Scaevola Koenigii.*

weatherworn, in need of repair even to the broken steps of the small reservoir and the pitted cement of the storeroom floors.

By contrast, on the beach and a little to the right of the yard sat proudly the large reservoir that Mark had built during the time we were waiting to come down to the island. But it was still empty; as we landed we were informed that it leaked but that all the cement had been used up so we would have to wait to repair it. A setback, though at least the old reservoir was full. Farther to the right of the yard, a path led to a long low thatched house full of bunks: the bachelor quarters. And beyond this, but once more on the beach, was "the big house," our house, between two old casuarinas, its steep roof covered with the gentle fall of their needles.

In the opposite direction, along another sandy path, *le camp*: four thatched houses with four small thatched kitchens opposite them and four small distant (the law requires fifty yards) privies. The camp is where the married laborers live. Between it and our house is a space of about three hundred yards, and this is the area marked on the map as the settlement.

The entire rest of the island is, from the Seychellois point of view, uninhabited wilderness, and goes by the name of *dans bois,* though certain much visited parts are separately identified. *Dans bois* is the area of the plantation, of the tall palms, of leafy thickets of cassia bush, of papaya trees. It is crisscrossed by footpaths that vary according to the work or habits of the island, past and present. One path leads to a former lime kiln (there are still bits of unburnt coral on the ground where the lime was sieved); another to a series of weedy ridges (a sweet potato patch); others, overgrown, to wells no longer in use. One can tell much about the life of an island by its paths, particularly the clearly defined ones. From the yard, for instance, a path almost a road runs straight to the edge of the part of the island known as La Plaine. This is the bed of the old trolley line that carried the heavy guano from the tailings to the yard. At its terminus may once have been some of the richest deposits, but now the plain is a really barren area, rock baked by the sun with only the hardy

At the *saline*

tendrils of camel's foot creeper snaking across it. Seven or eight years ago, we were told, there were still a few sooty terns nesting there, but laborers had set fire to the brush several times—besides eating every egg as it was laid—and the birds had given up the unequal struggle. The last link with Remire as a guano island went with them.

The plain lies in a shallow depression, looking almost like a filled-in lagoon. Its appearance made Mark wonder if he could let the sea in (again?) to make both salt pans and a turtle pound, but he decided it was beyond him, particularly as its seaward boundary is the highest part of Remire, windblown dunes of sand that rise to all of twelve feet above sea level. From the tops of the casuarinas growing along this ridge we can just see our nearest populated neighbor, D'Arros Island, twenty miles to the south.

The other clear, well-trodden path follows the eastern side of the island from the camp out to *la saline,* a cemented natural catchment area on the plain's edge which used in fact to be a salt pan but which now catches, and holds for a few days, rain water.

Here, whenever there has been enough rain to fill it, the women of the island happily gather, and the sharp crack! crack! of laundry being flicked on rounded washing stones sounds like pistol shots; and there is a lot of talking and calling back and forth, happy reminders to them of the cool rivers and smooth granite boulders of more civilized Mahé. Ordinarily we must use well water for laundry and the animals, leaving the reservoir supply for human drinking water only.

Less broad but still definite, the path continues past the *saline*, then turns toward the sea; at its end, dug into the grassy top of a dune and protected by a bower of *veloutier*, are the few unnamed graves of the cemetery. Each has its small black wooden cross, and a few small broken vases that once held flowers—imitation, no doubt (wild flowers are not considered suitable for such occasions, and there are none cultivated on Remire). As we walked around the island we went there occasionally to wonder whose bones lie rotting in the sand, who died in sad exile from Mahé, or from some far-off country. No one on the island could tell us.

And how old were the graves? Passed on from one careful Catholic tenant to another, some might be very old indeed. One cannot judge from the crosses, since they are replaced when the old ones rot. For how many generations has the custom gone on? Mark, who likes to absorb atmosphere as well as facts, used, as he walked around, to imagine himself a tenant of a hundred years or more ago, and one night he dreamed vividly that he met among the palms a gentleman dressed in the style of the 1780s—French, very courtly. He bowed but did not speak, and to Mark's great annoyance, dematerialized as Mark drew near.

How we longed to find some trace of pirates who may have used the little island as a hideout; of the French and the English, stopping to explore on their way to India; or the numerous freebooters, slave traders, legendary ship captains, and ships with stories themselves, valiantly wavering through storms off treacherous African Banks, or mysteriously set fire to. There was a past there—we were sure of it—but all so inaccessible.

Someone's grave

On the Way to the Island / 45

It was as though we walked on a film of time for whose opaqueness only ignorance or disinterest was responsible. In countries full of history one takes the oldness of the land and the parade of its past as known, established, almost for granted. But on an island like Remire? Its sparse history was at once more graspable yet better effaced, and this was irritating. Mark spent most of our first two weeks poking about for remains, any remains. He kept his eyes open for bits of masonry in the underbrush and old well sites; he beachcombed for ship's anchors and guns and bells. He hoped to find some fragment to connect with the passing of Arab dhows or of the Portuguese, and we both floated for hours above the reefs, looking for wrecks—an escape for us from unpacking the present. The present was so full of boxes, of the many new faces of our workers that still remained a blur, so full of new habits to be acquired, of our whole new life. Besides, there had to be some remnant of the past, if only we looked hard enough.

One day, we were at least slightly rewarded. We were swimming along the southern edge of Grand Brisant and came upon a piece of brass, then another. By the end of the afternoon, we had collected a nice weight in boat fittings of various sorts, of good quality such as were likely to have been carried on an expensive yacht, but no anchor, cable, or any other trace. Many schooners trading between Mauritius and the Seychelles were converted yachts; surely such a wreck would have been reported in Mahé. But apparently not. While we were in Mahé, we had of course read everything we could concerning the Amirantes, but there wasn't much on Remire. A *Pilot* book mentioned a deserted habitation and pumpkins growing wild in 1891: the government archives, the suicide of a manager in 1905; and we were able to collect a few stories about the place, all of them pin-downable to the era of the Seychelles Guano Company's concession in the early 1900s and to the subsequent tenancy of Dr. Lanier, of whom more later. And though we did read of one wreck, it turned out to be a false lead. So what yacht left its few brass bones on our doorstep we will probably never know.

V

But of course the present concerned us most. When we took over the lease of Remire, we took over what is usually called a "going concern." What sort of going concern Remire was, exactly, we had yet to discover. The previous lessees had presumably made some sort of money out of the place, but its recent history was gloomy financially—even a little shady—darkened by one partner's affable and conscienceless facility for cheating the other. Since the cheated partner, being occupied with other properties and deals, had left the clever thief to run the island as he pleased, and since the scoundrel had availed himself of this opportunity to peel the island of as large a proportion of its products as he thought he could get away with, and then declared them neither at the customs in Mahé nor in the books in his partner's office, we had no way of knowing even vaguely what the island could produce. Fortunately, as Mark said, we were after a home and a fishing base, and did not expect a really profitable copra estate. But still, until we could establish the fishing, we needed all the sources of ready cash we could lay our hands on, and could not afford to overlook even the smallest pig, the most rat-infested maize crop, or the most aged and thin-necked (a sign of drought and malnutrition) old crone of a coconut palm in the plantation. There was certainly plenty of runty pork wandering around loose, rooting up every taro, sweet potato and young papaya that might otherwise have had a chance to grow, and what edible plants they didn't demolish a flock of thoroughly wild and equally stunted chickens did. Everything had been allowed to go to seed and to weed, and wore a generally unkempt air, except for the compound area, which was, as before, swept clean of even a vestige of a blade of comfortable green grass, bearing adequate witness to this curious force of habit in the Seychellois and their idea of what is nice: even in green flourishing Mahé, courtyards are bare acres of dirt or, often, mud, with a few *potted* flowers along a firm little wall made of upturned beer bottles. It keeps the jungle out.

But on Remire, one could hardly worry about jungle. Thickets here and there, yes, but the live mowing machines had certainly kept everything useful, pretty, or nourishing well in check. Even so, the most recent manager, out of earnestness or lack of imagination, had evidently thought it necessary to spend quite a lot of the lessees' money on having the women slash and burn rubbish, in ways so careless that many of the palms had blackened stems, and much of the island, already only thinly covered and thus exposed to the continuous leaching of the sun, was rendered still more useless than before.

And the palms! We saw some efforts had been made at replanting, but in what a manner! Two in a hole here, one on the upper lip of a hole there, holes right under other palms containing young ones inevitably the losers in the battle for sunlight and space to grow; and then scores and scores of the oldest most miserable palms I had ever seen, with about three wispy pale yellow fronds and one nut each.

Why had these never been cut? We stared up at them, and they stared sightlessly down. Unanswerable. More than this, there would be a whole row (coconut palms are always planted in rows, even if the nuts came from such poor stock that they weren't worth planting at all) of young, quite handsome palms, and then there would be five or six of these sterile horrors, and then the replant would continue. Inexplicable. Yet despite this, there weren't many young palms to wonder at; most were middle-aged, and only a few really good bearers amongst them. A coconut plantation, in other words, that lacked both quality and quantity.

That the older palms were suffering was not surprising when we thought it out. After all, of Remire's sixty-two acres only ten are classified as "sand," while the rest is phosphatic sandstone; that is, sandstone into which guano has leached over the centuries, making it possible to break it with a strong hoe or pickaxe and thus "cultivate." Locally, this substance is called *pavé* and of *pavé* three of four grades are recognized as having different degrees of hardness, but they are all hard. (In spite of—

or perhaps because of—its thin covering of creeper and weed, it is even difficult to walk over; we were continually bruising our toes and heels on lumps of *pavé*, protuberances of *pavé*, unevenly eroded blocks of *pavé*, and were unable to travel over it at even half the speed of the laborers.)

To plant a palm in *pavé*, one must dig a sort of well, breaking through the hard pan layer to reach the water table six to eight feet down; unless you do this, the palm will die. But once the palm has been put in its hole and used up the nourishment of the filler added—mulch, guano scrapings, old leaves, or whatever—then it is literally in a flowerpot with no soil, a jail with only water to sustain life. The palms' desperate need for mulch made the burning-off the island even more shocking and unnecessary.

And not only had there been bad management of the coconut plantation, but most of the casuarinas (whose leaves form a valuable acidic mulch on our alkaline coral base) had been cut down as well. There were stumps everywhere, cut for firewood, for roofing poles—even, we discovered, for their supply of needles to burn inside houses as a way of clearing them of mosquitoes. And of the grand old trees that had been enough of a feature of Remire to cause the *pilot book for the southern Indian Ocean* to mention "conspic. tall trees," only six remained. Admittedly, there had been a freak storm five years before which uprooted many of the oldest trees, but there were in addition plenty of fresh stumps. Mark and I wondered if the government had given permission to cut them. Knowing the scoundrel, probably not.

And why was all the housing squatting complacently on soft land, while most of the palms and casuarinas were struggling to grow in rock? It seemed obvious that houses should have been placed on *pavé*, surely excellent foundation material, rather than on expensive (because imported) cement plinths in good planting land—especially when, on Remire, there is so little of it. The appearance of the island certainly bore out what we knew to be true: that in recent years it had not been organized from an agricultural point of view at all, but rather used only as a cheap fishing base by a series of absentee landlords out to extract as much as possible from it at the least possible cost to themselves.

The preponderance of *pavé* on the island is truly rather sad. Inevitably it makes Remire a "poor" island agriculturally, for in *pavé* only trees will grow, but even with trees if you do not have enough reasonable soil to grow good ones, you must have the size and extent to grow many. Any lessee of Remire has therefore always had to have some other string to his bow, like fishing, in order to make ends meet. We knew this very well before we came here, but still, as we walked around, we sighed a little.

One path on the island made us brood on our lack of topsoil at every stop: the old guano trolley line. As we trod its well-worn surface, we couldn't but think sadly of the time when Remire was still the haunt of nesting sea birds and covered with centuries of deposited dung, the time before she received the attentions of the Seychelles Guano Company.

The years before the First World War were boom years, as elsewhere in the Seychelles—not least because it was then that the Seychelles businessmen began to sell off the rich guano deposite of the outer islands. Remire was one of the most heavily exploited: Mark has calculated that nearly a hundred thousand tons must have been removed, representing a fertile topsoil we shall never recover; for now that we have trees and palms, which the remaining guano islands possess little of, we will never again attract the sooty and noddy terns and the boobies in the vast numbers necessary to build up a supply of this excellent, if hot, manure. These sea birds avoid the blessed shade of trees, choosing only the barest stretches of inhabited islands to lay their eggs on, or, better still, islands that have no human habitation whatever. With their long wings, the terns find it difficult to get off the ground if there is any high underbrush; they need a clear run, and the boobies, being about ten times as heavy, need an even longer and clearer one. They are on the ground in the first place because that is where they habitually nest; only the frigates and white terns nest in trees, and then, of course, the guano spills down the leaves and trunks, which burns the leaves but does not build up effective ground deposits in quite the same way, though over hundreds of years it might mix with fallen leaves to form a valuable mulch indeed.

We cannot really complain, however, about the guano company's exploitation, for it is owing to this that we have inherited a coconut plantation at all: under the terms of the contract with the Seychelles government, every island cleared of guano had to be completely planted up with palms. Good, new, young palms, all sprouting in their holes, well mulched, fed by the guano left in the crevices of the rock—even little Remire must have looked tempting agriculturally, then.

Or so we suppose, because after the company had swept the land (literally sweeping the guano out of the nooks and crannies and recesses of the bared *pavé*) and planted the coconuts and left, the lease was taken by a most remarkable man, Edouard Lanier. Lanier's tenancy was the only one to do any agricultural good to the island (until, we hope, our own). As with many of the characters of the recent past in Mahé, his energies were reflected by the double image of a multitude of business interests and experiments demanding an inquiring mind not often found in the little colony, and a multitude of legitimate and illegitimate children. Among his many interests was, for a while, Remire. He never lived here himself, but he would swoop down upon the islands from time to time, and always had a series of experiments going. The main one was the establishment of sericulture, to which end he seeded the island with a vast quantity of castor bean bushes that are still with us, growing wild in hardy clumps. And it is his turtle-pound wall that in ruined clutter sticks out from the southeastern side of the island. (Mark is determined to build one too so he can store turtles before selling them in Mahé.) And every plant we have brought with us from Mahé to try here—pepper, jackfruit, breadfruit, bananas, oranges, limes, chillies, cocoplums (a sort of wild plum resembling a beach plum but unfortunately tasting like slightly sweet damp cotton; children like it)—has been first tried by Lanier. This we were told by the old gardener who works here. But we cannot find out which, if any, of Lanier's essays succeeded. It is all hearsay of thirty years ago. Only the oldest laborers, men still linked to the slave days by the gold ring or a small red stone worn in one ear lobe, who were mature working men at that time remember now that such and such happened; and since the Seychellois conserves his life force by reducing living to the least possible work, the result of any extraordinary effort, like planting and tending something you are not sure will grow, is less memorable than the effort itself. In any case, between his time and ours, everything had died, or was burned, or cleared by careless labor and hungry livestock.

We were also beginning to understand, from things Mark's fishermen said—two of them had been with him before, while he was still in government service—that Remire was by no means the solitary, isolated island we had thought it. In fact, to hear them talk, it had been a sort of entrepôt for passing fishermen, a haven for boats illegally in the Amirantes—illegally because no one, unless in possession of a master's ticket, is allowed to take a vessel out of sight of land. But the banks within this range are fished constantly, and the tempting massed shoals of the Amirantes are still relatively unexploited; Remire is an easy island to make for from Mahé, and the law is impossible to enforce. The good anchorage made it a pleasant first port of call, a place to relax after the trip and before starting to fish in earnest, and boats leaving Mahé made a point of letting families of the people on Remire (and any other island they might be stopping at) know they were where they were going; on the day of departure, letters, bags of fruit, a bit of beer, a bottle of wine would be put quietly on board, and neither the police nor the owner or lessee of the island would be any the wiser. And once on the island, what more natural for the manager and laborers than to give these kind fishermen some coconut oil, a pig, a few chickens, some palm toddy to thank them for bringing contact with Mahé and their friends? And since the produce proffered in friendship and gratitude cost them nothing to give, they could afford to be as lavish as the manager in control thought they could get away with being. This, naturally, depended on how much control the absent owner or lessee was able, or bothered, to exercise. Most owners forbid unauthorized boats to land. But the case of Remire was rather special. The scoundrel was probably fairly aware of what returns he ought to be getting, but because he himself was operating outside the law it paid him to encourage—even comission—boats to call. How else could he get produce back without his partner's knowledge? Any reputable vessel had to have produce listed for customs, accepted as loaded by the captain—not much leeway there. So not only were the fishermen stopping on their own behalves but on behalf of the scoundrel as well, and as it was the established practice that payment would be in kind—rather than cash—pigs, ducks, eggs, chickens from Remire had been finding their way back to Mahé in steady streams. There may not be honor among thieves, but this system was working all right and would probably have continued to if the scoundrel hadn't got bored and decided to sell out his share to us. There followed a pause in activity, a watching-and-waiting time while we organized ourselves and boats still stopped casually. Then, to a sort of tribal gasp of horror, that Englishman was observed to be sailing down to Remire himself, with his wife, his children, that well-known Arab servant of his, and all his furniture and animals—obviously intending to stay.

The future of Remire became one big question mark.

TWO

Gappy, the "Great Disorder," Marcel

VI

IT WAS SEPTEMBER when we arrived, and it was cool and rainy, which was a pleasant surprise. The end of the southeast trades is usually a dryish month in Mahé, but we had been told that weather in the outer islands was quite different; we would have to learn what to expect, presumably, from the laborers, and we were soon being taught by Marcel—one of the few men Mark had allowed himself to inherit from the previous regime; we had heard that he was a good gardener: old, dogmatic (what is it about gardening?) but good. September, Marcel told us firmly, was a fine time for planting, so Mark was thoroughly happy. All the hundreds of seedlings we had brought we would have had to plant anyway, but Marcel's news was good to hear, and the rain was a blessing, saving us hours of watering time. We had a special hole dug for each fruit tree and special trenches for the pineapples, and for the rest we made ourselves a large garden. Mark contentedly doled out the vegetable seeds to Marcel while I painted names on pieces of bamboo. We also made seedbeds for the tobacco on stilts ringed with kerosene-soaked rags (to ward off the ants), and kept the women busy clearing and dibbling maize kernels in the sand dunes, while some of the men were put onto the heavier work of preparing the one fertile patch of land inland for the tobacco when it should be ready to set out. Mark was determined to get the plantation at least started by the end of the windy season so that he could concentrate on the fishing during the calm season to follow.

Once fishing began in earnest, he wouldn't be able to spend much time on shore.

The weather continued to hold, beautifully cloudy, with rain squalls passing along the horizon of the sea, if not over us. Every day Mark watched for the first shoots of corn, while in the garden under their little shelters, pumpkins, carrots, sweet peppers, garlic, ginger, beets, turnips, Chinese cabbage, lettuce, tomatoes, and beans were sprouting. The soil did not look anything like what either of us thought of as soil, but it seemed to be adequate, even without manure (the animals had not been penned long enough for the manure to collect or ripen).

The garden, and the sheltered area of the island which we had set aside for the orchard, became our oasis, where we could refresh our optimism for the future; looking at the coconut palms was too disheartening, and all the other work was progressing so slowly—or so it seemed in our enthusiasm and impatience (a little over a week is not a very long time)—and we were still in the throes of deciding what to "do" with the plantation: away with the coconuts and plant something Really Economic? What? Cashews? Vanilla? Perhaps just timber? Not large enough. But it had to be trees of some sort; nothing else could survive the *pavé*. But trees were always lengthy experiments: one had to wait so long for returns. Perhaps we should stick to coconuts after all . . . that was at least safe. And so the discussion would go.

Meanwhile, to mesh in with what we had to do, we began to form new living habits. Getting-up time in government service had been seven; now Ahmed brought out tea at six, after which Mark would go out on a tour around the island, and come back for breakfast. Then he would see the fishermen about gear maintenance or the manager about new plans while I taught Rory a little, worked on my drawings (I had a commission for some new currency designs from the Seychelles government), or went to the kitchen to invent something interesting for lunch. Lunchtime, in Mahé, had to wait until, or if, Mark got home from town, but now he found it more practical to eat at noon, like the laborers, so that while he was eating he would not be disturbed by requests from the manager, and have a siesta in the middle of the day. In the afternoons I wrote or sewed or took the children for a swim. Then Mark got up, checked on the work done on overtime or extra, had tea, and swam himself before going out to wander around the island again, either alone, thinking, or with me and the children. It was at this time of the day that we really noticed how different our new life was. One of the things that impressed us most was

Ahmed drawing our water from a well
in the *pavé*

Ahmed drawing our water from the well

the extra time we had for ourselves and the children. No cocktail parties: hours to walk around the island, noticing things, in the cool of the evening; we no longer had to go out to dinner or have people in: time to read to the children or talk to each other.

Promptly at six, Ahmed carried the hot water to the little outside bathroom and poured it into the washtub for the children's bath, then the children had their supper. After supper, stories until bedtime. Then, with them in bed, we had our bath and dinner. And for Ahmed it was equally pleasant. His work was finished by nine every night—no exceptions, no late hours waiting up for us. And no late hours on the town for him: the whole island shut down by nine, and except in the manager's house, no light showed through cracks in the windows, tight-barred against the night. It did not take long for this rhythm to delight us with its simplicity quite as much as it delighted the children: we were always *there*. And when we were out of the house, they could come too. No point of the island was too far for Ming's little two-year-old legs to carry her, and Rory, at four, was more than capable of tramping anywhere. Walks were great explorations—a visit to our solitary heron at Heron Corner (the place the heron favored); hunting crabs on the sandstone flags at the southern beach; and, constantly, collecting shells; trips to the papaya grove for Ming's favorite fruit; swimming lessons wherever we happened to be on our sandy beaches or in the deeps in the coral. They both became real water babies, though only Rory acquired a deep tan; Ming is, unfortunately for her tanning ability, red-headed like me, and became permanently freckled instead. In my mind, I could hear my mother and grandmother say, "Oh, what a pity to blemish that lovely white skin!" But of what use a white skin to Ming, destined to live all her childhood under the hot tropical sun? I had suffered enough, and wished her as hardy as possible. (With the result that most days Ming's face is as red as her hair, but it fades quickly and she never gets the terrible sunburns I do, no matter how long she stays out.)

The peace of it all was wonderful, in spite of worries about the plantation. Already, after only two weeks, we could feel the difference in ourselves. We seemed to expand to fill the island.

Beach news: where the heron took off
this morning

Thoughts we had had at first about subleasing a piece of island to this friend, a bit to another, were quietly dropped. We wanted our domain to ourselves. Oh, the laborers were with us in a sense, but we didn't know many; they were dealt with by the manager—these words were to come back to mock me—and we had long been used to living with and yet not with our fishermen, on various boats, on Um Sharifa, in all our camps. It was quite like the best of the time in the Sudan all over again, only more comfortably shaded and housed.

If it had not been for the radio, the outer world might as well not have existed. No sail even passed on the horizon; we floated all day in an empty bowl of ocean, busy with ourselves; then promptly at eight, we listened to the news, and again at ten to see if anything important had happened meanwhile, after which—satisfied that our lives lacked nothing—we went to bed. We found ourselves following the news in a way we had never bothered to in Mahé, not through envy or loneliness or the wish to be personally involved, but because we now had more time to read, to become well informed, and in this sense world events became a part of our lives with an immediacy that I never got out of reading a daily paper. [One of the British Broadcasting Company's best programs is their *Radio Newsreel,* in which they broadcast reports from on-the-spot correspondents in, if atmospheric conditions permit, the correspondents' own voices. This gives a sense of reality to the news. Another is a once weekly *Review of our Correspondents,* which lets these same reporters give more background and opinion from the various spots in which they are stationed: Paris, Lagos, Bonn, Saigon, Salisbury, Gibraltar. I cannot praise the B.B.C. enough for this type of newscasting. The Voice of America we found we did not listen to so much; after one is used to the British speaking voice, the American radio broadcaster sounds so slow and lugubrious; one feels it is primarily a service for foreigners who don't understand English very well, and not, like the B.B.C. Overseas Service, organized specifically for her expatriots and colonials abroad. A matter of taste. But we were, by chance, listening to VOA the night—our time—Kennedy was shot; distance and apartness had no effect on the shock of that, nor on Churchill's last lingering, nor on Adenauer's passing, nor on any of the other milestones that we see move by and recede into the past as clearly from here as anywhere.]

We had in fact achieved such a pleasant routine, and such a feeling of belonging, that it was hard to realize we had only been on the island three weeks.

Our lives had begun to acquire such fulfilled feeling that it was with real irritation that Mark found he would have to make a trip back to Mahé to see to all the loose ends we had left behind, and to get more provisions. Somehow we had badly miscalculated the probable consumption of even such staples as rice and sugar, and we were running low. We needed cement too, to mend the reservoir, to build new pigsties (so that we could get the pigs out of the mud in back of the yard area), to finish off our kitchen (Ahmed was having to wash up outside because the sink and drains were not installed), and to mend all those expensive plinths we disapproved of but could hardly replace with *pavé*-based housing overnight. The fishing boat's

Gappy, the "Great Disorder," Marcel / 61

engine was ailing too, and Mark wanted to profit by the last of the southeast wind to sail east-northeast. But he said he would be away only ten days at the most; naturally the children and I stayed behind, and the island became once more, as in the days before our arrival, under the control of our manager.

Gappy. F. Gappy. Gappy, our manager, a small furry rabbit (with teeth) that Mark more or less pulled out of a hat in Mahé to replace the scoundrel's old one. A change in regime, Mark reasoned, was best effected by a change in managers, and had taken the opportunity to send him down with some new laborers almost two months before we came down ourselves. Mark had liked his looks, and had, in Mahé, been impressed by his habit of noting any small loan or debt incurred by fishermen or laborers in the black notebook that he always carried (Mark is regrettably much too casual but knows a virtue when he sees it). The little man was, Mark had found out, an ex-policeman, and Mark thought this an admirably good thing, useful training for dealing with an island that had certainly not been subject to any appreciable discipline for a long time. His credentials were also good, and people from his part of Mahé spoke well of him; Mark therefore left the selection—subject to his own final approval—of the laborers to replace those whose contracts had ended, to Gappy, knowing that it was important for manager and laborers to get along. He had seen, he thought, enough on other islands of managers rendered impotent by bad labor.

Gappy proved to be an efficient organizer, and Mark began to congratulate himself. He walked quickly too, and when he stood up, he did not seem to have to lean against a doorway for support. He was stocky and well built, strong-looking. He also had a most engaging smile. This smile furrowed his broad light brown face to display a set of remarkably bad teeth, but his clear brown eyes were like a healthy calf's and looked at one from an honest sort of countenance. In between his black eyebrows there was a deep frown mark, but this must be, we thought, eye strain and not bad temper. He was forty, he said, married, with five children, but Mark was relieved to hear that he wanted to bring only his wife and his smallest child to Remire. The accommodation wasn't all it might have been. Still, we knew from hearing other planters talk that settled married labor (and, one supposed, married managers), though more of a nuisance to house, were a steadying influence on the usual type of youngster who went to the outer islands, seeking an easy life, little work under lax managers, free rations, plenty of fish, and a bit of money in his pocket to go on a booze-up at the end of his contract.

This latter type of man or boy is difficult to avoid hiring, however, for he is both cheaper to employ and more available than a family man: cheaper because he does not get "married" rations, nor does he require a whole house, nor does he come with dependents who will steadily pilfer or appropriate such fruits and goods of the property as are not under lock and key; and more available because a laborer's wife does not usually care for what is to her banishment to the outer islands, away from family and friends, and from her children if they are in school. Family, friends, and her children (some of whom may not be her husband's) are more important to her than her husband, and as she is not encumbered with any romantic notion of having to follow him whither he leads (especially if it is to one of those rough uncomfortable islands with no shops or social life), she makes her opinion quite clear to him. She does not need to worry about her keep, you see; a husband is legally obliged to support a legal wife, and rarely indeed in Catholic Mahé does the claim of desertion or disobedience to the marriage vows result in divorce

It therefore often happens that a married man either goes alone to the island or takes another woman as his housekeeper, or what the laws of the Seychelles delightfully call a "concubine." Of course, this is what she is, but it lends an altogether spurious oriental air to read of some worthy old bag thus described. She is nearly always an old bag because a young girl would not dream of leaving Mahé in the insecure position of a married man's concubine when, being young, she has other choices, or at least the opportunity of other choices, open to her.

More often than anything, however, it turns out that the married man is in fact neither married to his "wife" because of the tiresome legal ties (in which case she is called his *menagère*) nor living with her, but is temporarily living with (or on) some other woman and chooses to escape his complicated life by accepting employment in the outer islands, to which he will take yet a third. This he will do not because the Seychelles male is such a desperate philogynist but because he hates "doing" for himself. He works until the lunch bell. Who will cook his food? Who will wash and mend his clothes? As for sex: well, sex is usually to be had with a female belonging to someone else; it is the point of being cared for that is so important to him. (I would hate to be caught saying this is universal—or would I?) In any case, whatever female he brings, the poor proprietor is obliged to accept: one blanket law states that the owner or lessee must transport and house and give married rations to any woman the laborer descends with, while at the same time requiring the owner to see that the correct proportion of said laborer's salary is remitted monthly to his legal wife or Mahé-recognized *menagère*. There were times in Mahé when we clung a little desperately to the idea that a man who gets his clothes washed, his food cooked, and his sex, no matter the container, right at hand, is likely to be more contented and steadier to employ. Everything, from the men's lives to our legal obligations, seemed so complicated.

Eventually, during June, July, and August, we assembled an example of every category for the descent to Remire: a married manager, a married carpenter, a married mason, and a married laborer, all bringing legal wives; two fishermen practicing concubinage; two fishermen who were leaving *menagères* in Mahé; one fisherman who wanted to bring his wife but whose wife did not want to come and who didn't have anyone else on tap; one wife who left the young man she was keeping to descend with her husband, Mark's master fisherman, so that she could earn enough money to continue to keep her youthful lover; one married fisherman who was coming to get away from his wife and all women (there are the rare independent souls); five apparently wifeless and concubineless laborers; and one boy as general dog's body, officially the carpenter's nitwit-but-strong apprentice, too young for woman-problems.

All these people had to be taken by the hand to the hospital in Mahé for a blood test: the law requires that not more than five days prior to his departure to the outer islands a laborer must be tested for what the Seychellois politely refer to as dirty blood, *sang sale*. Since the schooner masters invariably do not know when they are leaving, and then never leave when they say they will, and since we were for those three months often within five days of a possible departure, we were forever having to round up people for yet another blood test. At this sort of thing, Gappy was very good—a godsend—but it was still a time-consuming affair. And futile. A case of V.D. is most often contracted during that wait between the test and the day the boat leaves, when the laborer has been officially signed on and has pocketed the advance of up to two months' salary he is then allowed to demand.

Gappy was also clever at rounding everyone up when it did appear the schooner was actually leaving; even on his own day of departure everyone who should have been was miraculously there, and Mark again congratulated himself on his luck. So Gappy and most of the laborers came down to Remire in the beginning of August, nearly two months before us.

VII

MARK had no sooner sailed off than the rain stopped. Even the breeze stopped, and the hot, still dog days of the change in monsoons set in. The first week he was away was for me a madhouse of gardening. I could not bear to waste seedlings, and Marcel, deaf to instruction, had planted whole packets of things, which were all now coming up. But Marcel had left with Mark to see a dentist. He had carefully explained that he only wanted to have the few stumps that were troubling him pulled out, not to get a whole new set put in: what good would expensive teeth be to him when he was bound to die soon anyway? So he'd be back soon, he said, long before transplanting time, and I wasn't to worry about the garden. Ha. I had to open up yet another garden patch—a lot of work, when I only had one of the laborers, a rather broody sophisticated fellow who said he wanted to return to Mahé on the next boat, to help me. Pressed, he explained that there were "things that weren't right" on the island, and would say no more, sulking. Anyway, he did work.

It remained brilliantly, remorselessly sunny, with not a cloud in the sky. Each transplant had to have a special leaf shelter made for it, and be watered endlessly by hand, with, when the variety of vegetable would stand it, brackish water carried from the least salty well. Since the large reservoir leaked, there was no question of using much rain water.

There was also the house to put in order. Three quarters of it was still depressingly full of boxes, and I gazed at them every day, wondering what I could do about them. Most contained books, and we had no bookcases, nor the prospect of any for a long time: there was much more important work for the carpenter to do. Looking at all these book-filled boxes depressed me for other reasons too. Did we really have to carry, dust, encase, pack quite so many printed words? Mark and I both love books and are proud of our library; we were forever shocked at the poverty of the usual civil servant's shelves. But we could have eliminated some things. Suddenly there seemed to be boxes and boxes of novels we had read and enjoyed but might never read again, and a great deal of out-of-date anthropology of more use to someone writing a history of anthropological theory than it was now to me; endless stacks of fisheries pamphlets, also out of date; and Mark had at least a hundred books on sailing, fishing, and hunting (some of which, I had to admit, he reads and rereads, getting more from his part of the library than I from mine), besides the serious histories and biographies that we wouldn't think of parting with (they'd be useful for Rory and Ming when—when they will probably be away at school and not here to read them). Of all this wealth, however, I had only seven books out: *The Concise Oxford Dictionary*, a French-English-and vice-versa dictionary, *La Petite Larousse Illustrée* (*"Un dictionnarie sans example est un squelette"*), *Modern Poultry Husbandry* (I would have liked a newer edition than 1948), Macmillan's *Tropical Planting and Gardening*, and, in the kitchen, the *Joy of Cooking*, which I used to jog memory for variations on a theme but which frustrated me by demanding so many ingredients I lacked; I supplemented it with the down-to-earth nature of the *Mount Kenya Cookery Book*, written in a more pioneering spirit and giving recipes for making soap and floor polish. (The Kenya book would never, for instance, ask *its* readers to "take one 6 oz. tin of tuna fish" in a land where most people, like us, start with it alive and thrashing in the bottom of the boat.) But despite our having little excuse to keep so many books, I loved them all just because they were books, and could never bear to throw one away, even my dead mother-in-law's little gems of *Being and Doing* and *The Flower Hours*, or something like that, by May something-or-other, full of wholesome uplifting advice.

By the time Mark's ten days had become two weeks, wholesome uplifting advice was something I needed. I think it was only then that the realization of just how cut off the island actually was sank in. Isolated, in the true sense of the word, suspended in an apparent vacuum—it was indeed a peculiar sort of life. We had chosen it, but I had not bargained on it without Mark, without the life line of the boat. The fishermen might talk of the good old days, when boats passed all the time, but now we never saw a sail on the horizon. I supposed (rightly) that our arrival had put a stop to that. But what if something happened to our boat on the way to Mahé? No one knew Mark was coming. No one would look for him. I could not look for him. What if something happened to one of the children? We had certainly thought about this before, as a risk we had to be prepared to take, but in the absence of Mark and the little boat, it seemed much more alarming. If anything did befall them, we could do nothing about it until our boat came back; we might sail the pirogue to D'Arros, which has laborers and a manager, twenty miles to the south—but they had no contact with Mahé either. Or failing that (I was really in the dumps), we might just sit here until some boat chanced by or one was finally sent to find out what *had* happened to us. When would anyone in Mahé get around to that? Six months? Nine?

And what would we do for food? I might think it romantic to live off coconuts, fish, pork, and fowl and think I was doing well too, but I was under no illusions about the laborers. No rice? There'd be an insurrection. As if rice were even nourishing, I said crossly to myself. Still, the panic about rice was already on; it was perfectly true: Gappy was pestering me for permission to go to D'Arros to try to get some "in case Mr. Carter does not return."

But as I looked at Gappy saying this, and said offhand, nonchalant things back, like "Mr. Carter is often late" and "Probably the engine is difficult to repair" and "You know how Mahé is for getting anything done" (which even the Seychellois say to each other), I realized that any private depressions I might have must be kept well hidden if not forgotten. To see Gappy panicking was very firming to my own resolve. If I had really thought out how isolated the life would be beforehand, I wouldn't be complaining now. That's the way it was, that's all, and there was nothing to be gained by worrying. And if I felt too muddleheaded to get down to any more drawing or writing, then there was plenty of other work to be done.

I remembered all the sea cucumbers I had collected, at the expense of a sunburned back. These were lying buried in sand, waiting to be attended to. I also had about ten pounds of turtle meat to experiment with, though no salt. Fantastically, the island was out of salt—another reason for Mark's having to go. I would have to find other ways to preserve it. Pemmican? It was so hot, and we had so many flies. Marinade (unsalted turtle meat cubed and dried in the sun, then boiled in rendered turtle oil for storage) I did not know about at the time, and no one told me. Mark, if he found he had to stay on in Mahé, was supposed to send the boat back for the turtles eking out their existence in the big pirogue and the brining pit filled daily with fresh sea water. Another reason to count the days. The men did not care if the turtles lived or died—or rather, they quietly hoped they would die—so I felt obliged to check personally on whether or not the water was changed. Twice I found it had not, and five times I was doubtful, but I was careful to call this to Gappy's attention in a tactful way.

For though I did not think very highly of my sophisticated garden hand's mental prowess, there certainly seemed to be some recalcitrant air to the island. With Mark away, I had time to observe the laborers more closely, to begin to tell one from the other, and to notice whether they were working, or not working, what time they started, where they went, and most of all, how they behaved toward me. I had, really, no official position. I gave no orders, except through Gappy, but I was potentially a dangerous spy for the owner (lessee, in our case, though distinction is academic from the laborers' point of view). They were very guarded. I didn't blame them. Mark and I could not help but be aware that as owners we were doing something not only unorthodox but unpopular and even distasteful in being so very odd as actually to live on the island. It wasn't just that we would probably interfere too much. Living on the islands the Seychellois *grand blanc* (white planter) almost never does, and it is as strange to him as it is to his laboring brother that a white man evidently possessed of money should want to bury himself on one of the outer islands, with no nice house, no parties, no car, no dancing, no films, no ships to watch in the harbor, no invitations to Government House, and no convivial boozing, of which all strata are so fond; further, no electricity, no running water, no flush toilet; a thatched house with sand all around it, no church on Sundays, no priest, no parade of pretty hat and dress—nor any shoes! Our children, in a land where in spite of the climate the number and fineness of their garments is socially a label, proceeded to go around in a pair of small cool pants, and sometimes not even that, while Madame herself (me) was (and still is) never seen in anything but old (comfortable) shorts and shirts. *Mon Dieu!* We made it difficult for them to respect us, and could only hope, we said laughingly, to awe them instead.

As it gradually became clear, however, that I had a reasonable command of the local *créole* (we had already, after all, been three years in the Seychelles), some laborers were quick to take advantage of the unusual situation, By situation, I mean that there existed, simply because we were in residence, two forms of authority on the island—owner's and manager's. Slowly, a very few of the laborers took to dropping around, for a chat ostensibly, but the time of day would always include a request, and the suggestion that they had already been unreasonably refused by Gappy. I bent over backwards not to interfere. But sometimes the request seemed so ordinary that I would drift down to the yard and ask Gappy if such-and-such was true, and immediately get for my pains his side of the affair, so replete with personal refutations and justifications that I had to protest myself perfectly satisfied, even though his reaction made me believe him in the wrong. I read myself no end of lessons, however, on Interfering Women, and reflected that no apparent single injustice, oversight, or omissional sin was worth undermining Authority, and Authority's form was Gappy, not me. But then I would notice the turtle water had not been changed, or that one of the laborers never came to work until nine o'clock, or some other glaring fault, and I would again feel obliged in the interests of the Property to, my version, ask, and Gappy's version, interfere.

Though Gappy was always scrupulously polite. But he would watch me out of sight, or nearly, and often I turned back in time to see him lean toward one of the people he was always to be found near, during the day, like the carpenter, or his wife's nephew, George William, and say something. Was it only my imagination that made me think that something was about me? He was altogether too servile at times, then suddenly he would be fearfully condescending. My attempts at tactful humor he understood not at all, for he had no humor of any kind himself —smiles were for other purposes, and his were now in no way "engaging," as I had thought them in Mahé. He had become oddly domineering. And obviously his sense of importance had grown and flowered in his role of manager of Remire in a way one would have thought impossible on such a small island, with such a small labor force.

But impressions are always subjective. I thought I was probably being unjust. It was his English perhaps: he refused to talk *créole* with me as being below him, or below me, or both of us. One must be fair, I kept telling myself, and give him a chance. After all, for him the whole setup was unusual. There were bound to be strains, and as yet Mark and I did not know enough to manage ourselves the complex-looking system of task (or *journée*) work, free time, rights and duties, and all the nuances of what to pay for what, and what laborer could be made to do what job best, and how often to change him, who got along with whom; this was knowledge we did not and could not yet have.

And even if we had thought we could do without Gappy, both of us had realized—and now I realized it particularly— that in the first year, getting the fishing going, Mark would have to be away a great deal, and that I could not have a labor force suddenly dumped in my lap. I had to get along with Gappy, and that was that. If things were slipshod, or if there was favoritism, or if there were certain people who never pulled their weight and were never disciplined for it—well, that was the way it had to be.

So I resolved to try to stay away from the yard and reserve my impressions for Mark's ear when he returned. But when would that be? I was careful to seem calm and unworried, but not so Gappy. Gappy was up in the air. Soon he was coming every day to the house and asking, "Madame, where *is* Mr. Carter? What is he doing?" And then, "I think, Madame, that he must have had some accident on the way to Mahé. Otherwise, he would have sent the boat back by now, would he not? Perhaps a sudden storm came at sea, you know." I would laugh, feeling

Evening, at anchor

slightly sick, and say, "Oh, nonsense, Gappy, Mr. Carter is all right. There is probably something wrong with the engine that can't be fixed quickly." And tried to believe it myself.

But Gappy was obviously upset. The *commandeur*, or Number Two, was constantly taken off his supervisional work to climb the tallest casuarina tree, and every night a lantern was, with much fuss, hauled up the casuarina directly in line with the anchorage, and in the evening groups of people would line the beach and stare out to sea. The master fisherman's wife went around looking cross and preparing-to-be-widowed, and the concubines were so often in tears no work could be got out of them. Even the carpenter was full of nerves and dreams at night, which he faithfully told me about each day, dreams of dark seas, shipwreck, calls for help. Seychellois take their dreams very seriously. The old woman I had known right away I was not going to like took to dreaming too, and each morning as she grated coconuts for the chickens, she would make lengthy pauses to rub her kidneys (she always complained of backache) and to tell a bunch of eager idlers the latest dream-prophecy.

I could not help but blame Gappy for this chattery despair,

and the consequent slackening off of work—it was hardly worth working if Monsieur was dead, was it?—enraged me so much that I banished my private thoughts and went around being cheerful and encouraging. All of them, I realized, were thoroughly enjoying themselves in an orgy of being Caught Up in some dramatic event (what a story it would make), and Gappy most of all. Under a specious anxiety for the safety of Mr. Carter he was no doubt thinking of the compensation due him for not being able to finish his contract, and no doubt he had put the idea into other's heads as well.

For when the little lugger finally did appear on the horizon, everyone except the carpenter and mason wore a damped expression that could only be described as disappointment.

VIII

THE DROUGHT lasted through October and November, right up through Christmas to New Year's Day, when we had a small shower. Under a portion of bland, cloudless sky we waited and waited, parched, desiccated, everyone on half rations of water from the small reservoir (we had mended the large one, but there had been no rain to fill it), while in the distance and all around us, black clouds could be seen emptying their contents on African Banks, or D'Arros, or into the indifferent sea itself. And it stayed hot, hot, hot, and still. The sun became a physical burden; precious body liquid seeped out constantly. We all greedily drank coconut water; just sweet enough, just cool enough, it is a wonderful restorer of energy but not long-lasting.

By the end of October, the whole island population was on edge. No one could wash many clothes, as the wells were being scraped for cooking water and for the animals; everyone had prickly heat, and work was an unholy effort. It was in this sort of mood that we passed our second and third months on the island, learning the ropes, sorting out the workers and drones, and gradually gathering in the threads of leadership—or so we fancied. If things were "not right," as the broody, restive laborer said, they were at least deceptively quiet.

Mark had returned on the twenty-fifth of October; his delay *had* been trouble in getting the engine fixed. "But the *Veritas* is all right now," he said, and after a day or so for the men to rest he sent her back to Mahé with the turtles that were still alive. The master fisherman had orders to off-load them and return immediately. As when he had gone himself, Mark put only a skeleton crew on the lugger, leaving most of the fishermen behind. We had a good contract for *bêche-de-mer*, and while the gogglers were collecting these flaccid "sea cucumbers" so beloved of the Chinese in soups and stews, the harpooners could spear what turtles they could see from the whaler, thus building up a catch for the lugger's next trip.

The fishing certainly seemed to be starting out well, though Mark was annoyed that some turtles had died. But he was willing to ascribe to bad luck what I suggested to him had an element of negligence, and even I had to admit that the rest of the things on my list were little things: little things here and there that, to me, pointed waveringly at Gappy as the source of the inertia and antagonism I had felt while Mark was away—but nothing definite. And I realized, naturally, that the observance of "little things" is one of those nasty female characteristics that get us into such trouble; but it is also why a woman can run a household, for instance, more efficiently for a given price than a man. A man is satisfied if what he ordered done appears to have been done; he does not want to be bothered with how or, within limits, how much it cost, or who did it.

Mark had left Remire moderately satisfied with the services of Gappy. His eye, on a loftier plane than mine, had seen the future more clearly than the tricky path beneath his feet, and in his tours of the island, Gappy's ready "Yes sir," and intelligent spaniel look had contented him well enough. Mark never expected his orders to be carried out in a day, or a week; slowness is in the nature of things in the proverbially lazy tropics, and though he mentally transformed the island into orchards, new wells, new water catchments, a turtle pound, new houses here, old ones whipped away, new plantations "seen" with a wave of the hand, he certainly did not expect any of it to materialize in one year, or even two or three. He was perfectly prepared to bide his time, especially when there were so many plans being set in motion at once.

But then, neither did he expect to return to the island to find nothing had happened at all.

With him Gappy was always so wonderfully enthusiastic about everything. "Oh, yes sir. What a good idea, sir!" And Mark had to depend on him for all the knowledge he didn't have: the number of coconuts that could be collected in a morning by an average worker; the number of bundles of grass an average woman could bring in for the pigs, and of what size; the number of coconuts a man, or a woman, could take out of the shells for copra-making; the number of building stones that a man could bring in in a morning's work by foot, or by pirogue, depending on whether they had to be broken or just collected, and what size they should be (one-stone size or two-stone size, four-stone size or two-to-one); the number of coconuts a woman could be fairly asked to grate as her morning's work. This knowledge, we reasoned, would enable us to give the labor force what is called taskwork: "Do this," they could be told, "and you're finished for the day, or you can start "overtime" work, which is paid more. The minimum wage for a laborer on the outer islands is Rs.15/- per month,* with free rations for a single man amounting to another 16/- to 18/-. These rations include rice, or rice and flour, or rice and maize, or all three, depending on what is available, sugar, salt, coconut oil for cooking, meat or fish (fresh or salted), and coconuts. Spices, tea, soap, and so on, he must buy for himself. For this wage and rations he must work from six to eleven-thirty in the morning every day except Sunday. In the afternoons he can do overtime work at, usually,

* Since raised. At the time of writing this book, Rs. 4.50 was equal to one American dollar.

double rates, or nothing, as he pleases. Taskwork, though it would mean that everything brought in would have to be counted or measured to make sure the task was complete, at least freed the overseer from trying to oversee everyone all the time between six and eleven-thirty for the men, and six to nine for the women (at Rs. 7.50 per month). It must also, we thought, be bound to result in a better average total of work each month, being a sort of contract for a job completed and therefore more immune to "go slow," female complaints, pleas of small wounds gained *dans bois,* unforeseen accidents, headaches, dizziness, and misinterpretation of orders (an all-time favorite, this last). If we were able to reduce everything to taskwork, we could consider ourselves really organized.

But to do this, of course, we had first to reduce each job to its monetary value to us, relative to the wages plus cost of rations we paid per day. For instance, if a woman was ordered to bring grass to the pigs and we paid her .25 a day, if she brought five packets we would in effect be paying her .05 in cash for each packet, plus another .05 or .06 in the rations her "husband" got because she was there. (Of course we knew we had to give the man extra rations whether or not his woman worked for us, but we were quick to make clear that women who did no work were *personae non gratae* even if there was nothing we could do about it legally; the only way of redressing the balance of the extra amount the woman cost us was to get three hours of work from her a day, and by having her, free a man for the heavier tasks the property required.) Only five packets of grass in three hours did not seem enough, however. What if she brought seven? Yes, that was better. We had to calculate what we would be willing and able to pay for grass per year per pig, taking into account the expected profit per pig and the fact that grass going in one end came out the other as fertilizer, which we needed—and will always need—badly. That part of the grass not eaten would at least get urinated on, defecated on, and trampled: compost. Since a woman was expected to work three hours every morning, we had to judge how long it would take her to bring in seven packets. Was this number reasonable? That is, could an average

worker finish this task comfortably within the allotted time? If
she worked with a will, could she finish it earlier? If so, how
much earlier? A task should be worked out just nicely: to enable
the person to finish it about half an hour early, if she works
efficiently, and so that a really quick worker might be able to
finish as much as an hour ahead of time. She can then go on to
something else as overtime, or "extra," for a quick worker is a
rare gem, and well worth encouraging. If, however, you find that
a slow worker is getting seven packets of grass and finishing half
an hour early, then you may be sure the task is not heavy enough.

In all these calculations there was no substitute for experience,
which we hadn't, except some other person's. Short of relying on
the laborers' say-so for something basic, like the size of rock that
was one-rock and not filler, pebble or maccadam—and they
were interested parties—we had to depend on Gappy.

"Gappy," Mark would begin, "I want this area cleared. The
women can do this sort of work, can't they?"

If Gappy said "Yes," then Mark would say, "But what shall
we give them? What's the usual task?" And Gappy would say,
"It's measured by a stick, Mr. Carter."

"What kind of a stick?"

"A stick ten feet long. You lay this on the ground, and they
must do so many by so many."

"Well," Mark would say, "for this piece here, which is about
eighty feet square—that's eight sticks by eight—how many
mornings' work does that come to for two women?"

"Oh," Gappy would reply, "they should do that in two mornings."

"Two?" Mark asked, a little surprised.

"Oh yes, Mr. Carter. They will say they can't, but we will
make them. It is the task."

Mark would come back to the house pleased. "If it's only going
to take me two days to get that lot cleared," he'd say, "we'd better
start on more of this sort of work—seems worthwhile. We can
at least get some root croops in while we wait for the seedlings
to take."

So the orders would be given the next day, at "roll call" at six.

After our tea and breakfast, Mark and I would go out to see how the work was progressing. Sure enough, there were two women hacking away at the undergrowth. They didn't seem to have got very far, but perhaps they were only being slow with the big-stemmed bushes. Satisfied, Mark would go on to visit other work. The next day the same orders were given, but it would happen that neither of us checked early. Later Mark would go, or I would, or Mark would send Gappy. If it was Mark or I, we would discover immediately that only about half the work had been finished, and that badly. If it was Gappy, however, he would either come to Mark, walking busily, and say, "Those women, Mr. Carter, they don't want to work. Look, Mr. Carter, the little bit they have done!" Or, a variation, he would say they had finished, leaving Mark to go out later and find that the area they had done was by no one's measure eighty feet by eighty feet.

"Oh?" From Gappy, with an air of astonishment. "But those women! I showed them exactly—"

"All right," Mark would say, "let's go out and measure it exactly." Which they'd do.

The next day, after roll call and orders—which Gappy, I had discovered while Mark was away, issued from the small veranda of his house, dressed in a pair of electric-blue and maroon striped pajamas and yawning, his straightish black hair curly and tousled with sleep—the women would report sick, or simply not report at all. This was where I came in. We had made a strict rule that anyone expecting sick leave with pay must come to be examined by me, or, if too sick to rise from bed of pain, to make sure I got the message to come to him, or her; otherwise, no pay for that day. As it was important to have everyone working, however, I made a practice of following up delinquents (these were nearly always the women) by visiting them at their houses. But in reply to my questioning, they would give only the standard responses of *"Mon pas connais"*—"Don't know"—to any query about the work, and *"Mon li corps faire mal"* to questions about what was the matter with them. This could roughly be rendered as "I feel bad all over," and is said with a hand racing around the body, lightly pressing several mysterious aching areas, while the face contorts into a grimace at random intervals.

I would then tell Mark, and we would consider the position. Was it in fact a fair task? We had so many to see to each day that it was impossible to put oneself in the mental position of every worker. And the ladies were certainly not above conniving to get easy work (we had already been caught several times giving tasks that turned out to be ridiculous and therefore "spoilt the market"). Now, while we were establishing precedents, we could not afford to let people get away with walking out on a job; yet at the same time, we not only wished to be fair but realized that we'd never get anywhere if we weren't.

But what puzzled us most was that if the task was too hard why Gappy should have deliberately made it so. What could he get out of it? If anything, it should have been the other way around: he should invent easy tasks to bring the laborers thoroughly to his side, and dupe us, the ignorant foreigners. This was what we expected; this was what all managers did.

We had the same troubles when we tried to give taskwork to the three lazybones—Sopha, George William, and J-J Umane. Mark wanted holes dug for young coconuts. What was the price for a hole in the sand, a hole in hard *pavé*, and for an in-between sort of hole, part sand but with large chunks of *pavé* in it? Gappy named the prices, was told to tell the men, came back to say they weren't interested. Why? "Oh, they are just trying for more money, Mr. Carter." Which we thought very likely, knowing them. So for the time being, Mark made them dig the holes in *journée* work, but they were very slow and tiresome to supervise. Yet if questioned directly about the prices, they just shrugged their shoulders sulkily and wouldn't answer.

Our plan for an efficient island with the laborers working at jobs and rates that pleased both us and them wasn't getting very far. In annoyance, Mark decided to put every able-bodied man on the property, excepting as always Carpenter and Mason —they actually went by these names—onto collecting rocks. We had, by some miracle, come to a working agreement on the price and size of a rock.

IX

WHY WOULDN'T ANY of the laborers do any extra work? If nothing else, one would think they should have been inspired by the fishermen, who were certainly earning good money. To be sure, if it is uncomfortably hot and sticky on land it is ideal fishing weather at sea, but what the fishermen were doing was hard work—by Seychellois standards, anyway. Up at—yawn—six-thirty, half an hour after the first bell (and half an hour after us), wander around, cup of tea, second cup of tea, cook some rice for lunch if it is an all-day trip; then wander down to the beach and squat there, while others gradually assemble. Payet, meanwhile (as master fisherman), and Berley have got the sail from the boathouse, the diesel and oil ready, the water tank filled. (Berley and Payet have Mrs. Payet to cook for them.)

With everyone arrived, someone wades out to the pirogue, slips its moorings, and brings it ashore. Sail, men, little bags, bait—the gogglers with their masks and flippers always last—file in, and they row to the lugger. By seven-thirty or so, we can usually hear her motor being started, see the sail hoisted, and watch her go off, the pirogue swishing along in her wake.

Sail up and Berley at the wheel is the signal for everyone else on board except Payet to go to sleep again, leaning on their lumpy bags or a coil of anchor rope and pulling their caps over their eyes. The fishermen, especially the gogglers, are the island's gay blades, and so tend to be rather tired in the mornings. Once they get to the fishing grounds, though, they put in some real work. Near the selected reef, the gogglers are dropped off in the pirogue, in which one of them will stay to paddle and keep near the others, collecting their handfuls of *bêche-de-mer,* some ginger-brown with white markings, some a brilliant orange, some golden, some (the best because they shrink the least in the drying) looking like black velvet with warts. The orange ones are the worst; great big beautiful creatures in the sea, at least eighteen inches long, they shrink to three minus their guts and ready for shipping—not worth the trouble it is to collect them. All of the holothurians are surprisingly heavy even in the water, and lifted out of it into a boat, like gooey lead.

Meanwhile, Berley, Payet, and the other line fishermen have taken the *Veritas* off to some favored bank, over which they will drift, bottom-fishing. On the way, Berley's lines, which are out over the stern, may or may not have caught a kingfish or a bonito, but no one worries. Trolling is never taken seriously. It's bottom-fishing that is to them the real art: how much lead, how far to drop it, the type of day (cloudy or fair), the amount of trace, the feel of the current, or a bite, or the different bites of the different fish. A large grouper must be hooked before he can back into his hole, there to swell himself immovably. A snapper is greedy, easy prey. He takes the bait with a rush and swallows it whole, then tries to pull down toward the bottom. Small rockfish, like the bare faces, nibble undecided at the bait, but they will often make up their minds in a hurry if they see it being withdrawn. The great art is to know when to withdraw it.

Other popular fish are members of the *Caranx* genus. The men will always stop and cast their lines if they see a shoal of them. Caranx are subsurface feeders—one needs only a spot of lead on the lines, just enough to carry them away from the boat. When a caranx takes the hook, and feels himself no longer free-swimming, he will lie broadside to the line, and because he is a deep flat fish, this gives him enormous leverage. Hauling a big one through the water is like hauling in a tabletop.

If the fishermen are in to a good place they fish on and on, paying little attention to time and none to food. But once they decide to stop, they stop. Lines may be left out to fish for themselves, but their owners squat, their plates piled high with rice and curry. And only when they have eaten will they drink their water: the first cup, to wash out the mouth, spat overboard, the second mugful down in one gulp, and then a third. Ritual finished, they discuss whether or not it is time to pick up the gogglers. Payet looks at the sun. They all take out tobacco and roll a cigarette. Silence. The waves slap the side of the boat as she gently drifts along. When the cigarette in Payet's mouth has become almost, but not quite, a butt, he will get up, stretch, and nod to Berley. Berley steps into the engine hatch, gives the motor a turn or two. Payet at the wheel looks around to make sure the lines are all in, then shifts out of neutral. Berley eases himself aft and slowly baits and sets his trolling lines again, leaving in them the small loop that will tell him of a strike.

The gogglers hear the engine a long way off, and by the time the lugger gets up to them, are ready and waiting in the pirogue: they haven't yet eaten.

On shore we usually hear the engine by about three in the afternoon. Weighing the catch, cleaning the *bêche-de-mer* of their lengthy intestinal tracts, salting the fish, occupies what is left of the afternoon; by five-thirty or six they can all turn up for their evening toddy except the man tending the smoking-and-drying fire of coconut husk under the by now rapidly shrinking little bodies of the *bêche-de-mer*. Only when they have been given a good start—the actual drying takes several days—can they be covered and left for the night.

Turtle-harpooning does not fall into this relaxed pattern. Turtles have to be searched for, usually in the *Veritas* because she can cover more territory. When one is spotted, Payet or Berely maneuvers the boat between the turtle and the open sea, herding it along the reef but not crowding it so much that it will dive. If it does, it will come up again in five minutes, but it may come up to seaward of the boat: a chance one has to take. If turtles were at all clever, they would do this intentionally, of course. While the hunt is on, the harpooner stands ready in the bows, his long-shafted harpoon in one hand, the line attached to the head in the other. The head of the turtle harpoon is unusual; not at all the barbed, pointed affair used against sharks and, in the old days, whales (we never see whales now, but there used to be a fishery for them based in Mahé). The turtle harpoon head has two round flanges—the first faired in to the penetrating point; the second, a simple collar that stops the point from penetrating farther. The flange at the base of the point keeps the

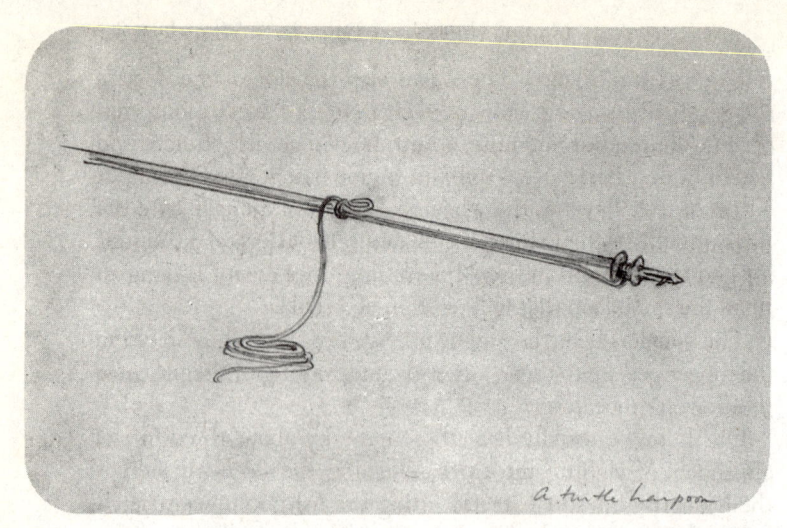

A turtle harpoon

head from pulling out. The turtle, harpooned from above, will thus be caught by the shell, the elasticity of which will admit the point but will then close around the small cylinder between the two flanges. In this way, the turtle can be hauled into the boat but remains quite uninjured except for the small hole in one of his plates which has to be cut to get back the harpoon head.

If it's a good turtling day (calm clear water, good visibility, several turtles sighted) an old empty oil drum will sometimes be attached to the line holding the first turtle harpooned, to act as a buoy the turtle can neither drag under nor get away from; the boat can then go after another. Or rather, the men will do this if Mark is with them. The Seychellois are noticeably more of the bird-in-the-hand school than Mark is.

During these first months, however, he did not often go out on the day trips, preferring to see to the property instead, but he did get in a three-day trip to St. Joseph in November; for mother-of-pearl shell and shark. The St. Joseph atoll, twenty-three miles from us, is a lovely long, thin loop of land enclosing a large shallow lagoon whose entrances are lined with mother-of-pearl shell buried under the sand. To gather them, the fishermen wade at low tide, little more than ankle-deep, feeling for the exposed lips of the shells with their feet. Since the fine lips are sharp as razors, this technique is strictly not for European soles, which, after a few agonized steps, are crisscrossed with burning slashes, but the men seem quite impervious. They feel a sort of tickle, I suppose, which they recognize, and bend down, scratch away the sand from around the vertically poised shell, and with a quick twist, pull the beard away from its sand-hold.

The tide coming in, bringing all the baby sharks with it (and it is very alarming to the novice to find oneself cut off from the boat by a wriggling herd of young shark, even if they are only a foot or so long and seemingly not interested in human leg meat), is the signal to give up shelling and return to the boat to rest up. A low tide in the morning is best because then one has time for lunch and a long nap, rocking gently at anchor before motoring over to an offshore bank for a night of fishing for the lagoon feeders' parents.

At about four-thirty the engine is started, the anchor pulled up, and the lugger chugs off to the chosen bank—chosen during an afternoon's desultory conversation on the wind, the likely wind, the swell or choppiness, the time of the year, and the strength of the current. To catch the really large shark, the head fisherman must plan to have the lugger just drifting gently along the edge of a bank, the *bordage,* by nine-thirty or ten at night. In this cool time, the deepwater shark rise with the upwelling currents of the *bordage* to keep their positively Spanish dining hours: not so much as an olive before nine, then the big feed between ten and one or two in the morning. There is, however, an earlier dining hour for the young—those averaging four or five feet in length—between five-thirty or six and seven, and it would be a pity to miss this.

But first to catch the bait. About fifteen or twenty decent-sized rockfish will be needed to start off with; after that the hooks can be baited with shark intestines or hunks of head. So the boat is anchored on the bank as for ordinary fishing, and the men start hand-lining. The first few fish will be cut up into quite

A shark receiving the *coup-de-grâce*

small pieces, to bait the hand lines; when each man has enough bait, plus a fish for dinner, the rest of the catch is cut into shark-sized mouthfuls and put in buckets in readiness for the night. Five-thirty sees the boat drifting over the bank, the shark hooks dangling just off the bottom. Suddenly first one man will get a strike, then another, and another. On both sides small shark are being hauled up to the gunwale, billied on the nose, dragged inboard, unhooked, thrown slithering into the scuppers. After the sun sets, the run slows down, and then ceases. The men busy themselves sloshing buckets of water over the deck to get rid of the slime and blood before nightfall, then set to work gutting, scoring, salting, stacking the shark while the fisherman detailed as cook lights the deck-side fire with some diesel oil, fuels it up with kindling and coconut shells brought from the island, puts on the blackened rice pot, and squats, fanning the flames now showing up bright yellow against the darkening sky. Berley, meanwhile, has started the engine, and Payet heads the boat back in over the bank for the later drift along its edge.

For this, more serious lines are prepared. Some have great broken-off pieces of crankshaft, or of the flywheels of old engines, broken ax heads, pieces of iron bar—anything heavy festooned along the rope above the chain so that the hook will drift deep down in the black water. Others will be weighted for medium depths—say, four to six fathoms (twenty-four to thirty-six feet)—while the heavier lines lie at ten to fifteen fathoms. Unless, of course, the big shark chose to come right up to the surface, snapping at their caught mates' entrails; then the men just throw the hooks over any way they come—baited, unbaited, weighted or not.

But these routs don't occur often. As much as an hour can pass with the men lying sprawled on ropes or sacking, their lines, before going over the side, passed between their toes to give the sleeper news of a take. The kerosene lantern on the wheelhouse roof flickers and glimmers, the glass chimney blackened with soot; Gros George (cook) has forgotten the kerosene again and the lamp is filled with diesel. Mark, his personal lantern by his side, squints at his detective story or science fiction. Then Berley stirs, leaps for the gunwale, starts hauling in. I don't know why, but the first bite of the evening and the first bite after a lull are nearly always on Berley's line. If it's a big one, another man will lash down his own line and help haul. A shark of fifteen hundred pounds or so will require three men and a fourth to see it over the side; some have to be roped around the tail and cut in half in the water before they can be taken inboard. Only stunned by the blows on its nose, a big shark is treated very warily until the knife thrusts into the gills and along the spine have made it limp and thoroughly dead.

With luck, two or three days and nights will fill the bow

peak with slowly rotting mother-of-pearl shell and the hold with the ammonia fumes produced by kenching shark bodies. Both odors are penetrating, and there is no escape from them except overboard. Payet queries Mark; nothing loath, they start for home. Fishing trips, if Mark is on board, tend to be longer than if just the fishermen are out, but a full hold is as good a reason as any to return to land; and besides, what the men have forgotten or run out of or not taken any at all of must be balanced by how much more money they think they will earn if they stay. When Mark goes he always takes an extra box of food, which he calls "cuddy rations" and hides aft in the little cabin so that they can stay out longer if he wishes, but when the men go out by themselves it is no use to give them extra rations: everybody just eats more and comes back because of *courants forts*—strong currents—the standard excuse.

Still, even unarduous as our fishing may sound by Atlantic, even by Mediterranean, standards, the fishermen were doing well, and the piled sacks of cleaned shell and dried deep-amber-colored shark were mounting up along with the number of turtle swimming moodily in their temporary containers, and the lumpy sacks of *bêche-de-mer*. By mid-November, the *Veritas* was again sent off to Mahé with the usual orders to make a quick turnaround.

X

BY NOVEMBER we had at last worked out the prices of the ordinary jobs, more or less by trying to make our estimated fair price agree with what we were willing and able to pay. To arrive at these figures, we calculated what the cost of the job might be in Mahé, then deducted certain rather small vague amounts we felt due us for having to quarter the laborers, repair the houses (frequently, because of the carelessness of the occupants), provide free fuel for their fires, reservoirs large enough for their drinking water as well as ours to be collected, and wells enough for them to be able to do their washing. We were also expected to transport them, their girl friends, their personal effects, presents from their families in Mahé, and all the things they could reasonably expect us to keep in the shop to and (except for the last) from the island free of charge, but we did not feel that any of these costs—one of the largest items in our budget—could reasonably be transferred to them. Having to pay for shipping was inherent in leasing or owning an island away from Mahé. In some compassion for an island owner's high transport costs, the law allows a ten-percent profit to be charged in an island shop; if the goods can be got at slightly reduced retail prices by buying by the gross or the hundred pounds or the dozen, then the added ten percent does approximately cover the cost of bringing the extra items to the island. What it does not cover is the bulky items like rice and sugar, which the labor gets as rations no matter what their price in Mahé, and which take up most of the cargo space on a schooner anyway.

Even so, you will say, labor sounds dirt cheap. Well, it is. But look at its quality. And then look at its character; moral, that is. One would have to be blind not to see that a Seychellois of the laboring class is simply not brought up to believe that A Job Well Done Is—not "Its Own Reward"; no one asks that these days—Well Paid. One or two good responsible laborers, Mark and I reasoned, would not only cut down on hidden labor costs already mentioned (by the simple fact that there would be only two of them) but would also save hours and hours of that most precious commodity, time. If they were just to do a job well for good pay and still stole from us, at least there would be only two of them to do the stealing, instead of thirty or forty, counting the children; children, for some reason, are particularly heavy finders-keepers of eggs and expensive copper nails.

Time: the time it takes the manager or his deputy, the *commandeur*, to check on the job that a man or a woman is paid to do but hasn't completed satisfactorily; he or she will either cheat on the quality or the quantity, or steal a part of that item he has the golden opportunity of legitimately fingering, or, if nothing else offers, let the how of the job so slip his mind that some totally maverick variation is introduced which puzzles everyone, and wastes hours.

Time, oh time! Every day each task of bundles of grass must be counted to see if there is the right number, checked for correct size, and opened to see that it contains the right kind of grass all the way through, and doesn't have some inedible bushier kind stuck in the middle. Each rock brought in has to be counted, checked for size or made up for by another larger one, and certified as the correct type of rock—not *pavé* instead of beach sandstone or coral, for instance. The filling of each measuring tin of lime right to the top has to be watched with a keen eye, and the tin itself examined for a large convenient hole in the bottom or an inch or two mysteriously missing from its full height ("because it was rusty"). That each coconut has to be counted goes without saying, and counting those that are issued for animal food or copra is obviously necessary as well. But each husk used for firing the calorifier (to dry the coconut) has to be counted too: the laborer has to be given a "task" of so many husks, not just the order "Bring enough." Each leaf for thatching has to go through the same process, so that the laborer can be told to replace unusable ones, some of which he has probably carried from the other side of the island—but why didn't *he* look at them? Each pig trough has to be filled with water each morning, and each pen swept and sluiced out with water; one or another of us nearly always found that one pen had been missed, so that the man in charge must be called back and told about it. If someone is put on to clearing work, there is always a part of the allotted area ignored or missed; if a group of women are weeding, one will go absent-minded and uproot a whole clump of the wrong stuff before she remembers—if she remembers. Or all of them will start enthusiastically weeding the right thing from the right starting point, but in the wrong direction. And if anyone is allowed near fish, fresh, wet-salted, or dry—well, it goes without saying that fish has to be counted before and after each stage it passes through. Fish is—no, I will come to what fish is in due course.

Fish isn't the end of the list of things that have to be checked on a property every day, not by any means, and Mark and I were beginning to realize that if we were not living on the island but stayed in Mahé where we "belonged," very little of this checking would be done. Gappy seemed to be willing enough most of the time, but somehow bad at it, or forgetful, or he himself misunderstood, or he would introduce his own variations. And this with both of us breathing down his neck! An owner who lived in Mahé, we saw, was not delegating his responsibilities to an agent—he was abrogating them altogether.

One would suppose, of course, that it is in a manager's interest to look after his employer's interests, to see that money is paid only for work completed more correctly than less and that stealing is at least kept to a tolerable level, because to be a good manager in this sense should increase his own value in his employer's eyes. But I regret to say that this is not the case. Managers have very little value in their employers' eyes, judging by the salaries they are given. And their answer to this has always been to live on the "perks," or perquisites, of their position. Even so, one would suppose that a local manager, having the advantage of living right in the middle of the hub of island activity, the yard, and being the intermediary between the laborers and the source of money would in general do a better job of management than the owner could. The manager should be up on all the vices, personal relationships, and past histories of the people employed on the island, and therefore should have some idea of what they will be up to next—in such tight quarters something is almost always brewing.

But in fact, what usually happens is that he is poor at discipline through being too closely connected, but good at getting his rake-off. The wise laborer will see to this as part of the vital, to him, developing of good relationships with the manager; a timid manager will find perks come to him even should he not lift a finger. The manager is, after all, the person who decides a laborer's pay every month by determining what "overtime" and "extra" is due him, and who also has the power to put him in the jail for a short time, or fine him up to ten rupees (all managers are Peace Officers).

Discipline of labor on the outer islands is therefore not usually the major issue that we had imagined, for a manager generally exerts only enough of it to produce the copra that keeps the owner happy, and sufficient salted fish, pigs, and poultry to make shipping them worthwhile. Eggs, for instance, are more or less considered a manager's perk; there is no way of preserving them used, so that as long as the manager and laborers do not between them eat so many that natural restocking is prevented, there is no check whatever on the number taken. Managers and laborers soon find ways of dividing the spoils which the owner does not demand and, indeed, often knows nothing about: the melons, pumpkins, papaya, vegetables, and fruits are consumed locally, and even the owner's fish is given out liberally in the interests, again, of good relations; the owner has of course to take the manager's say-so on how much fish has actually landed.

It really leaves only one thing that a Seychellois manager is lively on: the copra production. Coconuts to a Seychellois are *sérieux*—serious—not a joking matter. Coconuts are money. A planter's coconuts are to him the rent, and the food, and the whiskey. Coconuts are clothes, a car, and a little bit of *dolce vita* when the price is right. A planter will spend a lot of time trying to catch someone stealing his coconuts, when the theft of something with more intrinsic value goes all but unnoticed. It would not pay a manager to produce significantly less copra than an owner judges he should, knowing the number and condition of the trees at his disposal. He would lose his job. In fact, this is about the only way he would lose it. From what Mark and I have seen on other outer islands, a great deal of funny business will be tolerated for the sale of adequate returns in copra.

We are, and were, far from sneering at coconuts. Coconuts may be the lowest-yielding crop per acre known to tropical agriculture, but in relation to soil conditions, labor conditions, and therefore to actual cost of production, the return on the investment of planting one coconut palm is not at all bad. If the average is taken over twenty-five years, we have worked it out at about seven-percent return on capital invested. That is, for the first four years you get nothing, but after that returns remain fairly steady—bar droughts or *Melittoma* beetle or rhinoceros-beetle plagues—for the next twenty-five to fifty years with remarkably little output in labor of a difficult or demanding sort. Basically, a plantation in good heart requires only that the butts be collected off the ground, for which the ground must be kept clear enough to see them, and then husked, pried out of their shells, and dried: copra. The drying is done either in the sun or, more usually, in a calorifier, a long building with layers of wire racks on each side and a furnace pipe made up of old forty-four-gallon drums cemented together up the center. (The fire is stoked from the outside with a long stick.) The calorifier represents a certain capital investment, naturally, like the land and planting the palms, but it is a long-lasting and cheap way of evaporating the water from the coconut meat and takes no skill to operate. Coconuts, therefore, may not make you wealthy, still you don't really have to work for what you get.

There are certain key phrases in that last paragraph, though, which could not be applied to the little island of Remire. First, it is a very little island. Then the plantation was not in good heart. And many of the trees were already fifty years old when we got here. Could we ever consider copra as even a secondary source of income?

Nor, on the other hand, could the fishing be expected to carry the island. We could not afford to tolerate a lot of funny business—even with the best will in the world copra could not pay us to. We had to tighten up, the perk system could not continue: for while we did not then know all its categories, we were able to observe many, and Ahmed told us some. Besides, as soon as we began to know them—knowing them was inevitable on such a small island, in spite of the barriers of Gappy—the laborers themselves told us by their mood when we had gone against the grain by usurping one of their rights of the good old days.

XI

WE HADN'T GOT OVER any hurdles when we put all the men on to rock collecting—we had only acquired a not-too-costly breathing space to think about what was wrong and how to right it—so I can hardly say that the question of the Master's fish was the next hurdle. But it was certainly on the verge of a cause célèbre, with so many ramifications that I hardly know where to begin to explain them.

I should first explain that while the *Veritas* was away, Mark decided to concentrate all his fishing efforts on collecting *bêche-de-mer* near Grand Brisant; we had been offered a good price for them, and the quiet weather was ideal for the work. Consequently, only the small whaler went out every morning to deliver the gogglers to the reef and then keep pace with them while they dived. Of course, the gogglers took along their spear guns, and the boatmen were able to hand-line a little during slack tide, but by and large Mark's decision meant that the boat came back every afternoon filled to the seat tops with inedible matter but bringing only enough *bouillon* (as the Seychellois call the protein for a meal) for the fishermen themselves. Fishing for rations was done on Saturday, ration day, and the fishermen didn't waste more time at it than they had to, since Mark paid them on what they produced, in weight, or the required product. There was nothing left over. The pigs became vegetarians, and no fish lay drying on the racks.

After a week of this we began to notice that far from being anxious to earn more money through any sort of extra work, even rock collecting, all the men on the island suddenly became enthusiastic fishermen—not for one afternoon, but every afternoon. Work, confined to the morning hours, came almost to a standstill, but there was no way to force the men to do overtime. Realizing this, Mark thought that at least he might as well profit from their fishing; he offered to pay so much a pound for anything they cared to sell him. But there were no sales.

The pirogue, however, was in constant use. It gradually occurred to us that although Gappy always seemed to be plentifully supplied with fish on the pirogue's return, we, unless one of us was actually on the beach at the time, would get perhaps one or two small ones, or if the pirogue came in after dusk, none at all. Here I should explain that the men were obliged by custom to ask for the loan of the property boat, and all island owners or leasees are equally obliged to lend it—in return for a share of the catch. But the men were asking Gappy's permission, which was technically within their rights, and not Mark's, and Gappy never "thought" to pass the request on. Thus it often came about that we did not even know the pirogue was out, and only later would see Mrs. Gappy happily descaling behind her kitchen several large and toothsome fish, quite by chance, as one of us was passing to look at the pigs.

We then began to notice that the *farfars,* the fish-drying racks, were begining to fill up with fish whose tails remained undocked (all property fish had the finny parts of their tails cut off as a mark of identification). And on the beaches, behind the labor lines, there were rows of gunnysacks—ours, we had no doubt—with fish drying on them, which would disappear from time to time and reappear with wetter, fresher fish on them. And if some repair to one of the houses made it necessary for Mark to have a look inside, he'd see large, imposing gunny-wrapped bundles hanging from the rafters. And I, passing a kitchen, often saw the same propped high over the fireplace, where the smoke kept it dry and bugless.

Three years in the Seychelles had certainly taught us that (the government's rather stingy attitude toward its fisheries officer notwithstanding) fish to the Seychellois is a matter of importance second only to the coconut. It is the staple protein food of rich and poor alike. Fish, too, is *sérieux.* It is also cheap, partly because the fisherman selling fish does not need to depend on a middleman to do it for him (he can hire a stall in the bazaar himself, or sell it on the beach where he lands, or on the roadside) and partly because the Church brings heavy fire on anything that would raise the price of fish commensurate with the rising cost of living—like a thriving export trade in fish, or a fishing industry, which would necessarily have to be so based. The low market price, however, also removes the lure of economic gain from the actual or would-be fisherman, and this has resulted in fewer fishermen catching fewer fish, while the population goes on climbing.

A plentiful supply of fish in one's belly is therefore a dream of every Seychellois, and the fulfillment of this wish is one of the great incentives to *faire les îles* (to work on the outer islands). On the islands, as I have said, custom decrees that every man who has finished his day's work can ask for and expect to receive on loan a property boat, maintained at the owner's expense. The only stipulation, also by custom, is that a quarter of the catch shall be at the disposal of the property. Managers uniformly take this to mean the manager's share for his own personal use. And this plentiful supply of free fish is one of *their* incentives to come to the outer islands; after all, they don't even have to spend their own time catching it. For this reason, all managers are—one wouldn't wish to exaggerate—quite as keen for the men to go fishing in the afternoons as to earn more money by doing overtime for the property, by which they have nothing personally to gain. When the weather is quiet and the pirogue is out every day, managers can stack up an incredible surplus, which they can salt and send back to family or friends in Mahé. And the laborers follow suit with the rest of the catch.

The only chump who gets left out of this paradise is the owner or lessee. The man who pays the wages. The man who pays the wages of the man who has to repair the boat—pirogues are leaking patchwork quilts always in need of caulking cotton, copper sheet, *blanc d'espagne,* linseed oil, blacking, copper tacks, and wood, wood which has to be bought in Mahé and transported to the island or sawn on the island at cost in labor, and which, like all the other materials and labor the maintenance of a boat requires, must be paid for in hard cash. Oars too. Can't

A pirogue—a leaking patchwork of nails,
felt, oakum and copper sheet

have a boat without oars. But the oars are always left in the pirogue since who could imagine taking the trouble of bringing them into the boathouse each evening? Then it rains, or a bit of night wind results in shipped water. The last user of the pirogue never thinks to bail it, and no one else will because he didn't use it last, and the manager forgets, too—out float the oars. A new pair is needed. Who pays? Or the oars are used to roll the pirogue up the beach (when this is bothered with); then half buried in the sand, they are promptly forgotten and the tide takes them away. Who pays? It's not even as though oars make very suitable rollers; their diameter is not nearly large enough. But it's so much trouble to go to get the logs kept in the boathouse especially for this purpose. Unless they've been lost too.

To add to the financial burden this fishing vacation costs the owner/lessee, a manager and every laborer can and do expect that any vessel calling at the island will take whatever personal cargo they wish to put on board her for free transport to Mahé.

Since the owner is rarely if ever on board, all this is accepted as customary by the captain, who knows quite well that he will be supplied with free chickens or turkeys or pigs off the island in return for his kind favor. Quite naturally, the owner cannot, in Mahé, keep track of how much livestock he has at any one time. It would be hard enough even if he lived on the island, for birds are always escaping to lay eggs *dans bois,* sows lie on their newborn piglets, and other natural hazards may overcome the young of all species later (rats, drowning, congenital weaknesses, et cetera). So how could he prove any were "missing"? The most he can hope for, having had the expense of rearing them, is that he will eventually get his share, which is whatever a manager thinks suitable at the time a boat calls. If by estimating the probable increases over a given length of time the owner thinks the livestock production incredibly small, he faces the decision of whether or not to fire the manager, taking into consideration (1) the copra tonnage the manager produces and (2) the fact that another man might be worse in some different way. I have never heard of a manager being fired for not producing sufficient pigs or poultry—or dried fish either, for that matter.

Because even though fish is serious, as we are all agreed, the actual quantity, dried, that the owner is able to export from his island depends entirely on his manager's pleasure.

It is not enough, apparently, that everyone gets a free share of the fish brought in except the man who pays the expenses. The insidious piscine mentality common to all classes actually blinds the owner into conceding that when fish is needed for rations (don't forget the labor force is due a ration of fish or meat once a week in quantities carefully specified by law), the manager can and should send the men out in "property time" to fish—for the property. And since all their catch will be the possession of the property, they are not required to use their own fishing equipment but are issued hooks and lines from the shop. Three pleasant things subsequently happen. First, when the fish is brought in, everyone gets a liberal share: there's plenty of it, and the owner's far away, so how should be ever know how much is caught? Secondly, the manager gets a lot: he also is due rations, but the fishermen are so in the habit of his getting a quarter that he gets this plus rations. Of course, in return, he judges carefully the amount of fish there is and sees that no one is skimped, because he wants to be a popular little fellow. Thirdly, the hooks will naturally have all been "lost," but the line—well, first of all it will have to be dried. Cotton line cannot be put away wet. The manager does not want the bother of this, so he tells the fishermen to do it. By the time it is dry, perhaps everyone will begin to think of next Saturday, so it would be a lot of bother to reissue it all over again . . . in the end, hooks and line are appropriated by the man who used them. Because they have come out of the shop, however, they must be accounted for, but this presents no difficulty. They are marked down by the manager as "issued"—not to whom, but simply "For Property Use." So that when it comes time for any given laborer to leave, who can prove that once long ago he was issued one, two, or three hanks of line and will he please fork over now? And since everyone in Mahé uses the same type of cotton line, all bought in Victoria, who can prove that the line the laborer carries back on board the boat wasn't his originally? Any query of it certainly always produces the answer: "I descended with." Period, full stop.

We could see that we were really up against something when we began to meddle with "this fish business." We wanted a happy island. Everyone wants a happy island; otherwise, nothing gets done. "Go slow" and ill will are very tiring to live with, and must be circumvented. Fish, plenty of it, was one of the ways. Fish, as the Seychellois say, *"donne courage di moune"* (gives people courage—makes them strong and happy). Far from us not to realize the importance of fish, but it was very stupid of Gappy not to see that we got at least a share. Very stupid indeed.

It did not take us long to discover the basic system, mostly by observation—just "being" by chance on the beach when the pirogue came in—but we also locked up the salt. No one had ever locked up the salt on Remire before! Another perk for the manager and men alike. Salt melts, you see, and as long as some salted products find their way into the owner's hands in Mahé, and as long as the consumption does not become astronomical, how can he check on what it should have been? Yet salt is not cheap in Mahé, all of it being imported from the salt pans of Aden. By locking the salt up and offering it for sale in the shop, we made it hard for anyone who had borrowed the pirogue to keep us in ignorance of how much fish he had caught. We never demanded even a small fish from laborers on bad-luck days, but when one of them would come into the shop and buy five pounds or so of salt, I would alert Mark, and the pirogue would be impounded for a week.

It was a severe measure, this last, and hard on the innocent. But effective.

I am, however, ahead of myself: I had yet to take over the shop from Gappy.

XII

THE MATTER of the Master's share of the fish was particularly a thorn in my side. Time after time after time Gappy would get three or four fish to our one, if we got any, and even Ahmed often got larger fish. I would see Gappy's fish disappear heavily behind his kitchen, go home, check on what we had, look for Ahmed and find him down on the beach, cutting a hugh snapper in half for salting. "Ours?" I'd ask. "No, mine," Ahmed would reply, and I'd boil. I, in charge of feeding my family and in no position to *buy* anything even had I wanted to! But funnily enough, it hardly seemed to worry Mark. Oh, I was occasionally able to stir him into going down to the beach and scowling at the delinquents, and he observed everything that went on—Mark always does—but he seemed curiously loath to do anything about it.

"It will work itself out eventually," he would say. "I'm saving it up. Don't worry, I have my plans."

Naturally this wafer did not satisfy me, but more than this he would not at first say. Mark really hates telling me any idea of his that isn't fully fledged and out of the nest because he knows that I will helpfully pluck off so many of the weaker feathers that it will be quite unable to fly; therefore, he only reveals to me the ideas he thinks sturdy enough to withstand this virtual decortication—thinking, I suppose, that if the little thing survives, it must be a jolly good all 'round idea. Or conversely, he will sometimes deliberately expose a weakling to see if it either dies of the exposure or if some latent gene will arouse its will to survive—in which case, albeit greatly altered by the experience, it will eventually wing away in the open air. Be this as it may, the idea I finally discovered he was brooding was, to my way of thinking, a very middling sort of bird.

I said before that Mark is casual. This makes him deliciously easy to live with, as there seem to be so few things that really annoy him. His personality is conducive to relaxation, and he is always understanding. Like calls forth like, and I am a better person for being married to him (I think). It is a pleasure to please him because if he is (I think) being unreasonable, I practically always discover that it's something to do with his work that is biting him, and not one of the numerous things I know to be wrong with me, most of which miraculously don't, as I said, annoy him. Therefore I am able to be unself-conscious, reasonably sure that my sympathy will be entirely with him if he wants it, unmarred by the self-doubt and self-castigation that would diminish it, and dull the luster of our—well, love.

This time, however, something was biting *me*, and Mark was choosing to be entirely too easygoing for my taste. When does pleasant amiable casualness degenerate into "do-nothing" until nothing can be done? Mark's idea was, basically, that since fish was so important to everyone, he might well be able to trade a willingness to tread gently on this subject in return for an active cooperation in others.

"You mean, you don't want to put their backs up," I said.

"Yes."

"And they will understand what you are doing and stop fishing and start doing overtime for you because you've shown you're willing to give a little?"

"Well, yes."

"Ha, ha."

Mark looked offended. "What do you mean, exactly, 'ha, ha' in that tone of voice?"

"I mean that in this case, my dearest darlingest, I think you're nuts. What are we supposed to be making our money on? Fish. Who paid for the pirogue? Who pays for repairing it? Who's not even getting a tenth of his share in return? And who *is* getting all the fish? Gappy, Servina, George William, Sopha, and all the other 'boys'; even Ahmed has a stack of fish out there bigger than yours in the store!"

"Come, now. It's not that big. And the boys don't have all that much—"

"Well, they don't each have bales of it in fifty-kilo lots the way you're used to thinking about fish, if that's what you mean, but they're certainly trying to get there. And I don't think they're going to stop just because you're soft with them, either. You're just encouraging them to continue fishing you out of house and home!"

"Hmmm. Well, I'll think about it." And he went off for a walk.

Privately, I was almost sure this was Gappy's doing. Not only did he stand to gain fish by it but—and suddenly it came to me: power. Perhaps not even consciously, he was showing the laborers he was the boss, so indispensable that it was not even necessary to send any fish up to the Big House at all, or only one or two out of his bounteous good nature . . . or perhaps he thought that the lion's share remained his right even though the owner was here to claim it for himself? So far Mr. Carter had done nothing about it, had he? (This was not exactly true: Mark had spoken to him several times—but obviously not strongly enough to get through to Gappy, who could be very dense when it suited him.) Yes, the more I thought, the more it seemed possible Gappy really believed that the property share was his, and that whether or not we got any fish was of no concern to him. Managers always got it.

Meanwhile, I imagined, the poor laborers didn't know what to do. Nor, if they thought in such terms—and I was pretty sure some of them did by then—did they have any inkling which side to play. Gappy was still manager, wasn't he? He still gave the orders each morning. He still did their books. What went on between him and the Big House was—well, what was it? Anything? I don't think they thought about the possibility of our leaving in terms of Gappy ousting us, but could it be true that we would *always* be here? The Master would go off fishing; surely Madame would not stay here then. Besides, English people didn't last. Some of them had been on the island when an Englishman had lived here (actually an Australian), and he hadn't liked it, had had "trouble" which involved some fisticuffs with one of the laborers . . . he'd gone; "they'd" therefore got rid of one Englishman already, as they were pleased to see the affair. And after we left, Gappy would be king again. Could anyone afford to be on the wrong side?

Also, there was always the feeling of "we blacks" to hold them together, ostracizing anyone who came even temporarily to our side as a *maquereau*—a mackerel, a tale bearer, a white man's arse-licker, lowest of the low. In this situation, the few sensible people took refuge in a discreet silence, saying nothing to or about either party. But all the stupid ones were sullen and sulky, and harbored, as far as I could make out, strong feelings of being cheated.

Why? We checked and rechecked our calculations on the prices we were offering for work, and compared them with those Mark remembered from visiting other islands or talking with their owners in Mahé, and finally cross-checked as many as possible with Felix, the carpenter, who when pressed for direct answers could hardly avoid giving them. There seemed to be nothing wrong with our notions of a fair reward, and pressed further, Felix admitted this. Then he was quiet for a moment, pushing the stub of his flat pencil into his hair. I had got him by himself, for once: no hangers-on, and Gappy ostentatiously busy with papers in his house. It was nearing the end of the month.

"What price did you say, Madame, that Monsieur was offering for coconut holes?"

I told him.

"But I am sure I heard Mr. Gappy say—" and he named another, lower range of figures. "But I was probably mistaken," he said quickly, seeing my face.

"Perhaps," I said. "Thank you, Felix." And I went off to find Mark.

This was the clue we had needed.

It seems so obvious now, that Gappy was politely listening to Mark tell him one price for overtime or extra work, then transmitting another, lower price to the men, then returning to Mark with their refusal, which he accomplished by a helpless shrug and turned-down mouth, saying, "These people, Mr. Carter . . ." as though one could expect nothing but such foolishness from worms beneath Mr. Carter's and, by extension, Mr. Gappy's notice. Obvious—and, one would suppose, simple to correct. But we had little contact with the laborers who were being thus controlled; all our attempts were met by such sullen and insolent stares that neither Mark nor I thought we could persist without losing face. Nor could either of us believe that Gappy could get away with such a thing; especially not Mark, who had not had my advantage of seeing Gappy when he was being the Manager unhampered by the owner's presence. To Mark it seemed too childish a trick to be true, and one he could not fathom the long-term purpose of.

I had, however, managed to establish a little more contact than Mark. For one thing, I had been on the island longer, and for another, I had firmly retained the right (usually a manager's because the owner is not there) to dole out medicines. This made a bond with the women particularly, but also let me talk with the men while I treated their sores or cuts. And our children, run-

Afternoon at the camp

ning in the same pack as the carpenter's brood and Gappy's child, were everywhere. I was careful not to try to pry information out of them, but there was really no need, and probably the laborers learned just as much about us and the queer things *we* did. Also, my *créole* was far more fluent and understandable than Mark's (I have the advantage of possessing a natural ear for language, while Mark has to sweat it out by will power).

And I was, at this time, bursting with ideas on what the women could do in their spare time to their profit and ours, and actively canvassed for talents and skills among them that might be put to good use in creating imaginative handicrafts. I regarded the blank wall of their indifference and incomprehension as something they could be bullied or cajoled out of, and was not daunted. I also thought it a brilliant idea that they should band together to work their own communal vegetable garden. I would provide the seeds, they the work . . . and vegetables would spring from the earth in heavenly profusion. Which goes to show how little I knew, then, of the Seychellois character; a character I like and get along with now, by the way, by accepting it as it is and knowing that there is nothing I can do to change it.

I therefore often found myself down at the labor lines—the "camp"—visiting the women in their homes and discussing the garden or trying to find out which one could plait, or weave, or sew well. It took at least six visits and repeated docile *"Oui, Madames"* for them to make clear to me that a communal garden was out of the question. While Mrs. A might be able to make a garden with Mrs. B and C, it was certainly not going to include Mrs. D, who wouldn't work and would only steal everything ready to eat, or just before it was ready to eat and ripen it in the sun, à la Mahé, where each bit of property does not have the fortune to be surrounded by sea, as we were. And Mrs. A was a little doubtful about Mrs. B and Mrs. C because the other day . . . and as for skills in the handwork line, they all stoutly said they hadn't any. One of them, one day, thrust the handkerchief she had been embroidering behind her chair as I neared her house, and I was abashed at last. What could I do? Challenge her?

Yet it was in the course of these visits that occasional nuggets of information would emerge. "But why don't you want to do such and such?" I would persist if I was feeling particularly stubborn. And finally one of them, seeing I really would have to be given some answer other than *"Moi pas connais,"* would come out with "I won't do that for twenty-five cents an hour, it's too hard work."

"But Monsieur never said anything about twenty-five cents an hour! He told Gappy he would give you a contract and that you should tell Gappy what you wanted for the job and a price could be arranged."

"Moi pas connais, Madame." And communications shut down again.

At this point, after some conscience inspection, I enlisted the aid of Ahmed. I had not wanted to do this; his position as a stranger in the land and as our servant was difficult enough without asking him to spy for us as well. He was also sick, or sickly, with bouts of better and bouts of worse, and I had no idea what his trouble was. He kept complaining of aches and pains in the back and his eyes were lusterless. He had no fever, though, and some days would seem so much his usual brash cheerful Arab self that I thought he was only suffering from muscular strain. He had volunteered to dig holes for Mark since no one else would.

On one of his well days I mentioned to him that I thought Gappy was trying to make difficulties and explained how I thought he was doing it. Ahmed laughed and began to talk. I need have had no qualms about asking him to "spy," for the goings-on had been so obvious to him that he thought Mark must surely have some reason of his own for not taking action, yet. Ahmed's thoughts are always Machiavellian, and he was quite ready to attribute a devilish cleverness to Mark—which, under the circumstances, was highly flattering. Naturally I did not wish to undermine this useful version, particularly since Ahmed with the best will in the world could never keep his mouth shut, so I merely said that as Ahmed was more in a position to know the exact details, would he please tell them to me as he heard them. Marcel came in just at this point, but as Ahmed and I were talking Arabic, and I said to him, in Arabic, don't use names, we continued our discussion with impunity.

Any talk with Ahmed involves an immense amount of noise. I don't know why Arabs like to live at the top of their lungs, but enthusiasm of any sort turns up the volume, and this time was no exception. I think Ahmed saw himself in a fair way to render us services so invaluable that—I don't know what he thought, exactly, but he was very excited. I do know that Ahmed is superstitious and believes literally anything he is told; it's possible he was overwhelmed by the valorous and dangerous role of spy amongst people for whom tattling is a grievous offense, and who, as he does, believe quite matter-of-factly in witchcraft. Did he see himself laying down his life for us? Ahmed never believes anything by halves.

In any case, we were very noisy; if someone is shouting at you you have to shout back. Later, up in the house, Mark said, "What on earth was that all about? Ahmed done something terrible with dinner?"

The turtle pound nearly finished

Building the turtle pound

"Oh no," I replied, probably looking a little smug. "Just bits of dirt I thought might interest you." And I framed for him the picture Ahmed and I had pieced together.

Gappy, as I had surmised, had tried his tricks first on Felix. This is why he was always hanging around the carpentry bench. Then, briefly, on Armand, the mason. But Armand is a hard worker and loyal, and was by November busy building the dry stone wall of the turtle pound, which was like the Great Wall to all of us in effort and time; not only was he not inclined to stand around and chat with Gappy, but I suppose Gappy did not care to stand out in the sun all day, trying to talk to Mason either. And when Mason had finished his day's work, he drank his bottle of toddy, wolfed his food, and fell into bed. Felix's loyalty was composed more of innate caution than any real love of us or lack of time; he had no particular reason to join with Gappy, and was certainly not going to become involved in trouble. Felix hates mess. But since Gappy was the only person on the island for Felix to be socially acquainted with, and vice versa, Felix was not going to offend him any more than he would us. Where Mason would probably have told a persistent Gappy to bugger off, Felix Carpenter would just say "Ah" or "Mmmm" and go on quietly planing wood.

So Gappy turned his attention to those already indebted to him for their jobs—Servina and his pretty cheeky wife, Marguerite; and the three boys, Sopha, William, and Umane—to the pig feeder, the coconut collectors and the women. "Don't," he counseled, "do overtime work; they will get you to do it and then not pay you. They don't know anything, and expect you to work for a pittance, and will cheat you of that if they can. Why, last month—don't you remember—you cleaned *bambara* (*bêche-de-mer*)? Did you get anything for it? No. I assure you, I went over the accounts with Monsieur, and when I reminded him of your "extra" he said, 'No, he did it so badly I'm not going to pay him a damn cent!' Now, is that fair? *I* think you did it well and I told him, but Monsieur . . ." And so on. Gappy was always a good talker, and as black Seychellois are predisposed to think they are always being cheated of their dues by white Seychellois (and by extension any white man), his listeners would swallow bait and hook and become more recalcitrant than ever.

If any murmurs did reach them that Gappy was perhaps not always quoting Mark exactly, what credence could they give to that? Who said so? Ahmed. And who was Ahmed? Or I. Or Ahmed's friendly hanger-on, old Marcel. Should anyone wish to be like him? And Gappy was likely to know, wasn't he? He was on their side, wasn't he, against the employer who was trying to cheat them all? I don't know if any of them tried to analyze why he was on their side; if they had, they might have been just as puzzled as we were.

By mid-November there was some example of this "misinterpretation" every day—brought in by Ahmed or by me to be laid like a freshly killed rat at Mark's feet. But Mark, thus nagged by us both to Do Something, began to get more annoyed with me than with Gappy. He never said anything, but I could see him brooding thoughts about Interfering Women, American women in particular. He retreated into his British shell, and from the depths of this impenetrable structure, he finally snapped,

"Gappy is the manager I've hired. One must have someone to run the property while I'm away, and if all this nonsense is true, it should be perfectly possible to sort it out. Someone has got to be up at six to give the morning orders, check on the laborers, count the coconuts, and the lime, and rocks. I can't see you doing that sort of bloody nonsense. We've got to work it out, that's all. And for God's sake, tell Ahmed to shut up."

With which he stumped out of the house.

Mark's words crystallized my thoughts. Did we really have to have Gappy? In three years in the Seychelles had we so fallen under the spell of everyone's having a manager as a matter of course that we thought we couldn't do without him? To me it suddenly became obvious that Gappy was the most dispensable person on the property. Just think. We paid him one hundred rupees a month, and were obliged by law to pay that stupid old bag of his Rs. 12/- for being his "housekeeper." (All managers on the outer islands get their housekeepers paid for because obviously they can't be expected to fend for themselves; if the person he takes to be his cook happens to be his wife, it's his wife that gets paid.) On top of this, we had to give Gappy married rations, but without any hope of getting any work out of her ladyship in return. Oh no. That would be beneath her. All she did all day was to wander around looking for eggs (duck eggs—we had left the ducks loose) from my ducks and stealing them. My eggs. My future ducks. I knew she did this, because the Gappys so often had cake, egg cake. Rory and Ming were sometimes even given a piece.

But eggs—well, I couldn't really prove that my ducks weren't totally and mysteriously barren in spite of the cakes. Eggs were just one more item on the debit side. A larger item by far was the shop. Mark gave Gappy an extra twenty-five rupees a month for looking after it, which—on top of his ordinary salary—was supposed to encourage a manager to be moderately honest in the conducting of shop transactions. Most managers were. It is an aspect of the island more cut and dried than most: what goes in must be accounted for before it goes out again. But I wondered. That fishing line, for instance, that I saw strung up between the palms. And some people never seemed to buy anything. Was it chance that the names each month opposite the minute shop accounts were Servina, William, Sopha and Uname?

The fact is, and I might as well be truthful, Gappy's running of the shop was a matter of personal chagrin to me. I had already determined in Mahé that I was going to run the shop. Run the shop, I thought, and you have your fingers on the pulse of the island. Besides, who brought and paid for the merchandise? Who had to canvass the shops in Mahé to see the order was filled? Whose was the shop? It stood to reason I should run the shop. And it would give me a ready vehicle for getting to know the people. But when the dust of our arrival had settled somewhat and I made the suggestion that I take over, I ran into the blank wall of custom, Gappy, and Mark. And I had to admit, reluctant as I was to see it, that in the matter of prestige, the shop was a very important and importance-making part of the manager's work. Managership is symbolized by a key ring full of keys at one's belt and by the keeping of the books, and apparently any attempt to remove keys or books for any reason lessens its charisma. Of all the keys and books those of the shop were the most prestigious, and Gappy held on to them like glue.

But even more annoying, he made me, whenever I chose to enter the shop, feel surplus to requirement. As I walked in the door all talk would cease, some idlers would evaporate out the door, others stay to watch me, and Gappy himself would bustle out from behind the table with scales in a horribly proprietorial sort of way to attend to my wants. Naturally, faced with this sort of reception, I didn't stay long, and in fact took to sending Ahmed most of the time, which suited Gappy. But I did continue to trouble him on the matter of prices.

One of the justifiable complaints I had had registered with me personally while Mark was away concerned the prices charged for certain goods. Were these true? If they were, they were far over the allowed ten percent. So I asked Gappy if I might have the books and his copies of the requisition orders to check them. I did not say why. But I was quite unable to get my hands on them. Certainly it did not occur to me then that I was asking for one of the symbols of royalty; I merely asked for what I thought we owned. But Gappy very politely put me off from day to day so the books could be "up to date." I was given to understand, since Gappy had so many other things to do, that readying the books might take a little time. Why? I was instantly suspicious, but could prove nothing. And since Mark was gone and I was being so careful of Gappy anyway, I had no choice but to wait.

How did he manage to put me off day after day for three weeks? It sounds silly now. Probably because I had other things to do, even if Gappy's busyness was a mere excuse. The only things Gappy did during the time Mark was off was talk-worry about Mark and deal with the shop. Then when Mark was once more on the island, Gappy was still in and out of the shop all day long—and late the oil lamp burned beside Gappy, bespectacled and frowning in his house, transferring the day's transactions from the little notebook he kept in each laborer's name. As the shop was opened whenever anyone wanted anything, at no matter what hour of the day and no matter what other work Gappy might be overseeing, quite obviously the books could never be really up to date. And writing down a constant flow of small purchases occupied as much of his own time as the shop openings did of Mark's. Even Mark was irritated, and said there should be regular hours, twice a week, but Gappy said, "Oh no, Mr. Carter. They won't buy so much, and the more you sell them, the less money you will have to pay them when they leave."

This was incontestably true; Mark, appealed to in his pocket, let it go on. Nor would it have ever occurred to him that he might well take over the shop himself, with me substituting when he was away; Mark hates paper work, and was quite prepared to believe that the shop involved rather a lot of it.

To me, however, the running of the shop had become more than a desire; it became goal Number One in the end game of the elimination of Gappy. Remove the shop from Gappy, and the way would be clear for a checkmate: Gappy, minus the excuse of the shop, would have to start working, and I did not doubt that he would then be shown up in his true colors. From there, it would be an easy step to get rid of him altogether.

Unfortunately my Anschluss coincided with the end of the month. At the end of each month, Gappy went into retirement in his house and worked exclusively on paper until three days later when he emerged, looking worn with, he said, a migraine, but with an air of triumph over heavy odds as well. This really put Mark off, and he said I was mad to think of taking on all that "clerking," as he called it. I had to admit, didn't I, that Gappy knew all of the laws that had to be complied with in keeping the accounts?

"What laws?" I asked, annoyed. I regarded Gappy's end-of-the-month devotions as a transparent attempt to make Mark believe he was doing hard, terribly important work. This business of "laws" was nonsense. Gappy was so keen on laws he could quite well have made them up. Quoting law gave him standing—for not only did he know The Law, having been a policeman, but on Remire he *was* the law (all managers, as I explained, are automatically made Peace Officers, and Mark, knowing that he would probably be away a lot, had not bothered to change this privilege into his own name). "Laws, phooey," I said.

"Well, I'm sure that all these separate ledgers and notebooks for every last thing wouldn't be kept unless managers were forced to do so," said Mark quietly. "Besides, is it so impossible for you to wait until we do know the ropes? Rush, rush—we've only been on the place ten weeks and you want a revolution? Wait. Let things ride. We'll find out everything we need to know in due course."

"In due course, in due course," I felt like saying, "but at what cost?" Ten weeks felt like forever, with every day adding some new aggravation both annoying and expensive. But I was becoming really angry, so I said no more. Mark's quiet politeness told me I had gone far enough, and unloving thoughts are better left unspoken, in which form it is easier later to cancel or forget them.

It was lucky that I did hold my tongue. Looking back now,

I can see that I was omitting in my calculations one important point: to fire Gappy, we had to have so good a reason that there could be no question of paying him the salary for the ten months left in his contract. Though in my wilder moments I had thought, "anything to be rid of him cheap at the price," the fact is that at that point we did not have Rs. 1,370 in ready cash. Every cent was earmarked months ahead. Mark, of course, had not forgotten; he didn't think to bring it up because to him it was so obvious. He had "plans"—this was his plan—but he was waiting to be presented with The Way. If he did not find one, well, Ahmed and I could go on humming like hornets until we wore ourselves out before he would pay Gappy all that money just for the pleasure of being rid of him. We had to wait and watch.

Thirty days hath November. So it must have been on the twenty-ninth that Gappy went into hiding with the books; December 1 was a Sunday; the laborers would not have to be told their pay totals until Monday. (Another engaging custom was that this was always done in property time; Sunday was out, of course, even had it not been Church Day, and so were afternoons.) It therefore must have been the morning of December 2 that Mark helpfully offered to fill my tin with powdered milk from the bulk supply in the shop; I must have had something on the stove, Gappy was busy with the crowd clustered around his house (no one worked until it was his turn, naturally—nor after: the first one waited until the last had finished and everyone had a splendid morning of zero work all 'round), and Ahmed must have been busy somewhere else. Gratefully, I accepted Mark's offer and he walked off with the white tin under his arm.

Ten minutes later, he was back. "That," he said, "is the last of the milk."

"What?" I said, stupidly.

"It's empty. One hundred ten pounds of milk gone since we got here."

I continued to stare at him. I was sorry about the milk, but glad too. Mostly I was glad it had by chance been Mark and not Ahmed or I who had discovered the huge tin's glaring emptiness. It was so simple, after all! What better excuse could we have ever found?

"We mustn't assume anything," said Mark. "This afternoon we will do a complete stores check with Gappy. It's a good day. No work will be done today anyway. I'll think of some reason. An inventory of supplies so that we can make out our list for the *Marsouin.* That will do nicely."

The *Marsouin,* a motor sailer belonging to a friend in Mahé, was coming down with the extra cement and diesel that Mark had been unable to bring with him, and our Christmas mail. She was due sometime between the tenth and fifteenth of December. If what we believed was true—And how could Gappy hope to account for the absence of all that milk by the two-ounce and four-ounce purchases of the laborers? (Our own consumption I knew: we also had a "shop book," like everyone else; we had to be able to account for goods taken from the shop for our own use.) If it was true, then we would be free of Gappy in a matter of days. Christmas, which I had not been looking forward to particularly, suddenly seemed a fine thing, a season of cheer, with a reason to cheer. Our first Christmas on the island, and now it would be a good one. It was a deliverance.

That afternoon the contents of the shop, from aspirins to writing paper, were exposed to the hot sunlight of the yard, counted, weighed, listed, and put back in now clean cupboards (how I had been itching to *clean* the shop, if nothing else). We dug the sugar out of its barrels, put it in gunnysacks, lugged them to the scales, brought the sugar back to the barrels, and then weighed the gunnies; the same with the rice. The same with the flour, the lentils, the onions, pepper, curry powder, tea, and coffee. Everything else we counted by the tin or the pad, down to envelopes, sewing-machine needles, and fishing hooks. I loved each minute of it until I realized that it wasn't much use our doing all this if Gappy still held on to the books. Mark must get them. Gappy wouldn't—couldn't—put Mark off the way he had me. Besides, it was the end of the month. *Ipso et cetera* they must be up to date. What excuse would he have for not handing them over?

Mark came back with them that evening, and I started to work. Every one-ounce, two-ounce, three-ounce purchase had to be added up for each item, single sheets of paper added until they became a pad, single cigarettes until they became a tin, the way we had bought them. I had covered a fifth foolscap sheet when I thought of one thing I had never been able to get from Gappy: the list of the contents of the shop when he took over from the scoundrel's manager. We must have been mad, I said to Mark, not to have thought of that long ago. *Now* how could we get it out of Gappy without making him suspicious?

"That's quite easy," Mark said. "I'll get that the same way as I got the books. Stand there pleasantly until he gives it to me. But not now. It's far too late. You won't finish that tonight anyway. Let's get some sleep."

But I lay awake and worried.

XIII

TOTALING THE PURCHASES, subtracting these from the amount brought in Mahé, and seeing if I arrived at what was still in the shop took me the better part of five days. Not, I think, because I am so stupid and slow, but because of Gappy's horrible "legal" way of keeping the accounts. It wasn't enough that in writing things down three times he often forgot some part of a person's purchase, or put two ounces in one place and three in another, so that I had to check all three books for the average of a single item. Oh no. It was soon apparent that if three people were living together and bought between them, say, a tin of sweetened condensed milk (which they much preferred to the milk powder even though it was more expensive), a pound of flour, two pounds of sugar, and an ounce of tea, Mr. Gappy would "reason" that it was far too much trouble to write all these things in thirds in each book; so from the rough list he had taken in the shop, he would then transcribe, under each name, and in each individual book, "Purchases" and then the amount. *Commissions,* the *créole* word, was what he used, instead of the English in which everything else was written, so even that confused me. Commissions? Something Gappy had done for the person and was thus getting paid through the shop? When I discovered what it actually was, I nearly gave up. What had the purchases consisted of? On yet another sheet of paper, I sighed, and made a heading: "Anon." It's fortunate, I said to myself, that the Seychellois are so mistrustful one of another that they don't very often "share" purchases; the total amount of money these mystery goods represented wasn't much.

As I added and added long columns the picture of what was missing began to emerge. I could hardly believe Gappy could be stupid enough as to steal *"en gros."* Had he thought we would never check? And some of the missing things he couldn't have wanted: 13 tubes of toothpaste? 15 pads of writing paper? At least, not for his own consumption. We began to realize as we went down through the list of 42 razor blades, 225½ lbs. dried maize, 71⅞ lbs. onions, 85¼ lbs. lentils, 2 tins of Johnson's Baby Powder, 6 flints, 128 lbs. sugar, 26 ounces of tea, 24 ells of white shirting, 345¼ lbs. of rice (we had of course added up all the food given out as rations, but this huge amount was still unaccounted for), 168 Park Drive cigarettes, 213¾ lbs. of flour, 16 pencils, 4 toothbrushes, 123 Pall Mall cigarettes, 5½ lbs. sweets, 287 biscuits, 23¾ ells of navy-blue drill, and so on, down to the 40 lbs. of powdered milk left unaccounted for, that Gappy and his family could not have put away all these things for their personal use. Therefore, he must have forgotten to record them, except for the margarine which Ahmed reported they ate every day (the bright yellow tins lay around his kitchen), and at least some of the powdered milk, which the Gappys drank at the rate of two pounds a week but had rarely bought (until I was running the shop).

When all the accounts were prepared, Mark and I decided we would call Gappy up to the house and ask him to explain them, if he could. He listened, and was silent. Then he turned to Mark and said blandly, "Oh, I see, Mr. Carter. I have lost another job."

We made out the cancellation of contract agreement, and Gappy signed and Mark signed. Gappy said "Good afternoon, Mr. Carter, Mrs. Carter," took up his hat, and left the house.

Mark and I looked at each other. Well!

The most charitable thought was that he was both scatter-brained and stupid; the worst, that he had been "giving" largess for his own purposes. But whatever his reason, it had certainly been expensive. And the outrageous prices he had been charging on some of the luxury goods in no way balanced our losses; they only compounded his guilt in our eyes. Did Gappy think he could make up a deficit this way? That as long as the accounts balanced we would never examine the actual sales? But he hadn't even got the right amount of money; perhaps we had stepped in "too soon" and so upset his calculations. Or perhaps he thought he could embezzle for a year, leave when his contract was up before we got around to checking the stores? It was hard to see what he thought. What was more important was what we should do now. Should we bring a case against him? It took about fifteen seconds to veto that. In Mahé? "Justice" is expensive there. How much more did we want to be out of pocket for the obscure satisfaction of seeing Gappy in jail? We would have to go back to Mahé, appear in court at two or three or four widely separated intervals; meanwhile, nothing would get done on the island . . . nor, in fact, could both of us leave together without a manager to run things. So we had no real choice. We would be satisfied to get rid of him in a few days; let him steal from somebody else. But at least we would not give him good references, the way the others had;

references could be meaningless, we had realized, when the writer is in constant fear of being sued for libel. (In Mahé it costs a poor man nothing to bring a civil case; a lawyer will take it "on spec" in return for half the money his client will get if he wins. If the case is lost—well, it doesn't matter. The client can't pay, it will be proved, so costs are awarded, according to the inscrutable *Code Napoléon,* to the winner. A case of lawyer take all.) We had thought Gappy "looked" honest enough that his compatriots could probably be believed; now we not only knew better, but we knew better than to say anything as well.

The word that Mark had "accepted Gappy's resignation" spread quickly, and as if the floodgates had opened, sudden torrents of information against him poured in. The laborers at last knew who would stay and who would go. Gappy became such a villain that no one had ever known worse. He had been fired from the police force for stealing the chief of police's spectacles. He had stolen fish on St. Anne, pigs from Curieuse Island, coconuts from everywhere. He had nearly been caught for murder. He drank. He—I don't know what he hadn't done in his active lifetime. He couldn't have done all of it. Then the flow stopped, as suddenly as it began, and Ahmed got really sick.

Ahmed was at this time sleeping in the hospital, since there was no other accommodation for him, and word that he had fallen into a *crise* or swoon was brought to us by Marcel, who lived there too. I went to look. He was sitting on the bed with a crowd of interested people around him, all chattering and exclaiming. I could see at once that he was really not feeling well by the fact that he wasn't himself doing any of the talking, and so shooed most of the people out and started to ask questions. These soon revealed a flourishing case of gonorrhea which he had had for some time, and which had given rise to a pyelitis; I berated him for not telling me, when I had penicillin sitting up in the house, and asked him how long he had had it. He said, miserably, that it must have been that woman "they had all gone with" the night he arrived on the island with us, and who had left with her man the next day. Only Ahmed, of course, had not believed that he could get the clap from just one time. Arabs are strong men, not so easily infected. Or if he had, and he soon discovered that he had, he thought it could only be a "light touch" of it, and tried to cure himself with local herbal medicines, which nearly always consist of fusions of the leaves of various plants taken internally and applied externally. I am not sneering: many of the herbs are well-known *materia medica,* and every Seychellois suitcase I have ever seen open has bunches of dried twigs or leaves in the bottom, some favorite remedy he does not care to be without. Ahmed, who believes everything he is told with truly catholic faith, had been trying the gamut of the laborers' supplies or suggestions rather than admit to us his unmasculine weakness—Ahmed, who will say anything to either of us with nary a blush! I was more than annoyed. I foresaw that with the thoroughgoing infection he now had I would probably have to send him back to Mahé on the *Marsouin* when she came. And then he would have to sit in Mahé until Mark could afford another trip to get him. I sighed, and started injecting penicillin into his backside. This was on the fifth of December.

Ten days later there was no sign of improvement; if anything, he was worse, with severe pain on urination and still passing blood when he did so. I started him on the Achromycin tablets I had as a reserve. The *Marsouin* hadn't turned up yet, but it was far enough away from Christmas for us to continue to expect her: that is, she would still be able to make the round trip and get back in time for the holiday. We were, in fact, more worried about the *Veritas;* not to have returned by now, she must have suffered some sort of breakdown. And Mark knew that if she didn't come soon, she wouldn't come before Christmas. The excuse would be engine trouble, but the reason drinking.

I asked if he wasn't afraid they'd drifted, engineless, off toward the coast of Africa (it had happened to Payet before), but Mark said the *Veritas* was a good sailing vessel; she'd be all right. No, the thing that was annoying him was the contract he'd made with the fishermen. From our point of view, the terms meant that if they didn't work they got no money. But we now saw that if (as, for example, finding themselves in Mahé full of Christmas spirit) they didn't want to work and didn't care about earning more money for the time being, we really had no hold over them bar the boat. The boat could then be "tied up" with engine trouble—and what boat isn't half the time in Mahé, with the bad mechanics and lack of spare parts—and what could we do about it?

Mark cursed to himself but realized that it wasn't too serious. The fishermen we had left were doing well with the *bêche-de-mer*, and we wanted to stockpile a few hundred pounds of this anyway before sending it back. It wasn't as if he could have got rid of Gappy on the *Veritas*: no captainless boat may carry passengers. Gappy could have been passed off as a fisherman, but Mrs. Gappy and the little girl, hardly.

It was thus more important for the *Marsouin* to arrive to resolve the problem of Gappy; while we might worry about the *Veritas,* it was the *Marsouin* we longed for daily. We hadn't bargained, of course, on living cheek by jowl with a fired Gappy, and the situation was delicate. Every evening Mark would gloomily go through a list of things a disgruntled Gappy could do to us if he wanted to—set fire to the shop, kill the poultry, poison the dogs, set adrift the boats, bore holes in them, poison the pigs, put sugar in our fuel, and a hundred other deeds—so that during the day and often during the night, Mark would feel obliged to prowl around, seeing that everything was all right. And I, besides doing Ahmed's work, kept the children more in sight, and the dogs, and watched my young poultry and pigs. We had been finding remarkably little time for spearfishing and picnics and other idle pleasures before we fired Gappy, but now we hardly dared relax at all. No more trips to African Banks; we not only never left the island together any more—we didn't both go to the other side of the island at the same time. It sounds a little melodramatic now, but the precautions certainly seemed sensible enough then. It's not unreasonable to fear fire if all your worldly goods are under one thatched roof, or to fear foul play if you live among people who do not share your moral code.

Gappy was loose, of course. Mark did not see that he could put him into our little jail, and in order to keep him out of mischief, had continued, in fact, to employ him, on a temporary basis. Better that, said Mark, than Gappy brooding all day in his house. He also left him with a few of the keys: to the water reservoir, to the calorifier, to the cell, and some others whose functions, as far as we knew, were purely decorative. They did not match the shop and store keys, anyway, and that was all we cared about. The cell we used as a coconut store, and having this key kept Gappy busy counting in and counting out coconuts.

But not busy enough. What had we hoped? That he would take it all meekly? I could see the veneer of politeness growing ever thinner as the truth of his situation ate in like acid. Saturdays were particularly bad. I did the rations, and Gappy had to receive them from my hands. I kept the books. I held the keys. Mark gave most of the orders himself directly. It was unheard of. A manager treated like this, like a common worker . . . an owner being a manager! The world was upside down for Gappy. I think he quite forgot that *he* had been caught, and began to work the matter around in his mind so that we were in the wrong. He even began to tell Ahmed, handy and pinned to his bed in the nearby sick bay, that it was against the law not to have a manager and a *commandeur* on the islands; that a manager had by law to have all the privileges of an owner; owners could not tend the sick—this was the manager's job (the first one I had seized from him. I knew this rankled because I often found my dressings had been taken off and Gappy's cure-all, Mentholatum—Gappy was too modern for herbs, perhaps—applied to the wound instead), and so on. Gappy also adopted the convenient attitude that we had proved nothing; therefore he was not guilty, and therefore he was still manager and being wrongfully deprived of his privileges. He got the same amount of toddy every night as a laborer—was that right? He would refuse it altogether, and did. He was told to "give a hand" with the boats, with a log. Told. He, Gappy! Monsieur and Madame could demean themselves by working with their hands if they wished; it showed them up for what they were, poor whites, with no money . . . "That," Gappy reported to people, "is why they never want to pay you anything. They can't. You will work and work, and then one day the government will take the island from Mr. Carter because he can't pay the rent, and where will you be? Look at the way he is treating me! Imagine how he will treat you!"

Yes, Gappy was a good talker, and it was having its effect. We would not deign to change our habits because Gappy was a snob, but we could see that the "demeaning" things we did, the frugal way we lived, our interest in saving money, our fussing about fish, our anxiety to create an "economic" plantation (who ever heard of cutting down coconut palms deliberately!) made us seem either mad or poor, or probably both. If there was a cheaper way we did it that way, and if we could have gotten along with fewer people we would have (Mark had been rather outspoken on this subject); how near can you get? Then the clothes we wore—and look at those children! And living in a thatched house like any laborer too poor to afford nice sheet-iron roofing. Everything we did or didn't do could be turned against us. We were even seen carrying water, working in the garden, planting, and Madame looked after the chicken house herself! (I had to be sure of some supply of eggs.) Gappy used every item to good advantage. Even old Marcel was swayed, though he loathed Gappy for some special reason of his own. Still, we were very odd.

Strengthened by the reception of all this, Gappy became wonderfully convinced (and convincing) of his innocence and the injustice with which he had been treated. Things missing from the shop? Nonsense. We had falsified the accounts, said we'd sent down more than we had, used old bills from Mahé to confuse him, and made him give up his rights to his salary under duress and mental confusion. And why? Because we saw how he fought for fair prices for work, and thought that if we could only get rid of him we would be able to oppress and exploit the helpless laborers. As soon as he got to Mahé, Gappy declared, we would be made to pay, and pay well. He would sue us for libel and loss of career, and we would be bankrupt. Prison. Oh yes, depend upon it, he, Gappy, knew the law, and we would suffer, not he. And by extension, he made it clear that anyone who cared to cooperate with us now, or curry favor by spreading lies about him, would have him to answer to later. For who would take over the island next? Why, Gappy himself. With the money he got as damages from us. There was a happily ignored inconsistency: weren't we supposed to be too poor a cow to milk? But this didn't bother Gappy or his listeners, rapt in their dream of a white man ground into dust as finally and completely as he deserved, with the star of Gappy ascendant in the sky, bathing those who would follow him in its silver light. The thought of a white Englishman in jail was like the headiest of sweet ambrosias to them all.

Well, not quite all, we hoped. We liked to think that Armand, the mason, threw the ideas out as a lot of guff, but we never knew. And in spite of assurances of mine to the contrary, even Ahmed believed some of the things—about its being illegal not to have a manager, for instance. (Ahmed doesn't really think we *know* anything, and only succeed in "muddling through" with his help.) As for the state of our bank account, he supposed we would manage somehow. We always had, so far. "But," Ahmed would warn me when I came to see him, "you had better be careful about Gappy. I am sure he can bring the Sahib into court . . ." Ahmed, by this time, had improved a little, and being near the hub of excitement and nightly confabs at Gappy's house was enlivening his convalescence. He also felt very important. First, because he was—and Gappy knew he was—the receiver-transmitter of all *dicta Gappi;* and second, he now knew for a fact that he had been poisoned.

He had believed this for a long time, he assured me. And

now Marcel had confirmed it. I raised my eyebrows in mock politeness. "Oh, you may think what you like, Mem-sahib," he said, "but it is true. Only, I am stronger than these weak Seychellois. Their poisons can make me sick, but they can't kill me. See? I am already better!" He also admitted that this was why he had told me nothing about the V.D. He would not have succumbed to it if he had not been weakened by being poisoned, so obviously he had to use Seychellois medicines to rid himself of the poisons before he could come to me for penicillin, since everyone knows . . . His logic was like a chattering of monkeys, but I am always trying to "improve" his mind. "Ahmed, you said yourself you caught your dirty blood first, the first night you were here," I began, and we were off at a shouting gallop through the next twenty minutes, neither side making the least impression on the other. Laughing, I finally gave up. At any rate he was getting better, and that's all that mattered. "But who poisoned you?" I thought to ask him, just to see what he would say. "Gappy?"

"Ah," said Ahmed sadly, "I don't know. One of Them. Perhaps Gappy, perhaps not. Marcel says he knows but he dares not tell me."

Marcel was showing some sense, there. He never "mackereled" when he could see that it would bounce straight back on him. Besides, second only to his role as chief guard and informer (self-constituted), Marcel was happiest in possession of a Secret. This is one, as a matter of fact, he kept. I don't think Ahmed wanted to know, always supposing Marcel could have told him.

Christmas eventually came, but not the *Marsouin*. Nor the *Veritas* either, but by then we hardly expected her. Determined to put on a good face, we had decided that after our own fun with our children (luckily we had had the forethought to buy their presents before coming to Remire), we would give a party for all our employees, following a Mahé custom in which the staff of a plantation comes to the Big House to wish the Master well and be given some money and grog in return; we would show our good will by doing the same here.

Without the *Marsouin* we had no whiskey or wine to serve, but Ahmed made a barrel of *palmiste* beer with Marcel's help, and I made a huge bread-dough cake, not to put any fancy names on it, and we played our tape of Seychellois dances. A few people danced—thin Armand with fat Mrs. Felix, looking disdainful, Marguerite with George William, and Sopha and J-J Umane with each other, doing the same kind of prehistoric twist to every tune; Gappy danced with Mrs. Gappy, and Felix with his wife after Armand had returned her to him. Armand's shy little wife, Agnès, sat huddled in a corner, and the boys, when not gyrating, sat and looked about them belligerently. The fishermen came in late, in a bunch, and lined up on three of the Arab chests. I don't recall their dancing, even with *la belle* Marguerite; perhaps they couldn't: they were all quite stiffly upright and handled their heads gingerly. Earning better money than the land worker, they had been able to start drinking the night before and still reckon to have enough to stay drunk clear through Boxing Day. Servina, usually wildly jealous of Marguerite, was too drunk to care about anything, and was long past the fishermen's stiff stage. He must have brewed a *purée* and drunk the lot, for he had not bothered to dress and of his own accord stayed outside quietly, crying and swallowing more beer.

Mark and I kept busy urging down the cake and beer (sweet things with drink are very *comme il faut* in the Seychelles; we should have had bowls of candies as well if the boat had come, or if I had wanted the bother of making them in our hot climate), talking brightly about I don't know what, and smiling and smiling and smiling until our jaws set, wondering how long we were decently expected to entertain on a Christmas morning. We were trying to do the right thing—what was customary for once—instead of swimming against the stream. But by the end of December, with the weather still breathlessly hot and rainless, any attempt to jolly people along was doomed to be gloomy. By then, the rift was so wide that no amount of liquid hypocrisy could bridge it, which is saying something for an *affaire Seychelloise*.

XIV

BUT NO HUMAN RELATIONSHIP can remain suspended in time, changeless, forever. Malevolent or not, our employees were now at least face to face with Mark in the field and me in the shop. I am sure they did not like us any better, but they began to know us, while simple economics made them see that since private fishing was not a source of cash, they had to start doing something that was.

We had to swallow the fact that the hard core against us obviously believed they had forced us to raise our prices—only Ahmed, Marcel, and, to be sure, Gappy knew we had not changed them—and to ignore a lot of smart-aleck asides and a good deal of hand-on-hip demeanor from The Boys. But they were working at last, and this was what mattered. Gappy might say what he liked, but after Christmas had passed and the opportunity of getting out fast on a boat to Mahé had not materialized, the laborers had to assume we would be able to pay them, or that The Law would. Even for a Seychellois it is difficult to do absolutely nothing for more than a few days at a time, and the strike, having been à la mode for a whole month, was now a bit *vieux jeux* and boring, especially when the prices had "improved."

It was only sad that the weather had not. The new year was christened with a shower, but that was all. Everyone went around saying it was most unusual, the way people always do about the weather, but this did not serve to clothe the sun with clouds or call up the susurrus of the palm fonds that whispers the approach of rain. Under the circumstances, Mark decided that planting anything would not be practical for the moment, and as soon as enough rocks had been accumulated to keep Armand contentedly at work on the new pigsties, Mark laughed and shrugged and said that we might as well make what copra we could before a boat came, if one was coming. The sun would help us dry it, as it did the fish and the *bêche-de-mer*.

In its time and place, this decision, forced on us by the merciless sun, turned out to be inspired generalship. In one stroke we outmaneuvered and disarmed the enemy, already weakened by having to take our ability to pay them on faith. Copra. Set rate. Set tasks. Set jobs. Set work for the men, set work for the women, familiarity, normality, sanity at last! This was something they all understood, and everyone began to pull together for the first time, excepting, as always, Gappy. But now it was Gappy who was moving against the stream, Gappy who would not work, and Gappy who was by these facts pushed into the eddy of his house while the work in the yard flowed around him. We were overjoyed. It was like having let go a slow and wobbly ball down the alley by mistake and yet see every pin start to totter and fall in chain reaction from the mysterious angle of the blow on the king.

I think it was at this time that Gappy began to go a little mad. He would come out of his house, blinking in the sun, and go off at a trot to the side of the island from which approaching vessels are usually sighted. (Vessels whose masters know their way about the Amirantes never approach Remire head on to the anchorage, but go to the south of us and then round our eastern point to catch us by surprise, appearing broadside off our veranda, unannounced, and usually just as we are quietly and dimly drinking our early morning tea.) About ten minutes later he would be back, looking disheveled from having been to the top of a casuarina, and trot to the camp, to keep his finger in some pie of difficulty. He would shortly return and disappear into his house. A minute later out he'd come, and off to the other side of the island again, his long hair uncombed, eyes bloodshot, and talking to himself. Too pat to be true? Not at all. He was drinking. He told Mark as much, and admitted, with that disarming candor of which he was capable even in these circumstances, that he had always drunk too much—thus the migraines which bothered him so, and which accounted for the heavy consumption of aspirins now appearing in his shop account. When the sun rose too high for all this activity to be practical, the doors and shutters of Gappy's house would be quietly closed and peace would reign, broken only by the steady *clock-clock* of coconut shells being fractured with two harsh blows of a knife and the occasional cry of outrage when some of the livestock became too forward with the growing pile of thick white meats.

It was not until evening, when no one was working and idle ears were available again, that Gappy was content. In the evenings he was always at the camp, stirring and stirring, attending to his assembly line of trouble and using his considerable imagination and inventiveness to recoup his weakened position. We might be able to get away with things for the time being, but Gappy kept our terrible fate fresh in people's minds. It just wanted the passage to Mahé to bring it about.

Ahmed and Marcel were still in the hospital, in a good position to see and hear all Gappy's evening comings to his house for liquid inspiration, and goings back to the camp, and Marcel (who was in charge of the calorifier each night because, he said, he was an old man and didn't sleep well anyway) used to swear that the light burned at Gappy's until two or three every morning. Ahmed, enjoying the zest all this had given the quiet island life (I fear that any place will be quiet for Ahmed after Mukalla, his birthplace), used to claim he'd sat up too, seeing what went on and guarding our property with his life (Gappy might still want to set fire to something, might he not?), and generally vying with Marcel as to who could spy most. Both swore the other slept—snoring loudly, however, at certain critical moments when a shadow was seen moving around the fish racks (where the covered stacks of drying *bêche-de-mer* and fish were kept, now that the calorifier was used for copra; the heat would have cooked the salted products, so our lack of any suitable storage space meant they had to be left vulnerably at large all night), or suspiciously near the frail wooden window of the shop.

Every morning there was some exciting tale to tell me, for me to tell Mark, of dreadful disaster narrowly averted, or dark plots with this one or that down at the camp, until Mark and I weren't sure who was stirring up more unrest, Gappy or our two children (one in his second childhood), who did not, naturally, reserve their tales of nightly doings for our ears alone. Half the time, Mark declared crossly, the calorifier fire was already cooling embers when he made his rounds at midnight, and it was then he who had to build it up. No lively Marcel or Ahmed moved from their pits while he was there, making fearful noises with the long fire rake and shutting the oven door with a clang! A lot of nonsense, he decided, and pooh-poohed all the stories with a shrug.

I was more pessimistic and therefore believing. I could see Mark slipping back into happy casualness, where, providing his work was done, he was not going to check too hard on what else the laborers did. It was a moot point. I wanted our hands on the wheel, our foot on the brake or accelerator, and I thought it up to us to be sure we knew what the engine was doing. A tapping to the rear of the chassis? Get to it before the big end goes—that sort of thing. After all our troubles with the delegation of responsibility (to Gappy), neither Mark nor I had yet learned to take and keep everything in our own hands; I didn't really know how, and Mark didn't even seem to want to. Mark still thought he could run the island on some sort of "old boy net" of "you scratch my back, I'll scratch yours" and not like a concentration camp; I thought our control much too loose, and that any loopholes we left would be widened without limit by people wanting to get as much out of us—white and foreign—as possible, while giving as little as they could in work in return. Mark thought to please and to call forth a pleasant atmosphere by operating with a certain leniency, by being willing to allow a certain amount of illegal home-brewing of the stuff that cheers, by overlooking petty thefts in favor of crashing down on major ones when they occurred, and letting the people feather their nests slightly at his expense if this made them into contented laborers. I was afraid we would never make contented laborers of the lot we had on the island then, and until we could get rid of the ones we didn't want, it was up to us to be strong-handed:

just, but strong. "Let them feel the bit," I said, throwing all my searching metaphors away, "then they'll know exactly how far they can go. How do you expect them to respect us if you don't?"

But I was seconded too noisily by Ahmed and Marcel, and lots of people "suggesting" what he ought to do has as bad an effect on Mark as on anyone. Every time Ahmed said, "Be tough, or they'll walk all over you," Mark from the self-confident strength of his Britishness said, "Nonsense, I know exactly how far I'd let someone go. It may take quite a few things to anger me, but then, I am not very pleasant."

This was true enough, but did the laborers know him that well? And what about me when Mark was away? I did not have any particular physical presence; my anger was not that of Jehovah; and even though I myself used to feel occasionally that it was Ahmed and Marcel who were walking all over us rather than some malevolent stranger, the tight-rein theory still appealed to me. I was not, however, running the property, and a woman has to know where to stop even "suggesting." I read myself another few lectures and threw my energies into the poultry production instead. I also had quite a bit to do in the kitchen; Ahmed's condition, perhaps aggravated by his supposed wakefulness at night, was still not completely cured; this was another good reason for telling him to sleep and mind his health and let the Sahib look after the property. For, we said, if he was still sick when a boat did come, he'd have to go. To impress Ahmed with the fact that this was not to be a holiday, we declared our intentions of paying only his barest living expenses: we did not intend to keep our *bel Arab* in the wine, women, and noisy song, the *fantasía* of life that he so dearly loves.

Mark knew *he* would have to leap on whatever boat came— and one *must* come sometime; he'd feel more comfortable if he could leave Ahmed here with me. I said, "Nonsense, we'll be all right once you remove Gappy." But Mark still looked worried.

"It it weren't for the *Veritas*, I might put off seeing about the

France for a while longer (the *France* was the schooner we had bought and were completely rebuilding)—yet I'd have to go sometime . . ."

"Oh, don't *worry*, darling," I said, trying to sound confident. I too, however, hoped Ahmed would not have to go. Aside from the loyal male support I knew he could furnish me, he was, apart from the children, about the only person on the property who was still smiling. Oh, clear blue day succeeded clear blue day, as did the lovely nights full of constellations; often we would sit out on the beach the better to appreciate the great sweep of sky over our heads. But on the whole, we had become rather serious and dreary with our troubles. Here we were, we laughed ruefully—we who were going to Do Something with one of the outer islands—making copra and grumbling about deep dark plots against us by *"les noirs"* just like any other Seychellois.

Thus January passed into February.

XV

ON THE SIXTH of February, early in the morning, the schooner *Argo* arrived, and with it our long-awaited stores and Christmas mail, the Christmas supplies we had got for the island, and of course the beer and wine which we made a point of buying at this time but could not stock the year 'round—its mere presence in the shop seems to act like a gadfly in the minds of our improvident workers, who can't stand the thought that it is there, and not inside them. And because it's difficult to refuse to sell any to those in debt, the sight of others gurgling heaven down their throats being cruel and hard, it is simpler not to order it more than twice a year, a sort of enforced saving of their money for them.

Oddly enough, when "Sail-O" for the *Argo* was called out, I don't think either Mark or I knew whether to be glad or sorry. By February the property was at least chugging along, and we had almost got the feeling that no boat was ever coming and what did it really matter in our never-never land. But I think this was just reaction against our having to part, and particularly against the instant trouble the arrival of a schooner represents. We were glad enough to be getting rid of Gappy, but at the same time we disliked the disruption caused by a boat. Nor was *Argo Veritas*. We dreaded the news we might now hear of her.

The *Argo* brought us a huge bag of mail, which had piled up in Mahé since November, but there was no time now to begin reading it. Mark pounced on a letter from Payet and stuffed it in his pocket, took some business letters to answer in Mahé, but we couldn't do more. As on the day of our arrival, there were stores to check, copra and pigs to load, people to sign off. And while we were loading we found that each bag of December's copra had to be resewn where rats had eaten through the bottoms, and when we started to move the salt fish, we discovered the salt had rotted the palm-leaf fiber the bales were tied with. Only the sacks of *bêche-de-mer* went on board without trouble, and we blessed this. It more than repaid the nuisance it was to prepare.

Still, everything got done in the rush, and under the circumstances I was glad enough to have Ahmed see that the stores were actually entered in the shop when the inventory had been taken. We broke open boxes and counted everything in desperate haste; I then threw Ahmed the keys and dashed for home. Ahmed was used to doing small errands or sales in the shop after Gappy was demoted, for often I was too busy myself. This morning I certainly was. We had four hours, precisely, in which to accomplish everything. At seven we had been peacefully drinking tea; the children were playing quietly; we talked, making plans for the day, a day like any other day. By eight the *Argo* was creaking at anchor, with the first load of copra being rowed out and the captain, who dislikes disembarking his own dinghy, laconically waiting to be fetched by ours. By noon Gappy was packed and on board, Mark packed and on board, and Ahmed—he had to go, we decided—on board too. (But the captain said firmly that he had no room for the others who had wanted to leave: Sopha, William, and J-J. They had to stay.) By noon too all the stores were, we hoped, off, and all the goods for sale on, and I—I was left standing in the hot sun on the beach, the children still unfed, the dogs, pigs, chickens still unfed, and nearly everyone around me weary and hot, and, it seemed, half drunk already.

Grimly I opened the shop and looked inside. The large crate of wine was by the door, its packing scattered and half the contents gone. I stared in dismay. Ahmed! At that hour in the morning, selling wine, with the ship to load! This was what came of having the shop open for purchases any time of the day: this! Ahmed blithely turning over the shekels, not a thought in his head for the result—this was what came of no *rules*, I thought bitterly. Rules for drinking time, rules for selling times. Oh, rules, rules, order, peace . . . For as I was standing there, the pirogue had come back from its last trip to the *Argo*, bringing a load of tipsy laborers all promptly shouting through the open door for more wine. I banged shut the door of the shop and said "Later," then went to feed everything that needed feeding, myself included.

Strengthened, I returned to the yard to take the inventory of Gappy's house, into which Felix was busy moving, helped inefficiently by his children and mine. The inner room of the house, between the front and back verandas, where I had never been, Gappy had divided into two rooms by tacking up yards of blue cloth—some of the quantity missing from the shop, I surmised, neither "issued" nor bought but just taken—over a frame. It made an expensive wall, but at least he had left it behind. The kitchen revealed even more: it was full of feathers from the warm breasts of domestic birds, the small feathers that fly around so when you are plucking them, and in the space between the thatched wall and the rear of the stone fireplace was a solid layer a foot deep of empty duck-egg shells. But the gloomy pleasure of finding all this evidence was continually interrupted: just outside, under a palm, sat the awful trio of bad boys, shouting songs I mercifully didn't know or recognize, and punctuating them with hoarse, insistent cries of "Wine!" or "Open the shop, Madame!"

It reminded me of being teased at school. First I tried to ignore them. Then I told them to shut up and go away, which had no effect either. Then I made Felix tell them, but his mousy voice merely raised another rude laugh. My instinct was to be tough, tell them all to go to merry hell, and walk away, very dignified, to my lonely home. But that was just it. I was alone. What if they followed me there? I dismissed the idea of rape as ridiculous, but for months Mark and I had been discussing the damage that could so easily be done to us. I had no police I could call! Our house was of thatch—how easy to set it on fire. Our dogs too tame—how easy to poison them. Our shop door of frail timber—how easy to break it down. Our ducks and turkeys all on free range—how easy to kill them. Our pigs at their mercy. And now myself and my children too, had they the wit or the courage to consider real mischief.

It is one thing to sit calmly by the side of strong male husband and declare firmly, "One must be tough." It is quite another to be, suddenly, alone, depressed and tired. They were in a nasty mood, those three, and hadn't confined themselves to the shouts one repeats. I knew enough about the lower-class male Seychellois when drunk—or any man minus breeding and morals and plus a good deal of liquor—to realize that the deprivation of further drink at this stage was enraging them, maddening them. But should I take the chance and sell them what they wanted? Which was worse—half drunk and vicious, or drunk all the way, and then, what must come, oblivion? Most of them, not being able to afford heavy drinking all the time, have weak heads. Perhaps if I sold them enough more I would solve the problems created by their having got this far already.

Thus I thought and reflected. Then I consulted Felix, but he offered nothing that could be called an opinion, naturally. Felix, retiring by nature, was not going to come out of his safe protective say-nothing shell with Gappy barely an hour off the island. But I had already made up my mind. It wasn't wise to appear weak or indecisive even to Felix, for though Mark had told him he was to help if needed, he couldn't back me if he wasn't given something definite to back. "I have decided," I told him, "to open the shop at four P.M., and not before. They can then have as much as they think they can pay for." I explained the idea of reducing them to a stupor by, say, six, after which we could all expect to get a good night's rest. "But first we have to get this morning's sales straight. You do have a list of what Ahmed sold, don't you?" Ahmed always did dictate his sales to Felix (the only literate person besides Gappy and ourselves) if he didn't tell me directly.

"Oh yes," said Felix. "I was there."

"Oh," I said. And then, thinking to get the point across to him, I added, "It's a pity we didn't know Ahmed was being so foolish or we would certainly have stopped him." I looked disapproving, and Felix immediately followed the lead. "But now they are drunk already we might as well finish the job," I repeated, watching his face. He looked more for than against. "But I would appreciate your being there with me, Felix. We don't want any unpleasantness."

"Certainly, Madame," he said, pleased (as I'd hoped) by the implication that his presence would inspire order, though neither of us had had any evidence for so supposing so far.

At quarter to four, we entered the shop and checked the morning sales. Three bottles were unaccounted for, and I put this down to Experience, making a resolve that the keys should never be out of my, or Mark's, hands again. We dragged the box away from the door and wedged it in a safer place beside the table. Felix stood guard, ready to hand out as I wrote down. Then we opened the doors and started to sell. The men were quiet now, but like pigs whose food has just been put in the trough they all pressed forward eagerly, each afraid another would get more than he. I could see how three bottles had disappeared, and only wondered that it had not been more. The rest of the bottles were quickly sold. I then rechecked the stores that had arrived, and tired, shut the shop and started for home.

When I was halfway there I heard a scream—a woman's scream—then shouting. It came from somewhere in the back of the store-hospital building. I hesitated, and went on my way. We had had cases of in-fighting before which had seemed to calm down faster for lack of official notice. But soon someone came running up behind me. It was big, strong, fat Servina, who, though one of Gappy's "boys," could not really be classed with J-J Umane, Sopha, and George William. He was married, for one thing, and more cowardly-cautious. He was also stupider, with a great bull neck and a puckered frown, and very sentimental. A few glasses of beer reduced his great bulk to a squishy morass of tears and sadness. But at this moment he was excited in spite of the tears.

"Oh, Madame," he cried, "come and stop them! Come and stop them! They are hitting old Lenclume! Oh, it makes my heart grieve to see them hitting an old man like that!"

Lenclume is Marcel's other name. An anomaly about Servina was that in spite of Marcel's bad odor with the rest of the island, he remained childishly attached to him. I think they came from the same part of Mahé, if there was no actual family connection. I asked Marcel once, but he could be close-mouthed when he wanted, and I never found out. All I knew was that the link was a strong one: there was a provable return-valve leakage of information from our house via Ahmed to Marcel, to Servina, and thence to Gappy. Perhaps Servina also wanted to play both sides, for Marcel, after Gappy's fall, had been for some time in a position of power on the island even if it was mainly usurped. He had busied himself picking up all the loose ends of "authority" that we didn't apparently want to be bothered with, and to these harmless, to us, bits of ordering about and in-chargeness he had added a good many airs and graces of his own. I mused heartlessly that the beating up he was getting now was probably richly deserved.

I merely asked, however, who was hitting him.

"Barbé, who says he stole his rice, and William and Sopha, who call him a *maquereau* . . . oh, Madame, *come!*"

Reluctantly, I went. But the fight was over. Though the old man was nursing a shoulder, hard, he looked at me so blearily I assumed he could not have felt much pain. The attackers had fled the scene. Assault is as illegal on the islands as anywhere else, but since I had no direct power as a Peace Officer, I was grateful that the habit of guilty fear had made them run away. My spirits lifted, and I turned toward home again with a firmer step.

I had been home a few minutes and was in the kitchen, filling the kerosene lamps, when in rushed Maxime Esparon, one of our gogglers, a tall white blond fellow whom the others call "the white turkey." I looked up, annoyed. No one may enter our kitchen or house without permission—no more than they would enter each other's.

"It is I, Madame, who stopped the fighting," he announced grandly. I will always undertake your interests. I will be your guardian. You have need of a man's strong arm? Call on mine! Monsieur, before he left, commissioned me so, and so I will remain! Give me the key to the cell and I will lock them all up!"

It was obvious he too was drunk. I demurred against giving him the key. "Catch them," I said, "and call me."

"No, I must have the key! Don't you trust me, me who lays down my heart and arm at your feet?" (*Coeur* in the *de lion* sense, I am sure.) And more of the same. I saw promise of this continuing for some time, so I went up to the house, found an old key, and gave it to him. Esparon saw no difference. He went off proudly.

In another minute Servina had bounced back. "Madame, I will tell you this frankly, even though they call me a mackerel, you can't let Lenclume remain alone tonight to look after the calorifier!"

"Why?"
"They will kill him, that's why!"
"Who? Barbé?"
"No, Sopha and Big George." (The carpenter's apprentice was Small George. Big George at this time was George William, Gappy's nephew.) "They have sworn to beat him up again, good this time, when you are not around—late, when they can get him alone. An old man like that, *ça faire moi la peine* . . ." And he burst into compassionate tears again. "*Madame, quoi faire, Madame?*"

"Stay with him," I said. "You are his friend."
"*OUI, Madame!*" Light dawned. Satisfied, he went away.
Soon he was back. "But you will have to pay me for staying up all night when I am tired from loading the boat!"
"Yes, yes, we'll see about that later."
"*Oui, Madame.*" And he staggered off.
I lit the lamps.
"*Madame, Madame!*"
It was Esparon.
"*Madame!*"
"Yes, yes, I'm coming." I let the glass down on the last lantern and went to the door. Esparon had remained outside this time, at least. I joined him.

Immediately, he slapped his hand on his bare chest, covered with curly blond hairs. "I will defend your honor if they kill me," he cried. "For this job"—indeed, now that I was out of the kitchen I could hear a lot of background noise—"you need such a *brave* as I! Felix! Felix is a chicken. He knows his chicken-run, but he doesn't know fighting! Me, I—"

I interrupted. "What's the matter now?"
"Come, Madame, come down. You have to be witness. I will put them all in the cell. All! With my bare hands!"

I considered. It would be a good thing if I could get "them all" —whoever was so busy disturbing the peace—into the cell, and it was true that Felix was not physically strong enough to manhandle any of the cruder laborers; it was also true that since Mark had not made him manager (we wanted no more of that breed), his position was a little amorphous to carry much weight.

Esparon gabbled on. I left him, went into the house, got Mark's .22 rifle and loaded the magazine, then called the dogs, and the children (who thought this all a great game; I preferred to keep them with me than alone in the house, where there was no one to look after them).

By now the noise from the yard was really getting bad. I went down the main path, slowly, with my entourage; Esparon went on ahead to his house. I felt a little foolish, and hoped my appearance would cause the fighting to evaporate as it had before. It didn't. Coming around the last palm of the *allée,* I entered upon a set scene.

Esparon was just leaving the fishermen's bungalow, to enter right, looking bravely about him. Enter left, from the camp area, Sopha, hotly pursued by George William, hotly pursued in turn by Servina, running like a heavy bull. They disappeared around the corner of the manager's house, now Felix's. A scream, not a serious one, from Mrs. Felix. In a matter of seconds they had circled the house, whence exeunt left again. Meanwhile, I, leaving the children lower right, ran across to mid-left, just in time to see Sopha working away, filling an empty wine bottle with sand. He looked up furtively, but with a certain amount of defiance, and deftly broke the end off the bottle.

"Sopha, drop that!" I said. His attention was caught for the instant that it took George William to come down on top of him. "Get him!" I said. (Anyone with such a weapon in his hand was cell-worthy as far as I was concerned.) William and Sopha were now rolling on the ground, but William had a strong grip on the wrist of the hand holding the bottle; in a second, he had twisted the bottle away. At which point Servina promptly jumped on William and grappled *him.*

"Get off him, you fat oaf!" I shouted, excited myself by this time though our great fierce black dogs just stood beside me, wagging their tails. But Servina had rolled underneath with his momentum, and George William was now on top, though still in the bear hug of his opponent. Instantly, a sharp stone hit William squarely in the center of his back; he gave a howl of rage and I looked up just in time to see Marguerite about to follow this successful blow with a bottle of her own, though unbroken. I threw up the gun, jerking her arm aside (the gun wasn't loaded; I still had the magazine in my other hand). "What do you think you're doing!" I said sharply. This had created a diverson. Marguerite was in a rage, breathing heavily, and speechless for once. Servina grunted. "Big George insulted her." He was kneeling heavily on the offender as he spoke, and from George William's hand plucked Sophia's bottle as though he were picking a spray of mimosa, and threw it far into a thicket of *veloutier*. Sopha had got away, of course; he stood, glowering, at bay. "No bottles," I said. "No bottles on this property!" Servina let George William go; he stood panting, warily watching Marguerite. "You, Sopha," I said, "get one more broken bottle in your hand and I'll shoot you!" (Sopha had been the first to give the fight this vicious turn.)

"Shoot me, then!" cried Sopha. "Shoot me!" Quick as a weasel, he slipped in between us, grabbed Marguerite's bottle, and ran back toward Felix's house.

With this, the tableau broke up, and the round began again. While I thought about what to do next I moved quickly back to the yard, this time in time to see Esparon pulling back the rubbers of a spear gun; the figure of Sopha flashed by, followed as before by William and Servina.

"Stop that!" I called, running over to him. "Are you mad? You could kill someone!"

"I will kill them all!" Esparon disengaged a hand to beat his chest again. "Me—I am the *régisseur* here! Felix is a *poule*. I will put order here!"

Armand, who had been standing quietly by the hospital end of the store, his eyes goggling and his sharp mason's trowel clutched at the ready, rushed over to me. "Is that true, Madame? Is it true?"

It wasn't, but in this cluster of drunks, whom did I wish to offend? "Just give me that gun," I said to Esparon, "if this is the way you're going to help me! Give it to me!" I fear I stamped my foot and reached for the gun. "I will kill them!" From Esparon again, and he shook my hand roughly off the gun. Armand watched, bloodshot eyes still very wide, trowel raised, but no help. But someone was approaching. It was Berley, Mark's bo's'n. He rolled, but he was coming. Inexorably, he laid a heavy hand on the spear gun, and in the struggle the iron of the harpoon slipped out of its socket and bent double. With an effort Esparon shook Berley off, then gave me the gun. He glared pinkly at me, but he was sulking and therefore silent. Berley reeled silently away.

I had by this time loaded my own gun—just in case—so I now turned and shouted at Sopha again, who was passing, then raised the .22 and fired over his head when he didn't stop. The little pop was not very satisfactory, and I wished I had brought the heavy shotgun. Sopha heard it, though. "Shoot me!" he yelled over his shoulder. "That's right! Shoot me!" The sentence ended with a Doppler effect as he disappeared around the corner of the house.

Just then a terrific crash sounded from inside, and Felix, who had been standing by his steps so inconspicuously I hadn't even noticed him, went bounding lightly up them—only to come down them again, backwards, with his arms around Sopha. Through the open doors, I could see that the partition Gappy had made had been knocked down, and Mrs. Felix, though she was crouched on the back veranda, screamed every time the sanctity of her bedroom was violated by George William, who was charging back and forth with a section of the frame around his shoulders and his head in the cloth, knocking into things.

It was the perfect opportunity. "Armand!" I called. "Help Felix!" "Servina!" But Sopha recovered his balance, and breaking from Felix's grasp, ran off among the palms. At least, I noted, without the bottle. Just as promptly, Big George scored a final victorious crash with the frame, shook off the cloth, leaped down the steps, and ran in the opposite direction. Armand was wavering around, saying "Excuse me" every time he bumped into us; Esparon had followed me, now recovered from his mortification and protesting for his gun. This I held onto, firmly. I looked at Felix and shrugged. Felix shrugged. Servina staggered out from behind the house and burst into tears on Armand's shoulder. We were left, if only by default, masters of the field. It was over.

Before I went home, I gave Felix the real key to the cell and told him to lock up anyone he could catch, if he thought it necessary, knowing that he would catch no one. Everyone was far too drunk to act in the coordinated way required to gang up on one person; it says something for the hatred Marcel inspired that three people had united to beat him up. But I hoped the key would lend Felix some small aura that would help him maintain order, and so I left it.

Esparon turned up at the house an hour later, one last time. "Give me my gun now," he said. "I promise I will shoot no one."

I said no, that I would give it to him tomorrow morning if there were no more fights.

"But they will kill *me*," he whined. "I am white and they hate me! Give me my gun, Madame, *please!*"

After some altercation it got through to him that I meant it, and he left, much more offended than afraid. I was glad to be rid of him. With his officious boastfulness and dangerous interference he had only been a hinderance; at least the others, though drunk and vicious, had not pestered me with their airs and graces. Perhaps this was unjust, but I felt his mask had been stripped away to reveal a sniveling little man out to curry favor where he could, and more of a chicken than Felix when it came to actual fighting.

By nine at night there was not a sound to be heard, and I could at last relax. The children were sleeping peacefully, having taken the whole fight as a Punch and Judy, and perhaps they were right. But we were still drying copra in the calorifier, so before I could sleep myself I went down to the yard to see if the fire had been stoked for the night. I found Marcel asleep in his bed, where, Felix, told me, he had been throughout the excitement, Servina nowhere to be seen, and Felix himself, a long piece of white cotton cloth wrapped around him like a sarong, throwing the last few husks into the fire. I thanked him, impressed by his thoughtfulness, asked if all was well, and went home to bed.

It was hot, however, and sleep didn't last for long. By two in the morning I was hearing voices raised in Esparon's house; I envisioned the troubles starting again, and was prey to every sort of doubt or fear as I always am at that early-morning hour. I jeered at myself for thinking I could handle drunken men, and for being so stupid and weak as to have sold them any more wine, and felt very sorry for myself and that I had urged Mark to take Ahmed, leaving me no one dependable except for meek, quiet Felix. How humiliating to have taken such a chance. In spite of any action of mine the situation had been out of hand, and I had only made myself ridiculous. And what foolishness to have underestimated it. Anything could have happened, could still happen . . . I lay awake, listening to the voices. They are all cowards at heart, I kept telling myself. They wouldn't dare do anything bad . . . But I didn't really believe it. I only felt terribly alone and humbled, knowing that if anything did happen it would be my own fault.

When day came, however, nearly everyone was asleep, and those who weren't went sheepishly about their work. We picked up from where we had left off, and I drew strength from their complaisance. Gradually I tightened my hold on every aspect of the work until I felt in full control. I became almost glad that the Great Disorder, as it was soon called, had occurred. It cleared the air, and it made them all feel a little guilty: some reserve of gentlemanliness made them say to one another that it had been a shame to behave so when Monsieur was away—taking advantage of his absence, as it were—and there was a general feeling of wanting to make it up to me. Even Sopha laughed, for the first time ever so far as I knew, when I asked him the next day how his head was, and George William, after being sick on the foundations for our new house, smiled and laughed too.

Besides, they knew if they ever wanted to leave the island they now had to work: they were laborers indentured to us for the cost of the wine. Overnight the island made a disconcerting, but pleasing, shift to a hard-working, eager sort of place, each one ready to take up instantly the potential work Mark had left him to do. And I suddenly found myself busier than I had ever believed possible. There was no mooning over the absent beloved spouse this time. If anything, I wished as often for Ahmed as for Mark.

XVI

SO. I HAD THE ISLAND TO MYSELF. No manager, no husband: I not only had the opportunity to run it "my way," I had to run it no matter what. Principle One of my empiric methods soon formulated itself: the Keys Keeper has to run all day long. Principle Two: the counter of things even harder. My days went something like this, with minor variations: up at 5:45, dress, slosh water over face, down to the yard by 5:55 to give the orders at 6 A.M. Any unusual jobs, explain, supervise. Count out coconuts for animal food, and oil rations. Home again in time for children waking up, build charcoal fire in kitchen, make tea and breakfast, eat standing (as I'm wanted for weighing copra). Run down to yard, help Servina lift the sixty-kilo bags onto his shoulder for trip to shop, be in shop when he is and back at scales again for the next one. Cannot think of taking another man off another job for this, and I am strong enough. But it is hot work. Finish by 11 o'clock, give pigs their grass. Home again, find the grated coconut waiting for me to press for oil (the ladies say this is man's work and refuse to do it, so I must, as men are busy on more important things. After all, it takes only half an hour if one works fast). While doing this, I put some rice on the stove—the fire has died during the morning while I was cooking the dogs' food, so it has to be built up again. Then rush to the house, make the beds—can't sweep the house yet; there is the rest of the lunch to cook and it is already noon. Ring the bell for the children, fry some fish, run to the garden for vegetables for a salad, give the children their plates, eat standing again because I have to count the lime after the 12:30 bell. The dogs and chickens get fed first, however, even if it makes me late; I have finished extracting the oil-bearing milk from the grated coconut, and it is the "dry" coconut that goes to the chickens. I run to the pen with it, fill their water trough, then grab a notebook and go out to the lime kiln. We always make lime where there are no trees to get singed, so it is naturally a very hot and sunny place at 1 P.M. The tins are filled, marked down, emptied in a new pile, filled again . . . it is soporific. The score mounts slowly up. After an eternity it is three hundred and ninty-six. They have finished. How much? they ask. I tell them, and they grumble to themselves. It feels like more to me too; I wish they could or would count to themselves, rather than look at me afterwards as though I had cheated them. Stop at pigsties. The pigs are almost out of water, but it all has to be carried from a well two hundred yards away. I am too tired. Look for Servina, who is responsible, but he can't be found. Head for home. On my way Umane and Sopha ask me to count rocks, and I promise them at 4 P.M. At home I wash up breakfast and lunch dishes together, then dust and sweep the house. Now, with the property to run, I would give a good deal to have a servant, but this is impossible. Marguerite had to be fired from housework for theft, and Mrs. "King," the old nosy one who stood so commandingly on my front steps the day we arrived on the island, is now too busy, she says. She is paying me back for refusing her services then: my original sin. Mrs. Felix gets asthma and so does nothing for anyone. Armand's wife is expecting a baby in another two months, so she's out. There is no one else—Mrs. Payet and the concubines had taken the opportunity the *Argo* offered to return to Mahé and their men. But anyway, Ahmed will be back soon.

When I finish, it is four o'clock. I get my notebook and go down to the beach to watch rocks flung from one pile to another. This is harder than lime to count because of the various sizes, but quicker. It is very still; the sun seems just as hot as it was at midday. I count King's pile (he is called King because of his opinion of himself. He has been here a long time and is very barrack-room lawyery about everything, an unappealing type but more intelligent than the others. I find we usually get along all right. At least he can count, so knows I am not cheating. When I finish King's pile, I move on to Sopha's, then Umane's. I suggested they work together, but they are all too jealous, or wary of the other fellow not pulling his weight. Then I run along to see that Servina distributes the pig food evenly, then check on the day's tasks and on what must be done the next day. If there is time, I go out to the eastern corner of the island to see that the women have taken all the covers off the tobacco plants so they will get the night dew. If there is still more time, I nip around to the turtle pound by the beach to see how the wall is holding. Armand divides his labors between this and the new pigsties, depending on the tides. I come back by the site of the latter and down the old guano trolley line to the shop, which I open for people wanting things. When I get home there is the men's ration of toddy to hand out sometime between garden work (which must be done in the evening so transplants have the night to recuperate and water soaks well into the ground) and lamplighting. After the lamps, there is the children's dinner to cook, then they must be bathed and fed, read to a little, and put to sleep. I don't eat at night myself, usually; it's just too much trouble. I bathe, write down the day's notes on which the monthly payroll is based, listen to the news, fall into bed.

There is the bread to make too, though not every day, of course. Bread is such a great stand-by for a housewife in a hurry that it is well worth the time spent making it. Also, it can be mixed, kneaded, and baked in between doing a lot of other things; it's not a bit of querulous cookery one has to stand over. And there are the eggs to collect, and the chickens' night hut to clean, not that this takes long. But the incubator has to be fussed over every night, and the brooders, live and mechanical, must be cared for; having decided to increase the poultry population as much as possible, I can hardly give up the project in the middle, though I'd sometimes like to: thinking of all those feathers in Gappy's kitchen and of the birds found missing at each recount, I wonder whom I am doing the work for. But I go on doing it.

And on Saturdays there are rations to give out, which consumes two hours in the middle of the day (the poor children get a little hungry for their lunch on Saturdays). There is also the oil for rations to finish: once the thick "cream" has risen to the top of the pressed coconut milk, it must be skimmed off and rendered into oil by boiling. The whole process should be carried out every two days or the cream goes rancid, but there always seems to be a final lot to do on Saturdays; it is hot work, and slow, and the cream needs stirring, even on a low fire. Often Marcel drops by and does this for me if I am stuck somewhere else, which is nice of him. I don't *think* he takes any while he is about it.

My Sundays during this time I devote to an interesting but desperate struggle to make soap. Rain has at last condescended to fall, but now that we need it, there is no more soap in the shop; the brackish water of the wells uses it up incredibly quickly. So in answer to urgent demands I stand over the stove, mixing ash and water, caustic soda, and coconut oil in proportions I'm not at all sure of. The mixture rises and rises like some horrible witch's brew, filling the biggest pot I have to the brim. At exactly the right moment it must be whipped off the fire and stirred like fudge until it cools and sinks and thickens. Then, poured into a tin, all it makes is a mere two-pound bar. Secretly I'm rather proud of producing even this, but Marcel keeps coming in, sniffing and poking, and declares that no one will use what I've made because it "doesn't look right"; that is, like what everyone is used to. How many new products have met death trying to breach the same strong high wall? I feel injured, until I notice that the women, complaining of looks, hardness, roughness on the hands, and practically everything else, still snap up all I care to make and are always asking me to make more. After all, it does work (to my surprise too).

Gappy, the "Great Disorder," Marcel / 147

Miss Mark? Worry about him? I remember to give him a thought now and then; for the rest I am far too busy.

In this great push to get as much of the vital work the island needed done as quickly as possible, I found out the sad truth that having only one body, one pair of legs, one set of eyes is simply not enough. I could not be everywhere at once, and however unwilling I might be to do it, I had to delegate some of the work. "My way" was not an efficient use of manpower; my efforts to, I suppose, "show them" were wearing me out without making any telling impression on the workers; I had, therefore, to start to trust a little, and entrust a little, here and there, and into this vacuum crept, seeped—guess who?

I had rather it had been someone like Felix, but there was no one like Felix, and anyway we paid Felix too much to use up valuable carpentry time, on which the progress of all island building depended, by asking him to be a supervisor. Marcel, on the other hand, was very willing, even delighted, to do a few things for me, though he would not have put it this way himself. To Marcel, he already saw to everything anyway, and had been doing so for two months. I just hadn't realized who was holding me up. Not only me: in Marcel's humble opinion, saving his presence, the whole island would have fallen into the sea. Lapses from duty, you understand, never worried Marcel. His was a magic slate on which all that was good shone in golden letters ten feet high, while the space for bad remained forever a virgin blank.

Perhaps because of its association of wavy-haired slickness, Marcel seemed an odd name to attach to this unkempt old man, with his grizzled peppercorn hair and flat bobble nose, unshaven stubble on his chin, and his single-toothed evil grin—helped to pirate likeness by the earring in one ear and the piece of red flannel he had begged from me wrapped around his head. His shirt was always tied in a knot at about the level of his diaphragm, revealing a large expanse of crinkly brown stomach until his droopy pants of Wasco (a cheap type of blue drill that fades easily) began only just where decency rendered them necessary.

At this ambiguous level they were held by a drawstring, from which they depended very full and baggy, at some considerable outlay in material: Marcel did not agree with the current Seychellois rage for "tight-fitting."

His shirt, in spite of the fact that he might as well not have had one on, was a badge of great importance to Marcel. The social order of the island is visible in the matter of wearing a shirt: only the fishermen or the common laborers go without one. The *propriétaire* wears a shirt. The carpenter wears a shirt. The mason wears a clean undershirt on weekdays and a clean white shirt on Sundays. He, Marcel, would also wear a shirt. Being Marcel's shirt, however, it had to be different. No ordinary button-down-the-front affair with short sleeves, two pockets, and all that rubbish for him. No, his were very carefully designed by him (and executed by Mrs. King) as a pull-over-the-head type, with a boat neckline trimmed in Wasco to match the baggy pants, even though the cloth of which they were made was the cheapest variety of unbleached muslin we carried in the shop and looked like a dustcloth after two washings. For added distinction, the neckline had a *V*-opening cut in its front center, also carefully trimmed. The sleeves were cap sleeves, trimmed as well. As to the length of the shirts—well, one couldn't be sure. I never saw them worn the same way as other shirts, but only as I have described. The effect was far from the daring masculine undress of, say, a Josh White: this requires, note, a shirt front made in two pieces which are tied below the navel —not in one piece that has to be knotted on itself like an Indian mosquito net high above it, accentuating quite the wrong area: flabby stomach instead of virile chest. To Marcel, though, the effect was evidently both chic and fetching. I said before that Marcel seemed an odd name for him, but it turned out to be entirely appropriate. He was one of the vainest people I have ever met.

Marcel was also a loner. He had no real loyalties, no apparent ties. I am sure his attachment to Ahmed was a result of a natural leechlike instinct connecting him to the most plentiful source of blood on the island, and even Servina's interests were ignored if they interfered with his own. Once entrenched in a job, Marcel evidently made up his mind to be a one-man (at a time) dog. Only I shall steal from my master, said Marcel in effect, and anyone else I see doing it will probably be mackereled on. Naturally, Marcel earned himself much dislike on this score, but it also made him feared, an advantage of which he was well aware. For an old man, he got around a lot too. A person could never tell when he was safe from being seen by Marcel. How to know whether or not Marcel would mackerel? It was irritating enough not to be sure, but infuriating (if the occasion seemed to warrant it) to have to attempt a conciliation, which swelled the old man's head even further. He was loathed, feared, and, oddly, respected, in equal measure, and would have been well on the way to possessing the evil eye if only he had not spoiled the whole effect by drinking.

For Marcel drank anything, everything, whatever he could lay his hands on. Old sour toddy, lentil mash, sprouting corn-kernel beer—anything. And he would beg used sugar sacks for the purpose of steeping the precious residue of sweetness out of *them*. He always had a brew of something going, which he tended anxiously, tasting. And when once he had a good head of steam on he would be loath to waste it, to let it degenerate into a mere hangover for lack of fuel. He felt at his best when he was, not drunk exactly, but just past that stage and kept topped up. Then he really felt busy and efficient. But to remain in this nirvana, ah well. Like Pooh, with Marcel it was always time for a little something.

The evil eye, indeed. There were times when Marcel's eyes were so bleary he could hardly see out of them. Red-rimmed, watery old man's eyes, with yellow spots wobbling on a cornea latticed with blood vessels. When then he used to come to ask us something, his desperate attempt to stand up straight was almost pathetic. Almost. Because he managed somehow to combine this attempt with an air so full of self-importance and even assurance that I will remain forever astonished at his nerve.

The secret, of course, was that he was a good worker, the only good worker on the property aside from Armand and Felix.

He knew this well enough, and he also knew that the alcohol level in his blood notwithstanding, he worked hard, and he worked hard all day long, and didn't stand around haggling about the price first, or after, but instead got on with the job. At the end of each month he was amply rewarded. Nor was he a smart boy with a sullen look, like the dear protégés of the departed Gappy, who still showed a certain reluctance to lift a finger unless they could see—like having to pay for their wine—no way out of it. He was, he thought, worth his weight in malmsey, and in many ways he was absolutely right.

XVII

BUT HOWEVER MUCH Marcel helped me while Mark was away —and it was nearly two weeks already; how much longer it would be, I didn't know—he was never reliable. And however many jobs I was forced to relinquish to others or to allow to lapse for the time being, work for me always poured in to fill up the gaps.

I suppose any agricultural pursuit is like that, and on the whole, I can't say it wasn't a satisfactory feeling to get up early, at first light, and canter through the hours of the day so full of movement that the minutes, hours, days, and even weeks seemed to fly by under my feet, I also found that for the first time in my life I remembered everything, and noticed everything. I had to. My eyes were acquiring new skills. I could judge the weight of a bundle of grass at a glance, count coconuts quickly, estimate the amount of coconut water in a pail to judge how much had been drunk on the spot or spirited away for the making of hooch. (It was all supposed to go to the pigs, but it never did. I only complained when more than half was

Early in the morning Francine puts the fish out to dry

**Every morning the fish is put
out to dry**

taken.) I counted without counting hoes, spades, oars and kept in my head who had used what where last; and if anyone complained of being unable to fulfill his task of coconut collecting for the day "because no more had fallen," I was able to tell him where he had not been. I also memorized the positions of all the odd useful lengths of wood so I could forestall Felix's irritating habit of cutting a piece off a long beam when an adequate short piece was lying only a few yards away. And I could let my eyes range over the fish drying on the racks at any one time, and was able to tell if more than two or three were missing, and of what sort. This wasn't so hard as it sounds. The local hand-line fishing catches exclusively rockfish and only occasionally a tuna, barracuda, or snoek (a relative of the barracuda). These last being oily fish show up readily enough in a pile of rockfish (not oily). One only had to keep in mind what odd (in the sense of unusual) fish had recently been caught and how many, and then count the rockfish. If one big fish or, as I said, two or three small were missing, I would mention to the fish turner that I didn't see such and such—had he?

My reputation with the fishermen went up with this accomplishment, which was a good thing. Fishermen in the Seychelles are, like fishermen everywhere, scornful of landsmen and particularly of landswomen. But when Mark was away, I had to supervise the fishing as well as the property side of things. I obviously did not have to go out fishing with them, but I had been briefed by Mark on what to suggest they do, according to the kind of weather, and I had to weigh their catches, issue new lines and hooks if necessary, check that the boats were baled out, the oars in, the sails brought ashore and dried, make sure they took on board enough water each time they went out, to allow for emergencies. (Mark used to find it amazing how careless the local fishermen are of taking a sail, oars, and water in these days of mechanization—even old Payet, who should have known better. But by now we were resigned to having to think for them each time, every time.) For the rest, the fishermen were not so much the separate "do-nothing-on-shore" clique that they had been, since Mark kept removing men from property work and putting them on fishing and the reverse. The days of "this fish business" had taught us that we hadn't a man on the place who couldn't fish—just that some were slightly better than others. Only the gogglers—young, brash, modern—were still apart. But we were slowly eroding their unwarranted sense of superiority (we hoped) by making them do their share of boat work.

I was also becoming much more careful about the way I spoke in finding fault. I would only suggest, for instance, to the copra preparers that rather a lot of the coconut water had obviously been spilled, had it not? And what a pity to waste it. Tomorrow, I'd say, you must use such and such a pail, which will not tip so easily. They knew, of course, that all this was so much nonsense and that said coconut water was either swishing around their bellies at that very moment or back in their kitchens, waiting to be fermented into *bacca* (a sort of crude strong beer), and they knew that I knew. No hot denials could be made, no umbrage taken, however, at my way of putting it.

A few months ago, I thought to myself, I would never have

stooped to such deviousness. I always prided myself on my direct, honest, straightforward let-them-know-where-you-stand approach. But had I got anywhere? Besides, like any animal, I had to replace my lack of strength with cunning, and through watching and listening, and being always among them, I realized that only a little cunning was really necessary. The roundabout approach did not, as I had always thought, display weakness; it was simply good sense, or what Felix, in an odd flowery burst of language, called the "amelioration" of men; or just plain tact.

Orders, once the brash rudenesses of the boys had been reduced to politer behavior, became what was "expected" of them, or *"services pour le propriété."* And I learned to give them exuding (I hoped) an overwhelming air of confidence that they would be done. They usually were. But if the order was objected to, I also learned to shrug my shoulders and refuse to argue the point. If the man or woman wished his salary and rations, let him work. If he didn't work—well then, he could stay in his house and starve. Both Mark and I, I discovered, had been far too eager to Get Work Done; going around, urging people had put them in the position of being able to inconvenience us by making all sorts of conditions of acceptance—and before, they had quickly sensed our unsureness about whether a job was fair and how fair the pay was, and so played on this for all it was worth. Now I cultivated a couldn't-care-less attitude toward anyone making difficulties about *journée* work which their contracts obliged them to perform, and was mercilessly firm about its being completed to my satisfaction, while being, as I have explained, deviously knowing about affairs over which I had less control. Mark, I had learned, was, after all, right: one had to save one's energy to stand firm on a few principles and admit that so long as thefts and offenses remained minor enough they were best ignored. Discipline could be carried only so far before it degraded the disciplinarian.

When I did wish to exert discipline I had three methods, which were both effective and dignified. If a man did not appear for work and had no adequate excuse (reporting sick), I simply withdrew his toddy ration for that evening. No work, no toddy. For minor offenses, such as the perennial slackness over replacing oars in the boathouse, I waited until I had several people together—in the shop, for instance—and then began to tease the offender. I would ask him, when he had ordered his flour or tea, if he wanted a new pair of oars put down on this month's account or next month's. I always smiled when I said it, naturally, and never ridiculed—that would not have served my purpose. The man himself would look a bit startled, and say *"L'au moi, madame?"* ("On my account?"), and all his friends would laugh heartlessly at this uproarious joke on someone else. The idea of one of *them* having to pay for a new pair of oars was very funny, and the culprit who'd left the old ones lying in the sand below high-water mark would be poked in the ribs and slapped on the back until he too saw the humor and bravely told me I'd better put down two pairs on old what-his-name's account because the other day . . . and new shouts of laughter would break out, and a new victim would be poked and pummeled. It made my point. For a while the oars were better looked after.

If there was a more serious offense, such as a theft, or if there was any general order I wanted to make known, I called an *"appel."* After working hours, the bell was rung again to summon everyone back to the yard. They would have been warned during the day that there was going to be an *appel,* so most people assembled quickly, curiously. It was in the nature of an event. If one or two people were missing, those waiting would shout rudely for them and make ribald comments when they turned up. I would then say my piece, criticizing what had happened but mentioning no names unless it was necessary—that is, I could mention the injured party's name but not the offender; to mention the latter's name, in public, belonged to the final weapon of the *propriétaire* or manager—the "making of a case"—which then had to be reported to the police in Mahé. I could not make cases; I wasn't a Peace Officer. So it was my job to see that things did not get to this stage, by using the *appel*, which dragged everything out in the open in much the same way as a case but without individual accusations. After I had spoken, anyone else who wanted to could. Here was the audience; let him talk now or hold his peace. If someone did volunteer a statement or question, my subsequent strength, like his, would stem from the number of witnesses. And if the *appel* was used merely for a general order or statement of policy, each one of them bore witness that each other one had heard it. There was therefore no excuse for disobeying through ignorance; disobeyals became deliberate offenses, premeditated, and so occurred less often.

Unfortunately, no amount of *appels* could halt thieving, cheating on taskwork, cutting of working hours, idleness, bad days; no amount of teasing in the shop could cut the ice with someone really in the sulks; often they only helped by making the individual or crowd aware that I *knew* and by suggesting that if I could not blame one, I would blame all. No one cared for this. Because in this line I had another right-by-tradition: the right to search all houses and everything in them without warning, for stolen property. It was in everyone's interest to see that I was not driven to this, even if it meant a certain amount of stealthy mackereling. By instinct, the poor Seychellois is secretive and convinced almost to the point of paranoia that he will be stolen from if he seems to have more than the next man—more anything. He does not want someone passing his kitchen to look in. Perhaps that person—spotting something he does not have himself—will mark it and later remove it in the dead of night, when all good people are shut up tight in their houses. Even less does the Seychellois care for his house to be searched and his private treasures exposed to the public eye, so that though he concedes the right of the *propriétaire* to do so, he will endeavor to head the matter off. The *appel* gave him warning; he then knew what was in my mind and could consider what he knew—and whether or not it was on the whole worthwhile to reveal that knowledge to me. The fact that everyone felt the same way opened the ranks which had up to now been closed against us, and mackereling was no longer the offense it had been; it became, on the contrary, tacitly condoned.

One might think this would have created a horrible atmosphere of spies and suspicion, but it didn't. I began to think that perhaps the "closed ranks" which had so worried us had been more in our minds than theirs—no, that wasn't it; more likely that we were becoming something familiar to them, something accepted, and once the barriers of oddity and strangeness were down (with no Gappy to keep raising them), the Seychellois slipped into the more natural child-parent relationship, where no problem was too small to bring to me. Did one have to stick the ugly label of tattling on these confidences? Of course, problems always involved a complaint of another's behavior, and so it was telling of tales, but in self-defense or out of duty to the interests of the property. I realized at last that "no tattling" was an ideal of behavior not often found in actual practice. It was all very well for good saintly Felix to say *"nous Seychellois . . ."* and go on prettily from there, but in reality it was each for himself. It was left to Jean Nioz to voice a more likely truth. *"Nous Seychellois,"* said Jean with his crooked smile, looking out at me from under his cap and shooting his eyebrows up under its brim, *"nous Seychellois, nous jaloux. Nous pas oulez di moune gagner plus qui nous."* ("We are jealous. We don't want anyone to have, or get, more than we do ourselves"—the final "we" referring to the speaker or his immediate family.)

Of course, there are other more general reasons why there is so much petty larceny in the Seychelles. The long leap in way of life between laborer and *grand blanc* means that (as usual in these situations) a man can see his "master" eating or drinking in one day what in money would keep him and his family for two months. Nothing new about that, I'm sorry to say. The man might therefore steal out of the sense that some part of such prodigality was owing to him, or that out of so much wealth a little would not be missed. Secondly, the black Seychellois most definitely believes that the owner of property should look after it—i.e., lock it up. If it is not locked up, it is not valued by the owner; therefore, why should not he, a poor man, help himself? This applies particularly to poultry and pigs and other edibles that can be disposed of easily. Thefts of jewelry—hardly any. Even Mahé is too small. Thefts of clothing, radios, whiskey, and money—in town only. No, food is by far the most usual in the predominantly rural life of the Seychelles. Thirdly, he will steal out of a real desire to annoy, make poorer, or cause to suffer someone against whom he has a grievance. Grievances are definitely nursed here; though the smallness of the communities and the inward-turning of island life means, even on Mahé, that grudges are often hidden away or temporarily put aside, it only requires a bit of grog to release them to rise like genies uncontrolled out of the bottle. Fourthly, there is magic. Stealing for reasons of black magic or the practice of witchcraft is naturally caused by a nursed grievance—if the man is this type of person, and if he has an entrée to a witch or warlock. Often he has only to steal an article and never do anything with it— throw it away, perhaps—because he knows that the stolen-from will believe it was for witchcraft purposes and thus suffer accordingly. I say "man" here, but this is most often a woman's way.

But stealing for reasons of witchcraft did not involve us directly. Most thefts against us seemed to be committed for the first two reasons—that is, the laborer had reached the conclusion that either we wouldn't miss it or we didn't sufficiently look after it. We discovered that it was possible to retain edible goods or utilitarian items like fishing lines, chunkles, pliers, knives, and soap only by watching them or locking them up or a combination of the two. In the Seychelles, one has to be prepared for this, deciding which items are really worth the trouble. As compared to Mahé, however, we have the advantage on Remire that there is nowhere to dispose of inedibles and that there are only a certain number of people on the island to steal the live or growing goods, but that's all. Still, it is something and we are grateful.

One result of reaching this plane of acceptance was to make me much more tolerant about a certain give-and-take in the matter of our agricultural property. For example, rather than raise any sort of an issue with a person who cooks his food in coconut oil every night (the smell floats) but yet never asks to buy any coconuts or buys any of the oil in the shop, I simply charged him for, say, the moderate figure of twenty coconuts a month on his account. From twenty coconuts one can get two bottles of oil, and this is the average single man's consumption per month if he is thrifty. One thing: we know that since he has to grate the nuts, skim the cream, and render the oil himself, he won't—even though the nuts are free—bother to make more than he needs.

This being too lazy to steal very much is a great "saving grace." Here again the island gives us an advantage; in Mahé the single man would have his old mother, his girl friend, her brats, his brats by his other girl friend, and all the rest of his human ties pestering him for sustenance, and thus he would steal more. On the outer islands, with all these people out of sight and mind except one woman and one or two small children, wants are more easily satisfied and stealing is at least reduced.

XVIII

BUT MARK was still away, and all my musings on the advantages of being cut off—*eloignée*—from all the complications of life in Mahé did not dull the worry of being so completely out of reach of, and literally isolated from, Mark when he was not on the island. And even with Mark at my side, there were definite disadvantages to our isolation. To be completely self-reliant, one has to be such a jack-of-all-trades—and to have had so much experience. There were many times, even in these early months, I

Making charcoal

Watching the charcoal stack burn

didn't feel old enough to be living on my past in this way; we had to look after ourselves and our labor force so much more than if we lived on a plantation in Mahé, or near the services of a town. Without the frequent (or cheap) passage of ships and far from "centers of distribution," we were thrown back on our own resources for food, for mending our own equipment, which meant we must be prepared to make do in lots of areas where it is no longer necessary even in Mahé, and because we cannot either rely on regular shipping or afford to send our own boat regularly to Mahé, be inventive about substitutes; for tea (*bois dur* leaves), for soap, (my concoction), for tobacco (tea). Far from making us lazy, it is a life which offers constant challenges: if we run out of rope, we must twist it from coir (coconut husk) or our few wild sisal plants; if we need a pulley block, we must carve one; if we need hasps or hinges or angle irons, we must make those too, cannibalizing on other unused or unusable bits to do so. We throw practically nothing away. We could even keep ourselves in glassware by melting down the bottles we buy and reblowing them, if only we knew how to do it. It is a life in which the widest possible education in handicrafts, field crafts, and primitive pre-industrial-revolution technology is a practical necessity, and I only wish we knew more. Even when we have all the tools and materials we need, we are far from being able to deal with every emergency, and often have to leap across great chasms of ignorance to effect a repair.

Nowhere is this more immediately apparent than in the practice, by me, of medicine. This is a facet of life on the outer islands that has hardly changed over the last hundred years—or over the last million, for that matter. We have no doctor within call (no flying doctor service in the Seychelles, you may be sure) nor one checking in at three-monthly intervals, or at any interval, or ever, unless a touring government official happens to bring one along. True, that I have antibiotics at my disposal gives me an advantage that no one a hundred years ago had, but the rest of my doctoring is, perforce, only common sense. Without laboratory tests, diagnosis is immediately returned to the days of symptom-reading plus intuition; and when the intuition is not informed by any very great medical knowledge, my advantage of knowing the patient is counterbalanced by my ignorance quite as nicely as it was in the rough country doctor of the last century—more so. My ignorance may be less than that of my patients, but they do not suffer from inhibitions. They, happy creatures, can rely on hearsay, while I am only made miserable by fact. So since I am not a modern doctor, I often wonder if had I even the good herbal knowledge competent housewives used to possess, I might not be just as well off.

Still, I muddle along.

One of Mark's and my first really successful feats on the island was to fix the most ancient sewing machine either of us had ever seen. We both hit upon the two (main) things wrong within a few minutes of looking at it, and a little oil completed the cure. The owner—fussy old Mrs. King—was no end surprised to have her machine returned, working, the same day.

Having given this display of cleverness, unexpected in people otherwise so peculiar, a careful night's thought, Mrs. King presented herself at the house early the following morning with another request: we would please pull one of her teeth. Faith is a wonderful thing—very bolstering to the self-confidence—but not all that much. Mark, who gets shudders at the mere mention of teeth, bowed out immediately, but I wavered and finally decided that I could not be committing myself if I simply found out how strongly rooted it was. It was a little wobbly, but not pronouncedly so. I said as much, but Mrs. King, as always, had an answer ready. There are two kinds of teeth, she told me: ones with roots that go straight down and ones with roots that spread about. Hers, she said, was a straight-root one, and so should be easy to get out. I told her I would think it over, and in the end, decided against it. It was hard to tell how much she was suffering because she was always complaining about something; my appreciation of her health (and, I'm sure, hers too) was sadly impaired by her hypochondria. It's fortunate that most of our laborers are not like her. The practice of medicine is difficult enough for the inexperienced as it is.

Before coming to Remire, I had a very good idea of the sort of medical duties that would be required, having lived for years where our house was the nearest and, often, the only source of free bandages, potions, pills, and plasters. In Mukalla the doctors sometimes farmed out duties to volunteers too. I spent many months injecting veiled TB outpatients, boiling urine, and weighing babies. In the Sudan, in our tent on the island of Um Sharifa three miles offshore and three hundred miles by road from Port Sudan, if it wasn't us it wasn't anyone. But on Remire I knew, with a slight sinking feeling, that I would have to be better at everything, a serious devotee of first, second, and third aid if need be, and a midwife as well. This prospect was particularly terrifying. That I had had two babies myself (by so-called natural childbirth, because outside Europe and America this is the way everyone has babies as a matter of course—I suppose I must except military-base hospitals perhaps, but I don't know) did not give me any confidence that I would be much help to someone else. And all my reading only served, naturally, to underline the awful things that could go wrong. So in Mahé I went to the office of the Director of Medical Services and explained my plight, and was at once taken in hand.

In all, I spent about three months haunting the corridors of the hospital, and from the busiest doctor to the teaching sisters, from the harried nurses of the railway-station atmosphere of the outpatients' clinic to the busy staff of the maternity wards, and on down to the youngest of trainees, they all gave me time, and help, and encouragement; and they never sneered, as I had expected them to, at someone trying to learn just enough of their craft and knowledge with the hand as well as the brain and the eye to pass the stage of callow little-knowledge and get to the point of knowing what I did *not* know or could *not* cope with. They were very patient, and they seemed to like teaching me, especially in the long nights, sitting in the maternity wards between deliveries, rolling masks and talking over the last one.

I was also allowed, as a special favor, to watch a Caesarian section. Mark couldn't understand for the life of him why I should be so excited. "You aren't planning to perform any operations down there, are you?" he asked nervously. I couldn't give him any really satisfactory explanation except that by this time I was fascinated by everything that went on; I had discovered a natural bent, I suppose, and was greedy to store up as much knowledge and practical experience as I possibly could before the day came to go to Remire. And because our departure kept getting put off, I managed to be at the hospital quite a lot. It became much more important than anything else, and not only important—feeling twenty-five or so pregnant bellies a week kept its interest as well because no two were the same; and this applied to all the other "routine." Even people's pulses sound so different, one from another.

Oh yes, my eyes had a convert's shine, and it was possibly a salutary jolt that the life of the young girl having the Caesarian suddenly flickered out under the anesthetic. One moment, the doctor had been thoughtfully and methodically explaining his work and I had been all ears and eyes behind my mask; the next the rubber sack lay empty and inert. The surgeon reached up through her body and massaged the girl's heart for ten long minutes, but it was no use. To me, not being a Catholic, it was no particular consolation to hear, from the corner of the room, the baby's cry. The head sister of Maternity wheeled the child out of the room with tears wetting the edge of her mask (Seychellois nurses remain far more overtly sentimental than English ones in spite of an English training), and the doctors, after they had sewn up the corpse, went and sat together over a cup of tea. Everyone looked through or past me as though I were not there; it was the moment to go. I wanted to know *why* but did not dare ask. The show was over, and that was that.

But there were many good safe deliveries afterwards, though it worried me that I always missed the breech ones; since I certainly wouldn't attempt to turn a child in the womb, a breech delivery might well be something I'd have to deal with. With Agnès, for instance.

Every week since Mark's departure I had somewhat anxiously

been feeling Agnès's belly to assure myself that it was the baby's head I felt, upside down, in the right place. Agnès had been offered the chance to go back on the *Argo*, of course, but she chose not to take it. Her risk was now my responsibility. Well, I had until the end of April, if nothing went wrong. But the delivery loomed large and made my other medical duties trivial by comparison.

"I *know*," Mrs. Felix said to me one day, "that my children have got worms because last night they woke up and cried for water, and they never wake up for water unless they have worms."

"But you just wormed them two months ago! It's rather strong medicine, you know."

"They have worms. I was just saying to Felix that it is time we descended to Mahé to worm the children—if we cannot get the medicine here," she added thoughtfully. Mrs. Felix thinks life in Mahé is as nice as it is poor here, and is always after Felix to take her back. Any excuse will do, and I was loath to give her a reasonable one.

"It's up to you, of course, Graziella," I said. "Come up to the house this evening and bring some castor oil with you, and I'll add the chenopodium drops."

Surprisingly, chenopodium is a word they all know. I had no idea what it was when I was first asked for it; the doctor I consulted had given me Helmazine tablets, supposedly good only for round and thread worms, as the standard stuff to use, but the mothers were not inclined to place reliance on small white pills after the heady aroma of the chenopodium and castor oil doses. So I sent for the latter, only to find that the pills, finished by this time, had won preferment, which is something that happens with nearly all my efforts to please.

In any case, roundworm infestations seem to be the most prevalent. Our own children used to get roundworms in Mahé, but not here so far, though we continue to worm them regularly. We have all got over our horror that a child's intestines could contain these vermin in such an ordinary everyday sort of way. It is hard, if not impossible, to prevent a young child from picking things up off the ground, particularly fruit in one's own garden; no one can be watching all the time, and this seems to be the way the worms enter even the bodies of the rich and healthy, while the poor, particularly those with careless parents, can build up infestations great enough to cause the child to *vomit* worms as well. Ugh.

Sundays are worming days. Worm parades of mites behaving well or ill, according to the qualities of their mothers; mites scowling, howling, sullen, vacant, smiling, but mostly vacant. You! You with the big brown eyes staring at me. Do you think? Are you a sentient human being? Or just an animal that cries when struck and stares, mouth hung open, the rest of the time? At least in the Seychelles one cannot be accused of color prejudice, saying these things. Skins are brown, or black, or white in patches, or white all over. It's the vacant "to let" sign in the windows of the eyes that worries me . . . Good. He's swallowed it without twisting away quickly to spit it out. But not so the next one. Her reaction is instantaneous and violent. Her face screws up and she struggles wildly, until finally her nose is held and she is forced to swallow. The next one is apathetic-seeming but neglects either to swallow or to close her mouth, so that a minute later the oil is all on the outside, and so it goes, down the line.

The rest of the work consists of curing septic sores, dressing cuts and mangles (rocks dropped on feet and hands), and the perennial V.D. There are now two types of gonorrhea rife on Mahé, known locally as the "white" and the "red"—the important point being that the red is now penicillin-resistant, and requires streptomycin in a single heavy dose before it will succumb. As the men always know which they have got, I am not asked to make any personal examinations, nor is the acquiring of a case taken seriously. In fact, it is often the cause of some jocular pride to its owner. After his first trip to Mahé, old Payet kept me talking about his "foolishness" in the vainest manner all the way from the shop to the house, as if it proved what a gay old dog he really was. It is not recorded what Mrs. Payet's views were. I must say I think the passing on of V.D. to the partner of a marriage is one really justifiable complaint a husband or wife might make against the spouse's infidelity without being classed as a "nag." But Madame Payet preserved during the course of her injections a most dignified and unconcerned air, while I know I would be more than annoyed in similar circumstances.

XIX

LATE ONE NIGHT at the end of February, we all rushed to the beach. Late, I mean, from the Seychellois point of view. I think it was about seven-thirty. The noise of an engine was unmistakable, though we could see nothing. Then someone on board flashed a light, and a great cry of welcome went up from the beach. (I believe the arrival of a boat is the only event that brings everyone on the island together: it is the one thing that makes us all look, suddenly, outwards. Besides, it is understood that the arrival of a boat takes precedence over all other work, overriding Sundays and holidays, so that no one can be exempt from giving the boat his full attention even had he wanted to be.)

This was a small boat, though; no need to worry about unloading her. She could not be carrying much. The engine chugged away noisily and she came up fast to the anchorage, which told me there was someone on board thoroughly familiar with its location. Mark? Or just Payet? As she anchored we could hear them shouting, and above the other shouts I recognized Ahmed's long whoops. Ahmed can be heard halfway across the island through a dense stand of papaya trees, let alone over a hundred yards of quiet water. We waited. It took them thirty minutes to get ashore, and when they did, there was no Mark.

"The Sahib, Ahmed?" I asked.

"He's coming soon, *insha'allah.*"

"But this boat—whose is it?"

"Ours," said Ahmed. "The Sahib bought it."

"Oh? Who from?"

"Maxime Delorié. It's the *Gros Bouilloir.* Wait—I have a letter for you."

"Oh, good. Did you bring anything with you? Stores and things?"

"Yes," said Ahmed. "Lots of things on board, but a little wet; we had a bad trip down here."

When they had come ashore, I took them to the house and gave them some toddy, then put the children to bed before reading Mark's letter. It was, thank heavens, more informative than usual; Mark's letters are inclined to be full to the brim of how much he loves me, which is gratifying to be sure, but only rarely include information or news in the generally accepted sense of the words. This letter was a model of clarity, considering it had been written in a rush; it said that he would himself be down with the cement and diesel as soon as possible, that the story about the *Veritas* was that Payet and the rest of the crew had left her the first night they arrived in Mahé—not in Port Victoria, but in Anse à la Mouche, on the other side. Here Payet proceeded to unload turtles and fish with the pirogue, row them ashore, and putting them on the bus for town, he went with them, leaving one man on board. When Payet was out of sight, this man swam ashore and took the next bus into town, saying he'd be back that evening. Payet, once in town, sold everything to Lai Lam, collected the money, of which half was his and the crew's, half ours, and proceeded to get drunk. So did the others. So did the man (separately) that he had left on board. Meanwhile, the *Veritas* began to drag her anchor. More wind came up. She dragged farther. Night fell. The *Veritas* drifted onto a rock and sat on it, grinding a hole into her bottom.

In the morning Ernest, a friend of ours living on this bay, was much surprised to see "Mark's boat" apparently sinking in front of his house. He sent out a pirogue. No one on board. He sent a man into town. No sign of Payet. So Ernest got hold of our ex-partner, owner of the *Argo,* and the *Argo* came around to tow the poor *Veritas* away. When Mark got back in February he found her high and dry in Victoria—safe enough, thanks to his friends, but her engine, not having been cleaned of salt water since December, was a "write-off." He decided to cut his losses by buying the *Gros Bouilloir* and selling the *Veritas* for what he could get.

To do Payet some slight justice, Mark went on, Payet had confessed "all" in his letter, the letter he had sent down; and since it wasn't really his fault that no boat had come down to Remire before February, Mark was giving a chastened Tristan (Payet) one more chance. But this time he was going to keep a better eye on him—Ahmed's. Ahmed had seen Dr. d'Offay and was quite well again, so—Mark was sorry about this, but he knew I wouldn't mind too much because we had already discussed shaking him off our apron strings and getting him into more manly work—he was to start working on the fishing side. This would be a good channel for his energies and would give him a chance to try something bigger than cooking. I needn't worry about help with the housework, Mark added: he'd found Carmen, Ahmed's steadiest girl friend, and would be bringing her down himself.

As for Gappy, there had been no trouble at all. The minute they had docked, he'd scuttled off the boat and had got himself a job as a cabin boy on a schooner leaving the next day for far-off Aldabra. (The relief I felt on reading this made me realize that I had been afraid of what Gappy might do; the dispensing of justice in Mahé occasionally bends so far over backwards to protect the poorer man who might for this reason alone be the underdog that we could indeed have had the nuisance and expense of proving our charges. As I have explained, it would not have cost *him* anything to make a case. But evidently he valued his freedom and wasn't inclined to argue in the harsh light of court.)

Satisfied, I was just about to turn on the evening news when I heard Ahmed outside with Felix. "Madame, Madame," came Felix's quiet voice, followed by "Mem-sahib!" in Ahmed's idea of a stage whisper (because of the sleeping children).

I went to the edge of the veranda.

Felix said, while Ahmed nodded agreement, "Madame, I think I must tell you that King has just told me he heard Servina, Berley, and Barbé planning to go out to the boat tonight and steal everything on it!"

I turned to Ahmed. "Well," I said, "I'm sorry for you, Ahmed, but you will have to sleep on board tonight just in case."

Ahmed readily agreed and said he had been going to suggest the very same, and so had Felix, only I had taken their words from out of their hearts and laid them bare between us, and more of this sort of thing, which made me realize the toddy must have gone much too quickly to his tired head. I hoped he wouldn't fall overboard, and said good-night.

The next morning Marcel came pounding along to the house. Marcel is the only person I have ever *felt* walking on sand; even thick sand vibrates to the thump of his busy stride. The earth tremor this time was accompanied by the *clack-clack* of bamboos knocking together. Tapping the toddy palms had been added to his other duties.

"Madame! Madame! The toddy was stolen last night! All the bamboos are dry, dry, dry!" He glared at me, out of very red-rimmed eyes.

"So it was the toddy and not the things on the boat," I commented. Toddy-stealing I couldn't do much about. Except sit up all night, guarding the palms. If toddy was stolen, no one got any the next day; it was as simple as that. I counted on the wrath of their peers at being thus deprived to discourage the greedy ones. In my mind I passed on to other things. I wanted to get started unloading the boat. "Has Ahmed come ashore yet?"

"Ahmed?" said Marcel. "Ahmed never went on board again last night. He was sleeping in the hospital. Only getting up just now," added Marcel with an air of malicious virtue.

I went down to the yard, and got to the boathouse in time to meet Ahmed just stepping out of the small pirogue. I asked him if he had been on board all night.

"Of course," said Ahmed. "Where else?"

It turned out that Marcel was grieved with Ahmed for not bringing him a woman back from Mahé. He had, it was now revealed, sent a letter and fifteen rupees with Ahmed. Where was the woman?

This was the first I or, I'm sure, Mark had heard of the idea, but Ahmed confirmed that it was true. He had delivered the letter and the money, he asserted, but if the silly woman didn't turn up when she was told to, what was he supposed to do?

"Besides," said Ahmed, "I was much too busy. I was all the time at the doctor's, right up to the last day."

"Oh yes? What did he say?" I asked.

"She," corrected Ahmed.

"But I told you to go to Dr. d'Offay. The Sahib says in his letter you went to Dr. d'Offay. What happened? Who did you see?"

"I never went to Dr. d'Offay," Ahmed said firmly. "He could not have cured me. Look how strong I am now. No more troubles! No pain! No dirty blood! I'm all right now."

"But who cured you? Who's *she*? What did she give you?" I like to ask all my questions in one breath because with Ahmed I don't always get a second chance. This time, however, he was brief and concise, even unwilling to enlarge on the details.

"I went to the daughter of that *bonhomme du bois*. *Docteur* something they called him. I went many times, and now I am better. She even gave me some grasses to use here if I am ever poisoned again. She knew I had been poisoned right away, I didn't have to tell her! Her father left her all his medicines when he died, but she doesn't let anyone see what she puts on." (He continued at my insistence.) "You just lie there with your eyes shut and she puts grasses on your chest. I began to feel better right away. I had to give a man ten rupees before he would even take me to her," he added, his eyes large with respect. "You know the one I mean, don't you?"

"Yes," I said, "I know."

"I hope you really are better," I said sadly, and with, I thought, great restraint. "You will have to work really hard now, Ahmed, if you are going fishing."

"Mem-sahib! I am as strong as six camels! You will see. I will earn lots of money for all of us."

One thing about Ahmed: he never lacks confidence in himself.

The second nighttime arrival was Mark on the schooner *St. Louis*. All the fishermen were away turtling in the *Gros Bouilloir,* and we were having one of our odd northwest blows, which meant that the schooner had to anchor far off the camp area on the eastern side. No one heard the boat come in; this time it was nine o'clock and every one of the laborers was sound asleep. Nor did the captain want to disembark his own dinghy. "You can go ashore in the morning," he told Mark, not caring to strain his already tenuous command over the sailors by making them work at night. Mark shouted and shouted shorewards, causing Mrs. King to dream she heard someone shouting, she placidly told me the next morning, but with no other result. On board he stayed, and the next morning we were thrown into the usual rush of loading and unloading with as little warning as ever.

We also had to make up our minds whom to let go and whom to keep. Mark said he'd brought down a whole load of women for various people—why not get rid of some of the men? Sopha, William, and Umane had all "signed off," voluntarily breaking their contracts, while Gappy had been stirring them up, and Mark, after hearing the story of the Great Disorder, decided to make them stick to it. He also decided he could do without the contentious King, who had worked beyond his contract anyway. He went to tell them so they could pack. Then we settled down to weighing the rest of the copra and baling the fish, the sharks' fins, and so forth.

Just as we were hastily finishing the accounts, a group of people assembled outside. "Who's that?" Mark asked, annoyed. I went to see. George William stepped forward. Umane and Sopha were behind him. Oh dear, I thought, some sort of nuisance. But no.

"We have decided we want to stay after all," he said, "now that this island has improved—*commence goût.*"

Mark and I looked at each other and laughed. "I suppose," Mark said to me, "they've heard about Gappy."

Then he turned back to the men. "It's too late now," he said. "I've made up my mind. You will have to go."

It was rather a petty victory, but at the time it made us feel like emperors.

XX

THAT "WHOLE LOAD OF WOMEN"—with my mind fixed on all the work they'd do, I never thought about the complications they might introduce; so while I helped them settle into their houses, allocating beds and tables, and making notes on how many bunks Felix had to build where, I unsuspectingly took a good look at the new arrivals.

There was only one man: my sophisticated gentleman from the early days, Jean Nioz, who had asked Mark for a job again when he saw that Gappy had gone. He had brought a woman for himself much his senior; she sat very straight and stiff on her pile of luggage, her chin with its two small flat leather purses underneath jutting courageously outwards, while we decided exactly where she and the three other women were to go. Barbé, our blackest fisherman, had a wife completely white,

Gappy, the "Great Disorder," Marcel / 173

I noted with surprise, and seven children ranged the shades between. Maxime Esparon's girl friend was *café-au-lait-faible*, however. And Carmen, Ahmed's girl, who had brought her little boy by her "first man" and the baby "for Ahmed," showed brown and tawny in patches, a common type of pigmentation in Mahé, where even the cells of the body seem to get confused in the profusion of mixtures between ex-Africans, ex-Chinese, ex-Indians, and ex-Europeans, plus whatever sails in for a night ashore.

Mark had been pleased to collect these women in Mahé, even if he had had the work of making sure they went to a doctor and got on the right boat at the right time. He thought we should really test the theory that the *poulailler*, the créole word for a family man, makes for a happier island: for the quieter, more peaceful island it would have to be if I were to continue to run it myself while Mark was off fishing. Now that nearly everyone had a woman and a few children here, he was bound to be more hard-working, being no longer able to leave all his responsibilities incommunicado in Mahé.

When the fishermen came back on the *Bouilloir*, there were touching (?) scenes of reunion between Barbé and Léonie, and Maxime and Liliane, and Ahmed and Carmen. I was glad to see that Léonie and Liliane got along well together, for we had had to divide the fisherman's bungalow into two sections, one for Barbé and one for Esparon; it didn't afford much auditory privacy. But then, most Seychellois houses are built with partitions instead of walls anyway, for coolness. I had learned that Léonie was Maxime's cousin, so it was at least a family affair. The Esparons had the smaller segment of the house because they had only one child.

Jean Nioz and his Francine, who turned out not to be so old as I had thought her at first, had to share a house at the camp with two of the bachelors, Bo's'n Berley and old Shokrah. With a bit of tricky interior thatching, we managed to give each unit a separate entrance, but the kitchen went to Francine, while the men had to take over a tank we had been using to make lime in until we could get around to building another kitchen.

In the next house we installed Ahmed and Carmen; in the one next that lived Armand, his wife Agnès, his sister's second-oldest girl (brought down to the islands as a sort of nursemaid), and the three "small masons," as the little boys were called, who were so shortly to be joined by a fourth brother or sister (Armand said he was hoping for a girl this time, which made it unnecessary for me to ask Agnès which she wanted when I checked up on her progress: Agnès, amiable creature, never had and never will have a thought that differs from Armand's).

The next and last house out at the camp contained the Servinas, with three children, and a fourth just starting to show from within the shapely confines of Marguerite. It made her very sick, she said, and unable to work; I was not altogether sorry. We had had to put up with a good deal of her fiery temperament, either on her own behalf or on behalf of oxlike Servina, and the dampening effect of her pregnancy was a relief to everyone.

In the yard itself were Felix, his wife, and three children, now well (and peacefully) ensconced in the "manager's house," and Payet and his portly wife, who had returned to go on working to support her youthful lover in Mahé. The Payets had been mutually blessed with one son long ago. Now they lived alone in the small house Mark had made for them directly behind the boathouse, where Tristan could keep his eye on the boats and Mrs. Payet could keep hers on the fish. (Mark had worked out a new agreement to divide the profits and costs of the fishing with Tristan and Ahmed, by which the latter got a fifty-percent share of the *net* profit. Mark hoped this would have a startling effect on the efficiency of the whole venture, but it was of course still too early to tell. Ahmed had, it is true, gone off on the *Bouilloir* with Tristan and the others almost as soon as the boat had arrived from Mahé, which augured well, but the only immediate effect was that the drying fish, shell, and *bêche-de-mer* were looked after much more carefully by Mrs. Payet. She had always been paid to do it, but now that Tristan had a financial interest in preventing pilfering, he pushed her into a more Cerberus-like role over the contents of the fish racks.)

La belle Marguerite—pregnant

Also in the yard, under construction, was our experimental laborer's house, built of coral with its own reservoir incorporated. We had decided on a good compact design and were seeing how much it would cost. Our people eyed it admiringly as they passed. With its stone walls and aluminum roof it was a much superior article to the little thatch chalets of the camp area. Evidently only we thought it ugly and hot; our determination to use permanent building materials had overweighed our aesthetic sense, while our pockets had not allowed us to make it as large as we would have liked. We were, in fact, using the plinth of Gappy's old kitchen, and making Felix another kitchen of thatch. It was not really a family-sized house, and we had therefore promised it to Marcel, as our oldest and most hardworking *serviteur* other than Armand and Felix. (Ahmed, as a "married" fisherman, could not qualify.)

As for our own new house, the foundations still lay, exposed and bare of walls, very far from finished. Everything on the island took precedence; with only one mason and one carpenter, this was natural enough—especially since we would have been quite content to stay in our shaggy weather-beaten barn, reserving our money for more important things—if we had been permitted to do so.

With what virtuous airs did we talk of friends of ours who "went farming" and were so foolish as to fix up the house first! With what superiority did we sit in our chairs of an evening, moving them slightly away from the latest leak in the roof, and think of the money we were saving. And then, it is such fun to plan a house. We had "built"—on paper—so many houses in so many places since we were married that we now felt quite experienced—on paper. My secret fears that something awful would happen when we started to commit our latest ideas to stone seemed to be shared by Mark, however, for I noticed he was just as loath to begin as I was.

But circumstances pushed us along. We were forced to realize that the old house could not continue to shelter us forever. What are a few leaks in the roof to hardened campers? But when the roof itself looks lovingly and saggingly at the floor, who wants to be in at the consummation of their passionate longing to meet?

Still, we were loath to leave our banded walls of thatch. They made a fine background for our hanging carpets, and created (we thought) a pleasing air of elegant rusticity. With these walls, a well-waxed floor, and the gleaming Arab chests, our Victorian furniture did not look so out of place after all, and we took real pleasure in entering the cool polished haven of the house, where the gray-brown thatch was so restful to the eyes.

The interior thatching, we vowed, must be repeated in the new house, but for the outer walls we planned to use coral—only the whitest, like the houses in Bermuda—cemented with coral cement and built thick for coolness, Arab-style. The roof would certainly be thatch—it is the most attractive and coolest roofing the tropics offer. To me it is infinitely satisfying to look up to the tall ridge and let my eyes follow downwards the patterns made by the leaves close-packed against the poles. And it is just as attractive from the outside: a thatched house seems part of the palms and trees that surround it. We could only hope to repeat this visual pleasure with the new one, while at the same time giving it the tricky virtue of durability. Perhaps building it of *pavé* and coral would make it even more a part of the island. We would have to see.

But as the piles of rocks gradually became absorbed into walls and fresh piles were landed interminably on the beach, we realized that we shared with Edward the Confessor some of the problems he had had to contend with to build his great abbey. We too had to move each rock by manpower, ferry it across an expanse of water, and heft it up the shore. The process seemed so lengthy and expensive we often wondered if it was worth it. But when the weather changed to a time of northerly blows and rain squalls, and we all shivered in the bathing hut and made many a cold wet trip to the privy beyond the chicken run, we could hardly wait to get into a good solid unromantic house with plumbing. Wind makes thatch walls flap so as it whistles through them, and can blow very cold on tropicalized persons.

XXI

AS USUAL, whenever Mark comes back from Mahé, there were at least two hundred new plants of various sorts to set out, dig holes for, mulch, and make netting cages for to protect them from our live predators. But once again, and at last, it was desirable planting weather, with some rain falling every day, and on some days a blustery cool wind made work, on the land at least, a pleasure; it wasn't much good for fishing. Mark had gone to St. Joseph's atoll for mother-of-pearl shell (there was a tempting price being offered in Mahé), but I wondered how much work he was going to be able to get done.

Over the next few days the wind increased even more, and as I had suspected, he came rocking back. But he had got a load of shell, and when the weather calmed he was off again.

So our life began to settle into a pattern, with Mark as *chef de la pêche* and me as *chef de la propriété*, happier than it had been because less troubled, except for the private sadness we felt at each necessary parting. We had at least a feeling of getting somewhere at last, and of earning money, which began to remove some of our most pressing worries.

With the rain, the island began to blossom again, and this renewed our confidence in being able to live off the land.

Our chickens became plump and tender, and we could see beginnings of improvements in the breed in the fluffy balls of chicks being blown about beside their mothers. Our pigs were increasing steadily too, even though their feeding was causing as much trouble as ever: feeding the pigs is classed, as we found out, as the *dernier ouvrage* on an island: when a laborer has sunk so low, there is no further he can go. This was not at all our attitude, of course; the pigs were important, and we were willing to pay generously for their care, providing it was done well. But it never was. It made our first homemade hams and bacon seem like bars of gold in terms of effort taken to create them, and we savored them accordingly.

And with the rain, finally, our enslavement to the last crop of the noxious weed began to end. Marcel informed us that now was the time to "let loose" the tobacco, and every evening the oldest of his green children would have his special old curved knife thrust down their sides to loosen the earth, and their little leaf hats taken away. After he had prepared each one to embark on its new life without him, he stood gazing at it with tender care, fond as a father and just as proud. In spite of his cantankerous boozy ways, Marcel, we thought, was really a good old man at heart and did take his work seriously as something to be done for its own sake. Where would we ever find another like him? It was lucky that he had obviously resolved to stay to the end of his days. He was an admirable thatcher too, skilled in the handwork that only the old men still are—with a few exceptions. Jean Nioz, for instance, who had been in the army, was also busy on "repairs to houses," starting with his own living quarters and, to our surprise, doing it well (a sojourn in the British Army is practically guaranteed to make a male Seychellois so dissatisfied with his birthplace that nothing being good enough for him, he in turn is good for nothing).

Having Jean to do thatching repairs freed Marcel from what had been, until now, one of his chief jobs, and Mark turned once more to thoughts of plantations of sugar cane, manioc, and sweet potatoes, all of which could safely be grown outside the confines of the garden. In between fishing trips he would show Marcel and me where to put what, and how much of it, and he left instructions with me that on good planting days Marcel was to have as many of the women to help him as he wanted.

Each evening, therefore, Marcel and I could consult on the work for the next day, and Marcel would say he needed two helpers, or three, and I'd tell Felix, who had offered to transmit the day's orders and had been gladly accepted. The laborers also accepted this arrangement. They were used to going to the house in which Felix was now living for their orders, and it seemed natural to continue doing so. Only Marcel dissented.

Old Marcel and his tobacco babies

A tobacco plant doing well

There would be no intermediary for him! Importantly, he came up to the "big house" each evening, not so much to receive his orders as to confirm with me what he wanted to do, and to arrange how much help he would need for it. I didn't mind, though; as long as the planting got done, he was well worth humoring. After all, it wasn't as if his sense of self-importance could be much increased no matter how many favors he received.

And we were anxious to profit from the wet spell while it lasted, for we had no idea of when a drought might hit again. We became as weather-conscious as any farmers—and, like them, often found reason to complain of the weather whatever it was. Local lore wasn't helpful: nearly everyone told us something different. Our one certainty seemed to be that we never knew what to expect next.

That this is pretty well true of all tropical weather made it exasperating to read in friends' letters their wonder at our

Old Marcel and his tobacco babies

having taken up tropical life particularly from the point of view of the weather. How, they asked, did we stand the eternal sameness? They never wondered if we found the weather trying, or anything like that. They supposed, reasonably enough, that we didn't have any.

This is most definitely not true. Oh, I am not trying to horn in on those established opposites of winter and summer that govern so much of the world's thinking and living, and which exiles from temperate climates are said to long for (we think about snow too), and whose rhythmic contrasts year after year are supposed to inspire one with a quickened sense of passing time so that one doesn't just waste it lolling about the way everyone does in the tropics. After all, we do live almost on the equator, in a part of the world safe from typhoons, and where, as everyone knows, the sun shines hotly all year 'round, the climate hardly varies, nights are not longer in winter, woollies are never needed, no seasons worthy of the name disturb the even flow of the days, and one year is supposedly indistinguishable from the next. I admit that at sea level this is mostly true. But what everyone forgets is that in a climate of few changes, small ones appear magnified: even a three-degree drop in temperature can make all the difference between too hot to do anything and almost bearable, while another two degrees below that is refreshing and inspiring "spring in the air" or, more logically from our point of view, a "touch of frost." Let us say that we started at eighty-eight degrees (read in the coolest part of the house; the kitchen is often eight degrees hotter!). With our very high humidity (usually ninety percent) this is hot, thoroughly tiring, sweaty weather. I know it is not so bad as Port Sudan, or the Persian Gulf, or New York in July, or Texas, but here we have no air-conditioned escapes. It is still and breathless; the sea is like polished glass; nothing moves, except the water from one's thirsty body following the rules of gravity, steadily downward in endless trickles. Now drop the temperature three degrees—or better still, four, to eighty-four. We begin to feel chipper. A job that took an hour a few days before can be done in half the time now. The whole day suddenly seems longer. And then, if it is eighty-four degrees in the middle of the day, it will be eighty or seventy-eight in the mornings and evenings: positively bracing! Very early or very late, we are even chilly.

Once you are attuned to the climate, you see, little changes mean a lot, and the temperate-climate sneers that this is so only because one's blood had been thinned to the wishy-washiness of near water does not alter the fact that it is a very valuable adaptation for appreciating changes in tropical weather.

But temperature changes are basically trifling. We have much more obvious contrasts too, only they don't come in well-ordered seasons, and the fact that the weather has a limited temperature range to play about in doesn't mean that we are allowed—except during a drought—to suffer much boredom. It seems to be our fate either to grill rainless in what we were assured in Mahé was the wettest time of the year, then suffer deluges of rain when we want to be out fishing, or to have such a Ping-Pong game of sun, squall, sun, squall, sun that we can make few plans of any sort and the island's work proceeds at the jerky pace of a rundown clockwork toy.

The very waywardness of our weather makes preparing for it almost futile. Remire is such a small island that we never in any sense think about going out or taking a walk; we just are out, or we just slip up to the pigpen for a minute or go along to the cemetery to collect some purslane for a salad. But in that minute or two, out of that blue sky, rain can fall in sheets with only a second's warning in the rustling of the palms. One minute you are plodding along, sweat streaming from every pore; the next minute you are drenched with colder water, shivering in flimsy clothing, with no shelter worthy of the name of water-repellent to head for.

And the wind is just as variable. A day will start out with gusts whipping up whitecaps out at sea and high spray of the reef which by noontime has changed to a slow crawly sort of mood, and by night to such perfect stillness that the mosquitoes (very susceptible to breezes, thank goodness) hang in clouds between your eyes and your book, not to mention their other irritating activities near ears, neck, arms, and ankles. How can one possibly concentrate in such weather? It lifts you up and casts you down in a matter of hours; and in the brooder house, if you lower the lamp and open the doors for fear of roasting the little dears, you are sure to have to rush back to protect them from a sudden squall. Small chicks, quietly scratching by their mothers, their wing feathers just starting to protrude, will be lifted clear across the yard by a sudden gust and then wetted before the hen can collect them; the hen herself, after she has collected her brood, will cover them with her tail feathers blown so hard over her back that her fat parson's snitch is all bare.

But if a good stiff breeze, not a gale, comes in sunny weather and holds steady for a few days, we become wind-conscious. A fine sailing breeze, I will say to myself if Mark is out fishing, thinking of all the money he will be saving by not using the engine. Or if Mark is here, we begin to dream to each other of all the uses to which we could put wind: making biltong, or whitefish Norwegian-style; windmills to pump our water, making our own salt with windmills to pump sea water into the pans, wind-driven electrical generators, fresh-water pumps to irrigate our crops . . . Then the wind dies away and it is hot and still again, the sea like glass, and the whalers, drawn up on the beach with masts unstepped and sails stowed because it's been too squally to go out, are pushed back into the water without erecting masts or sails, there being no wind to use them.

Of all our bad weather, it is the squall-born heavy rains that are the most trying to live with—even though we could not live here *without* rain, and complain furiously when we do not get enough. Rain is like medicine to us—necessary, but to be endured rather than enjoyed. Unlike Mahé, where it rains a lot, the outer islands are dryish places. We have no mountains to catch the rain, nor even very high trees; what falls on us would have fallen on the sea had we not been here, so that we can take no credit for getting wet, and nothing we can do could increase our rainfall. If we could increase it, we would be able to do a lot more agriculturally, but as it is, we are sun-oriented and sun-dependent, and very much take its steady hot shining for granted, so that when, with little or no warning, rain falls, we are in turn surprised, thankful, annoyed, wet, sodden, cold, cross, and depending on its force or duration, often find we are financially less well-off than before it started.

Whenever it rains hard, therefore, we can think of at least twenty good reasons why it should stop.

In the first place, there are the boats to worry about. If any of our small boats are out far, the rain blots the island from view. Will they get back safely? If the *Bouilloir* is out, she and the fishermen will be all right, but will the fishermen catch any fish? Will they stay out until the rain is over, or will they scuttle back (wasting fuel) because of the discomfort on board? And when will the rain end? On board any boat, this is a question passionately asked. In a dinghy, after the first half-hour, the body is given over to misery. In a larger semidecked boat it takes only a little longer. Wooden decks in the tropics are rarely well enough made, seasoned, or caulked to be waterproof. Anywhere on the boat is soon as wet as anywhere else; hands are numb and white and wrinkled, and the fish which has been caught looks about the same, since the salt is leached out of it as soon as it's put in. The figures of the elderly Payet and Bo's'n Berley are studies in wet ex-army duffle coats; the cook in a tarpaulin sits huddled by the deck stove that won't light, even though the wind produces promising little gusts of black smoke from under the diesel-soaked wood. No tea again. Up in the bows lies Ahmed, wet but asleep under the recently downed foresail, while beside him huge Rogile, his pigeon-toed size-thirteen feet dangling over the hatch cover, sits gloomily looking out over the gray sea. No one will do any line fishing—fish aren't to be tempted in such weather, so it's no use getting even colder and wetter for nothing. Which means that Mark, whichever boat he is on, sits in the stern, fuming. Saving his presence, Tristan would have headed for home an hour before, but no power on earth can make a sea fisherman fish when he's sure he won't get any.

If, on the other hand, the boats are at anchor when the squall hits, we worry far more. There's nothing like a good squall to make us realize how exposed we are, with our toy boats bobbing on the heaving waters, moored by bits of string to tiny anchors in the coral far beneath, and ourselves mere insects on our low foothold above the level of the sea. Even a six-foot rise would send us swimming for our arks and leave the Seychellois—who, with the exception of the gogglers, can't swim—clinging to the palms with the birds of the air. A humbling thought. So the boats become even more of a life line when we hear of tornadoes or earthquakes and tidal waves in other parts of the world, and a man is dispatched in every lull to check the anchors and keep up the bailing, while two sleep on board at night, worried over by Mark (in our last bad storm, they slept so soundly the *Bouilloir* dragged her anchor three hundred yards without either of them waking up).

The *France*—as we had left her
when we came to Remire

But if Mark happens to be away, it is much more worrying. Especially since changes in our weather can be so abrupt.

When Mark returned from Mahé early in March, depositing a whole shipload of (as yet) untroublesome workers, he had known he would soon have to go back. Our schooner, the *France,* was coming along well, but was at the stage where he should be there himself to supervise the work. By the middle of April, therefore, he was wondering when he should leave and hoping that a fishing boat would call in, offering him a lift, so that the *Bouilloir* could continue fishing in his absence.

Then the engine of the *Bouilloir* broke down, a spare part was needed, and Mark decided he would have to go immediately to D'Arros to catch the schooner *Arne,* expected there shortly. He would have to be rowed (it was still, quiet weather, so still that even the light sail of the dinghy was useless), and Mark took all the fishermen and gogglers with him, to have a turn at the oars.

"A damned hot trip," he said, "but I don't dare wait another day." He looked around the horizon. There wasn't a cloud in sight. The barometer was steady at "fair."

He left in the afternoon, planning to row through the night and arrive in the early morning—which I could only hope and pray he had, because by morning a fierce northerly gale was blowing. I woke up to the restless sound of the palms and the first heavy drops of rain; soon the rain was lashing across the island, and the little *Bouilloir,* moored in the teeth of the wind, was being thrown and tossed, then brought up short on the martingale of her chain, with every wave. Obviously she would have to be moved to the other side of the island—but how? It was no use waiting for the fishermen to get back (D'Arros lies southeast of us), but what was left on the property could hardly have been described as sailors. I now regretted having paid so little attention to our marine affairs, for even had the engine been working well, I knew I'd never have been able to start it. Diesel engines are heavy, we had no electric starter, and this engine was not in its first youth.

In a short lull a man was sent out to inspect her moorings and bail her; there wasn't time for more before another squall hit. I decided that she would have to be rowed around *inside* the reef at midwater, whenever it stopped raining enough for this to be feasible. The tubby *Bouilloir* is not an easy boat to row, but on the other hand, I wouldn't have dared raise a sail in such weather, nor would I have dared take her outside the reef and then over it again with the crew, all pretty unwilling, at my disposal. Tactfully I consulted Felix, and finally he agreed —*if* we could get the anchor up, and *if* we could have a rope on shore (like a horse-drawn canal barge)—to undertake this perilous voyage. Poor Felix! Felix gets seasick the minute his feet leave land or something connected with the land like a tree or a house, and the rest of the "crew" weren't much more promising: one thin mason, two frail old men, the effete Nioz, brainless Servina, fortunately as strong as an ox, and two boys neither bright nor strong. All the women had to be ignored as possibilities; the ladies of the Seychelles do not go in for messing about in boats, and so were even less useful than I.

We waited anxiously for three days for midwater to coincide with daylight and a lull in the storm; then after a struggle to get the fouled anchor up, we fairly steamed around the corner of the island with the wind at our backs, dragging the rope with its gaggle of women behind us, dropped these appendages off the camp, and rowed slowly on, putting her anchor down just off the sugar cane plantations on the southeastern side. It was none too soon. The engine cover had broken loose, and the engine had got thoroughly soaked with rain and bilge water because we had not been able to keep her bailed out; so everyone came ashore with a feeling of a job well done—even a bit elated at its ease—including Felix, who had only been sick three times.

But the continuing deluges of rain, even in the lee of the island, swamped the engine every night, and it was, in fact, two whole weeks before the fishermen could get back from D'Arros—two weeks before we knew if Mark and those with him had even arrived there safely. I had to laugh at my early vapors when Mark had gone off to Mahé on the *Veritas;* as Defoe moralizes in *Robinson Crusoe,* if you think you are badly off, Providence will always show you that it could be worse. But, correspondingly, experience is toughening. I worried far less than I had before, having become more fatalistic or simply more inured to the hazards of our chosen way of life. Probably I thought nothing more could happen than had happened already.

But discounting the worry of caring for boats moored virtually in the open sea—and we have a good anchorage, as island anchorages go—we seem to be fretted by weather all out of proportion to the actual strength of the storm. Probably the prevailing temperature does make one careless and therefore vulnerable. Our work is done outside to keep cool, and not having to protect ourselves from hail or hurricanes makes us lazy; our buildings are more shade than shelter.

Therefore, when it rains, there is a rush to cover the fish and copra, *calipée* and *bêche-de-mer,* and another rush back to the house to roll up the carpet and pull furniture away from the latest leaks; and if the rain goes on and on, any work in progress —from laundry to pig-food cooking to carpentry to charcoal-making—virtually ceases, while construction, involving the use of lime and cement, halts entirely. Even conscientious Felix only works at half speed, though with the same amount of effort, at his bench hastily moved in under the boat shed (damp wood sticks to the saw). Nor can he continue his main job of the moment, which is outside, and so has to do fill-in jobs. There are plenty of these, naturally, if only we could think of them when it starts to rain, or if we could be sure Felix was going to be available to do them: a lot of wet air blowing about is generally the signal for Mrs. Felix to get another attack of asthma.

And in the rain, our baby turtles in their cement rearing pens almost get drowned by fresh water, and a complicated system of siphons has to be kept working, both in order to keep the salt level high enough to maintain their natural bouyancy and to keep them inside the tanks, not floated out over the edge. Raising baby turtles from eggs hatched on the island is Mark's pet project, and nothing can be allowed to happen to them.

Our normally rather hot kitchen, hotter than the surrounding air because it is fly-screened, is quite all right for rain (except that we are deafened under the aluminum sheeting of the roof), but when the water is being blown, fly-screening has little stopping effect, and there seems to be no quiet windless place to light the lamps at night: every corner is well-supplied with eddying drafts. If one builds for good air circulation, in bad weather one gets it with a vengeance.

Of course, we made an effort to design our new house sensibly, with bad weather in mind, but the greater need for draft and coolness cannot be gainsaid. Inevitably, there will be areas of the house, like the veranda, that are just going to get wet; at least the roof won't leak.

But as for conditioning the property and ourselves so that rain is not a state of emergency, I think it is impossible. All our resolves get promptly forgotten when the sky clears up to that brilliant blue never-rained-in-my-life look that so persistently deceives us too.

XXII

EVER SINCE MARK'S DEPARTURE I had been hoping he would return before Agnès gave birth, but it was not to be. By the end of April, I mentally prepared each night to hear Armand's soft voice at the window, and so it happened, one midnight. It had been arranged with Mrs. Payet, who looked comfortingly large and capable, that she would help me; when Armand came I sent him back for her at once while I moved our children into my room, set up the camp bed, lit the fire from the evening's embers, and tried to calm my nerves.

I was hurrying. Experience in Mahé had taught me that the working-class Seychelloise never arrives at the hospital until the very last stages of labor, and I was pessimistically convinced that my plea to Agnès to warn me when she began her pains had been ignored. Sure enough, Agnès's sighs as she climbed the steps and slipped onto the bed showed there wasn't much time. While Mrs. Payet established Agnès's clothes on one chair and herself stolidly on another, I washed and shaved Agnès and had barely time to remove the towels before the baby's head appeared. Soon a girl slithered into my hands, and with what I hoped was a mask of icy calm, I prepared to tie off the umbilical cord. Madame Payet remained seated. Bored? Ruefully I heard the teaching sister's soft Irish voice assuring me "Oh, there is always a *sage femme* on the outer islands, and all you really have to do is stand around and give moral support." However, I was glad enough that neither Madame Payet nor Agnès was in a position to see how my hands trembled as I tied the cord, such a slippery cord, and fumbled for the scissors to cut it.

"Will you wash the baby now?" I asked Madame Payet coolly, and she rose majestically from her chair to take the small bundle while Agnès and I waited for the placenta.

An hour later, after cups of tea all 'round, little Wendy, as Armand had asked to call her, lay mewing softly on Rory's bed; Agnès was asleep, and Madame Payet gone home with all the soiled linen. The room looked spick-and-span; there were no signs of trouble. But cursing myself for a fool, I stayed awake the rest of the night, thinking of the awful possibilities so vividly described in *Medicine for Nurses*. Twenty times at least, Agnès and her baby were scrutinized before the welcome daylight finally appeared. Thank goodness, I reflected, Marguerite had decided to have hers in Mahé. One success had by no means bolstered my self-confidence, and had put me in no mood of elation—rather the reverse.

· · ·

Besides, preoccupied or not, I couldn't help seeing that the peaceful lull of quietly running things, with the planting (and therefore Marcel) given priority, was coming to an end. It had been a mistake to think that Marcel would not be spoiled by a few privileges; even gentle Felix had begun to make guarded remarks, and presently Agnès and her visitors opened my eyes yet more. Each time Marcel turned up with some request for equipment or help, or to give a progress report (his way of making sure I knew he was hard at work), there would come a sound like the hissing of snakes from the women, whispering. It was impossible not to sense the change in atmosphere when he was around, and I wondered what he had done.

I suppose it was inevitable that Marcel's empire, built only on the intemperate foundations of Marcel, should come to an end. But in fact drink for once had nothing to do with it, and it still remains very curious to me that this sexless old bag of bones and leather managed to stir up such a hornet's nest of feminine rage. Perhaps it was the rain? Fertile nature around him? Youthful plants blossoming in his care? Babies in mine? Who knows? What is certain is that Marcel, presented with the opportunity of having women working under him on unfrequented tracts of Remire, was making the most of it. Starting with verbal descriptions of his prowess, he finally progressed to lewd suggestions of the strictly graphic type most Seyechellois find fetching coming from manly youth, or a rich old man, but that this —— should think . . . ! Dignities never before apparent were ruffled, and squawks of protest were poured into the ears of apparently credulous husbands or official keepers of the insulted flesh, who then came hotly to me to register complaint.

Naturally this was tiresome, but I became seriously annoyed when the women, sure of their weapon, proceeded to go on strike until I did "something."

It was difficult to find anything to do. Nothing could be proved, one way or another: Marcel had never tried to take on more than one woman at a time and even then only, so far as I was told, verbally, which meant there were no witnesses and no question of actual rape. For all I knew, the stories could have been complete fabrications designed to Get Marcel, and I tended, if anything, to believe this was so. For Marcel himself mined unsuspected veins of gravity and self-respect, firmly denying every charge. He was old, he said calmly, and loved drink better. That was certainly true! Besides, was it likely that Marcel could force his attentions upon anyone? The wenches we were employing may not have had brains, but they were strong and active and more than a match for him physically. What should I do about words? Everyone used the same ones. The fact that what these suddenly-ladies regarded as a compliment from anyone else they thought an insult coming out of the mouth of a toothless old man was, well, just too bad; I could hardly put him in jail for that.

So, quietly, round one to Marcel. The trouble passed, at least on the surface. He was blessedly silent for nearly a week, and almost mouselike. The women went back to work, and with a little arranging, we managed to keep everyone apart. Eventually, the men started to call Marcel "Taureau" in good humor, and Marcel apparently accepted the name equably enough, saying nothing in return, and smiling silently to himself.

But Marcel, you see, really believed he was a bull. One Saturday, after work, he came and announced that upon the arrival here of the next boat, he, Marcel, must return to Mahé for the purpose of acquiring a woman. A man, he said with great dignity, cannot be expected to live alone. And having been failed by Ahmed, he would obviously have to go himself. If he didn't get the one he had in mind, he said, there were plenty of others. He grinned toothlessly. Plenty of women, he emphasized, who would be glad to partake of such a home as he could provide.

From this time on, Marcel started to fix up his house. And (for money) the women he had so vilely insulted turned around and helped him. One embroidered pillowslips. Another made curtains. A third a brush and a mat for the floor. Marcel bought a cast-iron brazier in the shop and got to work thatching his kitchen, the frame for which had been up a long time. These efforts were observed, and he became the butt of island humor.

"When is she coming, Marcel? Is she pretty, Marcel?" To all of which he would smile quietly and keep his thoughts to himself.

But Ahmed had seen Her (the one to whom the down payment had gone). Fat, he said, like a barn, like a lime kiln, large and solid and strong. Pockmarked. Feet in slippers so worn on one side that the feet walked in the dirt with the shoes beside them. One tooth. (Like to like.) And dirty! This impressed Ahmed most. He may have lived all his early life in the filth of Mukalla *suq* with a stairwell full of goats, sheep, chickens, and droppings, but he is, like most Arabs, very clean in his personal habits. This female, said Ahmed, had a great smear of what she had been eating on her cheek, and that part of her ungainly body not covered by her sacklike garment was grimy and gray.

This information soon went the rounds, and everyone became even more good-humored. The women had won a complete victory and could afford to be generous. On the day Marcel finally set sail for Mahé he was cheered by the entire island, with much slapping on the back, handshaking, and *"bonjours"* (*Bonjour* is said instead of *au revoir*). He went on board the boat with a small box containing his best clothes, including a new pair of sandals bought in the shop and specially saved for this occasion, a fifty-rupee advance, and the little piglet we had given him under his arm.

But in Mahé, he got drunk, I suppose very drunk—for we never saw him again.

THREE

Liliane and Léonie— Feline Disturbance

XXIII

THE TWO WOMEN who had been the chief attractors of Marcel's aged lust were Léonie, wife of Barbé, and Liliane, mistress of Léonie's cousin Esparon. They were still sharing the former fishermen's bungalow at the time of their "strike"—long before Marcel showed any intention of leaving—and this was where I visited with them to talk it over. The bungalow has a long continuous veranda used by both families, and the ladies were ensconsed in deck chairs like dowager queens, sewing busily and only disturbing themselves to flounce to their respective kitchens to throw more wood on the fire or stir their curries with downcast modest eyes. It was wonderful to watch, which I did for a while. Since they were the injured parties, it was up to me to speak first.

Liliane was a firmly built feline sort of girl whose face no one ever looked at. Even I, supposedly unblinded by her sexual attractions, can hardly say what her face was like. It was so nothing compared to her hips and her walk—this last was enough to enrage a man, and did, many, during the time she was here; equally, it kept her keeper in total and abject enslavement. The reason we were presented with the honor of employing the Esparon *famille* at all was that old Payet had taken a fancy to Liliane. While we were still in Mahé, a friend of Mark's had asked Payet, "What are you thinking of, taking that one to Remire?" (meaning Esparon, who had a reputation for being the laziest of fishermen) and Payet had replied, frankly, that he like the ——. We got the story from Ahmed. Poor Payet. By the time Liliane got to Remire, Mrs. Payet was well in control of her erring husband, and though she may have been sending back all her money to another man herself, she was not going to tolerate any divided loyalties on the home front. Payet never got (so far as we know) more than his hand near her bottom, for a playful smack while the dragon wasn't looking.

Not so some of the others. Some? I think nearly all the fishermen and at least two property men, and even, we suspect, the gentle quiet Felix, one dark night. Felix was always so very Against Liliane, while she was here.

But to go back to the veranda. Liliane sat in front of her door, and Léonie sat before hers. Even in their poses, they were opposites. Liliane sat neatly, with her feet tucked beneath her, her breasts well braed into sharp points beneath her dress, her waist cinched tightly by a wide plastic belt; Léonie was all arms akimbo, legs any old how, so that her seat was more saddle than chair, her breasts very obviously not constricted in any way, but all of this not mattering very much because with Léonie (speaking for myself, anyway) one's eyes were drawn first to her face. The rest was so carelessly put together, so obviously (beside Liliane) not made anything of, so negligently clothed—buttons missing, shirt awry, hair awry, skirt pinned on, patched, but the patches hanging to one side, revealing to all the world the holes they had been meant to cover. Admittedly, these were working clothes. I wear some pretty old stuff myself, and I am relatively affluent. But this day neither Léonie nor Liliane was working, and Liliane was dressed in raspberry-red, with an orange headband, lips bright and shiny, her black hair teased out into her Sunday look, which was a sort of bushy halo around her head (ordinary days, she wore it in short pigtails). Léonie, on the other hand, was as she always was, a patchwork of gray whites and gray-grays, so that it was only to the once-fine beauty of the face, tanned the palest of browns by the sun and lined only a little by childbearing rather than thought, that the eyes were drawn.

Léonie, for all her tatters, looked a lady, while Liliane looked like exactly what Marcel (in his only counterattack, long after the event) had assured us all he *knew* she was (so, he pointed out, why shouldn't he have asked for it too?).

Instinctively, therefore—by which I mean acting on prejudices formed by appearances—I had mentally discounted the likelihood of Liliane's virtue being in question through any

Liliane and Léonie—Feline Disturbance / 199

verbal assault of Marcel's, and addressed myself to the older, more matronly Léonie for her side of the story. I knew I would have to listen to all of it; their feelings were to be soothed only by the chance to pin back my ears, and the plantations were waiting on their pleasure.

Léonie at once took up her favorite position of bedraggled dignity. "I won't repeat what that disgusting old man said to me, Madame. It wouldn't be right. Never! Never have I heard such things! I'll say no more!"

With which she proceeded to tell me in lurid detail every phrase and gesture, using such idiomatic *créole* that I understood nothing anyway, while Liliane, not to be outdone, came over from her end of the veranda and talked to me busily at the same time. About all I comprehended was Liliane's trump card (Léonie had run out of breath), in which she revealed with a very knowing look that Old Lenclume had assured her, Liliane, that "First he would sleep with you, Madame, and then Léonie, and then me—" A frown flitted across Liliane's face. "Then he'd do all the others, if he felt like it!"

I laughed. "Oh, really, how can you have taken such silly nonsense seriously? Marcel always talks just to talk, like any other old man; he's old enough to be your grandfather, and stupid in the head. Why flatter him that you take him or his silly words as even possible? You should have laughed at him! And now," I went on, "you'll stay away from work? He'll think you're frightened of him, or think he can do what he says!"

Both of them looked indignant, but not so positively as before. "Ah, Léonie," I said, before they could think of saying anything, "really it is a compliment, and to you too, Liliane. You see how much temptation you cause even to an old man just by being so pretty?"

Liliane, who had a good idea of her powers in this line, did not change her expression perceptibly, but Léonie looked up at me quickly, then down, while a wonderful simper of pleased vanity spread over her tired face. At which point I collected the dogs and went away.

. . .

I don't think it could possibly have been pique at the bedding order that caused Liliane and Léonie to begin to fight so disagreeably; much more likely it was just proximity. But their rows began to make life difficult for everyone, and especially for me—and Mark when he was at home. Ours is the house nearest the fishermen's bungalow, and Liliane had a very shrill, carrying voice. If it wasn't at war with Léonie, it was stridently calling "Max-*zime!* Max-*zime!* or "P'tit Max-*zime!* (the name of the child—a whiny cowed little boy who liked nothing better than swatting my baby ducks with the end of a coconut frond), as the case might be. I decided to remove the voice and the sparring partner at one and the same time by again changing the housing around. But it proved difficult. There could be no question of moving Felix, or Payet, or Servina and Marguerite; nor Armand; nor Ahmed, with Carmen and two children, and a third brought down to look after the other two, and a fisherman, Rogile, camping on the veranda outside. The only hope was the end house, sheltering Francine and Jean, and Bo's'n Berley, and Shokrah, a decrepit old man Mark had had as cook on board the fishing boat until we discovered that he had nearly as green a finger as old Marcel, at which point he was promptly transferred to property work.

But what could we do with the bachelors?

At this time, as Marcel had not yet decamped, there could be no question of either taking his house away or moving the other bachelors in with him; he wouldn't have stood for a lot of dirty old men in *his* house. On the other hand, we had been long wanting to do something for Jean and Francine, both of whom were good workers and merited better housing. Could moving the disputatious Liliane and family into half of their house be construed as "something better"? I thought not, and had this idea forcefully confirmed by Jean, whom I felt obliged to consult.

At this point of stalemate, Mark at last returned, full of good news on the *France*'s progress, but horrified to hear that it had taken the fishermen two weeks to get back from D'Arros—the bad weather had been so localized that he had no idea our storm had been more than a passing squall. And now he'd brought the *Bouilloir*'s spare part only to be faced with the probability that her whole engine would have to be sent to Mahé and overhauled; another debit to be chalked up on the account of weather. Alongside this serious matter, the housing question didn't seem so important—problems never did when we were together to deal with them—but I presented it to him anyway, and he finally decided that we would have to continue to suffer for the sake of peace, and put the Barbé family in with Jean, shifting the bachelors back to the hospital. I was very unenthusiastic. Mark had taken half the hospital away to increase the size of the store, but I had managed to get what was left repainted white and had put the beds and mattresses into some kind of order. And wouldn't half of a house be too small for all the little Barbés? But Jean, Mark said, was adamant that he wouldn't live next to the Esparons, while he was perfectly willing to live next to Barbé; and there were, Mark reminded me, more than enough bachelor bunks in that house to sleep all the little Barbés. We had no choice. The Barbés were moved and Léonie in her rags swept out of the bare little battleground for the last time, her nose in the air, leaving Maxime and Liliane their empty victory.

From then on, Maxime and Liliane lived as social lepers, in palpable isolation. Léonie, always friendly and talkative, a great sitter on others' verandas, saw to the pulverizing of what little might have remained of Liliane's reputation with the ladies of Remire, and found it no great labor. It was as natural that women should be wary of Liliane as they were unafraid of Léonie. If Léonie's clothing revealed perhaps a little more than it should, it was always by accident or inattention or a lack of mending: her sewing was reserved for some intricate and useless piece of embroidery which I had to admit contained beautiful work, wish as I might that she'd mend her clothes first. Léonie had a disarming personality too; even women as jealous as the Seychelloises are could take no exception to Léonie. Besides, she was beginning to swell with an eighth Barbé; this always appears to put a woman out of the running for a bit.

Liliane, on the other hand, never seemed to get pregnant, but remained and remained the same slim threat. It is a tribute, of a sort, that she was so universally disliked, and that her Max-*zime*, really an amiable enough fellow when sober, clever with his hands, good with animals, not a bad harpooner and fisherman (when he was not asleep), was so despised for her sake. Liliane could not have been described as white to our way of thinking, but both she and Maxime were classed as such by everyone else: poor whites, low whites, whites who "didn't know how to live"—like white people, that is. Whereas, Léonie, the very caricature of a poor white, was never, even behind her back, so insulted as to be called one. Léonie, who lived in a disorder as total as her dress, while Liliane kept her house so painfully neat and her person so groomed and Max-zime so white-shirted, and Little Maxime so shirted and shorted as well! Little Maxime was not either allowed or asked to play with the other children, of course. Every time the poor lonely child strayed toward the yard, where we had put up a swing and a seasaw, he would be called back sharply by his mother. I felt very sorry for him, even guilty; our own children played with the others half the day, their blond and red heads standing out clearly amongst the black ones, but never with Little Maxime. And when he took to coming around to our house, Rory would casually let him hold a toy and give him some of whatever there was—a cookie, a slice of bread. He certainly did not exclude him. But soon he and Ming would run down to the center of play in the yard, where Little Maxime was not allowed to follow, leaving him sitting on our steps, sad and alone. It made me feel guilty not because our children were mean to him, but because *I* then did not want him around either. A turned-inward child given to tormenting ducks and breaking things in an innocent innocuous way could not be left to wander my house at will, and I had no time to spare for him. So from our house he would also be "sent home."

And now even Liliane's attractiveness seemed on the wane. Men who had enjoyed her once or twice did not return. The mechanics were too difficult. Wives were suspicious, and Maxime, with no friends himself, was always at home. Men who used to get Maxime drunk at their own expense in order to have him out of his house, were no longer willing to bother. Their isolation was complete.

Into this situation walked Alex, muscles rippling, sneering smile on his face, heavy-lidded eyes half open, like a sleepy black god.

We were expanding our shark fishing, and Mark had brought back two more fishermen from Mahé. One was a pleasant curly-haired quiet fellow; the other was Alex. Alex was old Shokrah's nephew, but it was impossible to think they had actually come from the same family. Shokrah looks more Indian than anything else, and everything about him is old, long, thin, bent, crooked, flat. His color is light brown, topped by a fuzz of gray hair mostly attached to the skull just above his ears. He is very quiet, while still having the energy to complain in a resigned sort of way, like Eeyore, about how God, life, we, and all the others treat him.

Alex, however, was black, black, black, and shiny all over with animal energy not at all used up by the amount of work he vouchsafed to us and quite belying the sleepy look he affected as attractive to the opposite sex. He was always just slightly insolent to Mark and me, but he was a good fisherman, and fishermen are not so easy to come by that either of us cared to chuck one out for being cheeky. We ignored it. He seemed to get along all right with the others, with Rogile, Justin (the other new one), and with Ahmed and Carmen too; all three of the young fishermen were now sharing Ahmed's large veranda. Carmen was like a little queen bee these days, dressed in novel fluffy garments, looking very pretty—she is a pretty girl anyway, with clear brown eyes and snub nose and freckles on a face framed by straight black hair which she keeps combed and clean. But don't mistake me: Carmen may have gone around looking like the pussy with the bird inside, but no one could be so crude as to make lewd comments to, or about, Carmen. Carmen was Ahmed's, and that was that. The fact that she and Liliane were sworn enemies was owing to Ahmed's having sampled the latter flower, and not to the fact that one of her drones suddenly upped and left her hive for *chez* Esparon.

Or so we suppose. In any case, it happened quietly enough one day that Alex moved into the empty part of Esparon's house and established himself there as Esparon's nearest, dearest, and only boon companion, whom Esparon defended to the world as such; let no one say there was any funny business about sharing Liliane, said the white turkey, fanning his feathers and drumming bravely. "We're just very good friends. Are people so jealous of me that I can't even have a friend?" he asked me once, as he was working in the pig park. ("Park" is the créole expression for any enclosure containing mammals, birds, or reptiles: turtle park, duck park, chicken park, pig park.) "Here I am, working at the *dernier ouvrage*, which Monsieur and Madame have given me, but I still hold up my head. Words cannot hurt me," he added. "What do I care for these ignorant savages? Alex is my friend."

It's a pity, I moaned to Mark, that they're such snobs about pig keeping, whatever color or kind of man we try! What do we care about his morals, or how he arranges his life, if only he'd do his job well!

Esparon was working with the pigs now because the other fishermen had refused to work with *him*—except Alex, of course—and we had decided to give him the chance to "prove himself" by doing the pigs for us, or back to Mahé it would be. The reason the fishermen gave for kicking him out was that he did not pull his weight, but of course Esparon chose to think his former buddies were persecuting him because of his interesting *ménage à trois couleurs*. In feeling sorry for himself, and tight with rage at the gross untruths told about his Liliane, he imagined that the others cared what he did and they watched him constantly, avid for scandal.

He had a point. Remire is hardly such a bustling metropolis filled with amusements that a lively source of gossip can be ignored. But he could not accept, naturally, that the clique of the fishermen really did not care if Alex had Liliane or not, but only that Esparon never did his share of the work. Nor would he accept that we had given him the pigs to look after because he was good with animals, rather than because we, like the others, wished to humiliate him.

Poor put-upon pink young man, with his sandy-haired man's body housing the same small spirit that will animate his son after him. How hard it is sometimes to be born with a white skin.

XXIV

LÉONIE, YOU MAY BE SURE, made the most of all these goings on, but the very tranquillity of whatever arrangements Esparon and Alex had worked out between them did not offer really good material for active scandalmongering of the sort Léonie liked. She was a reporter with no news, but a daily column to get out all the same. What could she do but invent items to fill it? Leaving the now dull subject of her cousin's household, she began to nose around on the subject of marital infidelities in general, cozily confiding in first one female and then another which man she had seen going to whose house, and when.

Needless to say, it would have been much better for Léonie had she left this dangerous topic alone. Being the leader of a fine cohesive group all anti-Liliane (Léonie never blamed her cousin for anything but his weakness; clearly he was bewitched) had been satisfying, but in setting herself up as the spyer-out of all immorality, she was taking unjustifiable risks from the point of view of her own safety. She made women already suspicious more so, and the men furious. She fastened their attention on something no one ignores anyway; she liberated dormant jealousies; Pandora-like, she let loose a host of malevolence, and inevitably she could not remain unscathed herself.

Though I suppose her own heavy love affair might have gone on unnoticed much longer if Mark and I had not decided both to change the housing around again and to call a halt on the Barbés' intemperate spending in shop. These two blows robbed Léonie of her cover and her independence of choice, and deftly whipped the carpet from under her pose of virtue all at the same time. It was such accidental inflictions of bad luck that used to make even thoughtful sober cynics believe that gods were angry with them. What Léonie thought, I never found out. But I will have to hand it to her that she faced the situation with a certain brazen courage one could not help but admire.

By May, rain came less and less frequently. The last of the tobacco was harvested, the potatoes and sugar cane were growing well, and the new trees had either taken or died. It was time to stop planting new plants and start taking care of the old ones, and Shokrah had this work well in hand. Whatever we had set out had to be well established before June, when the harsh, salty southeast wind would be blowing across the island. This, Mark decided, was the time Marcel could best be spared for his trip north to Sabine country, and so when a fishing boat opportunely turned up, Marcel was allowed to leave.

Two weeks later, the fishing boat returned, as it had promised, with some extra stores for us but without Marcel, and Mark was angry enough to reallocate his house then and there to Jean Nioz and Francine. They had been kept cooped up in a part of a house long enough, and naturally it would be far better for the Barbés too. We were piqued about Marcel's faithlessness but saw no reason this disservice to us should not at least alleviate the housing problem for others, so little did we know.

Once the move was completed, it became immediately obvious to the interested inhabitants out at the camp that Jean, though professedly the best friend Barbé had in the world, always seemed to call at Barbé's when Barbé was out. And if Barbé was away fishing, Jean seemed to be helping around the house a great deal, or to be collecting coconuts in the vicinity excessively early in the mornings (collecting coconuts for animal food was one of Jean's "extras").

This way of managing things lasted for about a week, then abruptly the roles were reversed. It was now Léonie who sought out Jean, and in doing so, first made *us* aware of their passion —we are always the last to know anything, needless to say. The change in roles of seeker and sought coincided with our official closing of the Barbé shop account.

On the fishing boat a few luxuries absent from the shop for some time had arrived, along with the less glamorous staple goods, and at once I realized that the Barbés were grossly exaggerating the extent of the credit we were willing to allow them. Oh, to be sure, they had been warned three months running to reduce their account, but they had many children and I had been soft about it. The children always looked so badly fed that I hesitated to enforce the law that a man may only spend up to two thirds of his salary in the island shop. I was forever worrying about their children. I gave them iron and vitamins. I tried, as far as possible, to see that they got milk, and vegetables, and turtle liver whenever it was available. But nothing worked. They remained potbellied, anemic, whiny, wormy, sad mites, dressed in rags and a constant affront to me personally. Still, I continued to hope, of course, and part of this hoping was expressed in a willingness to believe that the extra purchases their parents made—or, rather, that Léonie made, since Barbé himself never entered the shop except for his bits of tobacco, cigarette papers, and matches—were "for the sake of the children."

But when the luxuries like sweets, embroidery, cottons, and cloth for dresses went on sale, I saw that Léonie was both improvident and silly, that Barbé had no control over her whatsoever and didn't care how much he was in debt to us either, and that the only way to make them economize was to close their account.

I didn't like doing it with Léonie pregnant again, but at least we tempered its severity on the children by calculating to the last penny how much bought provender they should consume a month (vegetables and fish were free) and allowed the Barbés to purchase these items only. Tobacco: out. Matches: in. Coffee: out. Peanuts: in but in specified quantities. Sweets: out. Sugar: in but limited. Oatmeal: in. Milk: in, of course, but powdered milk only since this was cheaper. Extra rice: out (the ration is very generous as it is, and the children ate far too much just plain rice—as do all Seychellois even when there is no economic necessity). And so on, and so on. All this was carefully explained to Léonie, who looked at me blankly, without apparently either caring about or particularly understanding what I was saying, but also without being annoyed at what I secretly felt was too intrusive a role for us to play in her life. It occurred to me that perhaps she had been cleverer than I thought and had been putting by extra supplies against the day when we could not be milked any longer, but this thought was quickly proved untrue. It would have been out of character, anyway. The Barbés very obviously felt the pinch as soon as they discovered we really meant what we said (it took two or three visits to the shop for this to penetrate), and this pinch was then promptly transferred to Jean Nioz.

On the paths, on the way to the well, amongst the papayas, almost anywhere the lovers met, and meeting, stopped. She, a packet of grass on her head, talked to him, eyes shining, while he rolled a cigarette and pulled his cap to ever better angles over his right eye. Strands of her stringy hair lay damply across her face, a mousy brown. Soft? His was peppercorn-tight-black. His shoulders were broad, well developed, with muscles evident as the sun shone on his black skin; the rest of his body tapered down through a wide belt, the brand of those who have been in the army, into khaki shorts, and on down to the thinnest legs imaginable. Her dress gaped in front, revealing pale flesh, and at the side, to accommodate the swelling burden she carried, dropped a little low for comfort, a large safety pin strained to bridge the unbridgeable, but her legs were still fair and firm —one could see more of them these days, as the dresses got shorter and shorter in front—and the coquetry of her glances showed that she, at least, believed herself beautiful and beloved. It was as though the new life within her supplemented rather than detracted from her magnetic charm for her lover; she was like fecund nature, a wild unfettered fertile growing nature, untamed like the earth under the brush and clutter of an old plantation, spawning, giving birth, accepting and giving and accepting and giving again in a profusion unhindered by any thought of order, or even of its own eventual exhaustion in the act of nourishing so many starveling weeds. He—he was hypnotized by the embrace of such a tranquil, thoughtless, careless love, and almost of his own accord, he gave her—sweets, love, tinned milk, love, flour, love, fish, my love, a stolen chicken (we shared in this giving too), and even tobacco for his love's husband.

Barbé's being a fisherman made it easy for Léonie to be indiscreet, but when he was at home she was not exactly careful. She was, however, totally successful. I know (because it would be so unlike her) that she had not thought out any plan of action once she no longer had her lover so conveniently in the house and now was forced (by a certain hardness she had encountered in us) to acquire the little things that make life pleasant from her lover as well as the big things; rather, Léonie, all instinct, untroubled by conscience or thought, simply went her own way, brushing past words, gossip, reports, her crying children with such a magnificent air of—well, innocence, that all fell away before her.

"Should anyone tell Barbé?" they all asked each other. "Though surely he must know! How can he be so blind?" But Barbé, when he was told, only vented his rage on the person who told him, after he was calmly assured by Léonie that such things were ridiculous for her to have done, pregnant as she was. "Besides," Léonie said, "Jean is your best friend. Is it not natural that he should help me while you are away? And Francine is my dear friend. I am always with her. People are malicious here. It's that Liliane, starting stories about me to make her own —— not look so bad." (I happen to know this because Léonie told me as well, by way of making a further complaint against the vicious Liliane.)

Fortified, I don't doubt, by Barbé's bland acceptance of all this, Jean too began to be more self-assured, less furtive; what I might harshly judge the now impressively sluttish appearance of Léonie did not seem to put him off in the least. The more there was of Léonie, apparently, the more he loved her. It was all quite out in the open now that they were lovers, and it became a matter of common speculation that Léonie's extra weight might just as easily be Nioz *premier* as Barbé *huitième*. Rumors went around that it had all started in Mahé before they came, and I, remembering Jean's refusal to share with the Esparons the house he'd been happy to see cluttered with Barbés, thought it might well be true. One really had to hand it to the old girl: all this time.

But naturally the more open Jean was about his relationship with Léonie, the harder it was on his worthy old bag of an official concubine. The threat of discovery in everything excepting, I suppose, the actual act, having been removed, Jean became positively insolent to Francine. And if she spoke back, he shook a stick at her as well. Poor Francine. She was almost continually in tears over That Woman, subjected to public humiliation and private devastating flash floods of impotent hate and rage, knowing full well that whatever overflowed the barrier of silence might earn her a good thrashing. Jean had become very masterful all 'round, it would seem, and perhaps in a corner of her mind she stuck to him the harder for it.

On his part, Jean had no intention of actually replacing Francine with Léonie. Not for him the responsibilities that Barbé shouldered so uncomplainingly—the expense, the clutter, the many visible results of unions with fair Léonie crawling about the floor. For Jean the icing only. Knowing this, I don't think Francine would have minded too much as long as Jean had stuck to pure sex; after all, she must have been aware of that for a long time. It was the presents of cloth and food going to That Woman which made old Francine cry so hard. She herself got none of the perquisites due a kept woman. On

Liliane and Léonie—Feline Disturbance / 211

the contrary, she was expected to share the expense of feeding and clothing herself and Jean while Jean fed and clothed that woman, and that woman's husband, and that woman's children with a liberal hand which had been long unknown in his own household. Bitter. Bitter indeed. While Barbé the cuckold chose to think all Jean's giving was for friendship's sake.

Or perhaps Jean told Barbé that his own credit was good in the shop now; let Barbé pay him back later when his was better. Whatever his reason it must have satisfied both men, however; they were still the best of friends.

It did not particularly satisfy us. Jean Nioz's credit in the shop was soon as bad as Barbé's. When I first warned Jean he raised both eyebrows up to his hairline, a quirk of facial expression he had, and seemed to examine me for an ulterior motive. But there was none. Mark and I did not intend to feed the Barbé family through him or anyone else who had not the credit to undertake the job, and that was that, though naturally I did not say this to Jean. "Form" must be followed, and speaking out the truth would only have brought on an argument obscuring and intending to obscure the main point, which was financial rather than moral. I merely told him to cut down on the spending, or else.

In fact, we make a point of steering as clear of moral shoals as we can, and interfere in a situation (unless by accident) only when the extent of a laborer's debt or a stoppage in the progress of work threatens the Interests of the Property. But of course, the distinction between reasons for our interference is of little concern to our employees: Jean was prepared to concede that in the shop we had, perhaps, some rights, but he was sure that it was no business of ours whatsoever that he should administer such corrective discipline as his woman (Francine, that is) might require. One night Jean, already suffering from the blow to his pride of purchase power, got so fed up with Francine's aura of furious suffering that he actually did thrash her—and hard. And Francine, bruised, lay on her bed for two days, groaning, refusing all food, and refusing even more firmly to come to work.

We decided that on the whole, things had gone far enough and that a little "putting of order" was called for. We confined Léonie to her house and its immediate surroundings and told Jean that if he did not start to work hard and get out of debt we would feel obliged to charge him, officially as well as unofficially, with disorderly conduct and assault.

At this, Jean started to become sulky. For some time, the quality of his work had been suffering; nor had he been doing any overtime. He was too much occupied for that. But now instead of improving, thus pleasing us and earning more money at the same time, he became even lazier and took on a truculent, insolent air as well. He chose, apparently, to believe we "had it in for him," or that he was being persecuted by righteous hidebound morality—anything but the unpalatable truth. A Seychellois male or female subjected to a little unsavory discipline loves to think himself victimized, even hated. "People have been telling stories against me" is a favorite. "Everyone hates me." "They are jealous of me." Thus Jean.

Naturally, he had to be warned again in the shop, and finally his account was shut too.

This enraged him, but he still had Francine. Her account was still open. She should pay now. Had he not done her the favor of bringing her here with him? She, a woman no one would look twice at, living with such a magnificent as he —she ought to be flattered that he still kept her on and didn't throw her out in the ditch where she belonged! However, Francine, though sorely tried, still had enough spirit left, plus a very good sense of her rights, not to be amenable to force. And Jean sensibly realized that beating her up would not be the way to get her money. Beating her up would involve us, and this made Francine feel strong. No. He would swallow his pride and pretend to be sorry. No. That wouldn't do either. Why should he? Ah, he had it. He would get sick. Francine's soft heart would refuse him nothing then. He would be quite sick, with pain, a deep pain.

Of course, this would bring Madame down on his neck. But

Jean, wise and worldly, knew there was nothing I could do to prove he *didn't* have a pain.

In all his calculations, he was perfectly correct—as far as he went. But we were suspiciously unconvinced, particularly when the pain diminished enough in the afternoons (after working hours) for him to make it as far as Barbé's house, taking parts of the extra flour, sugar, cocoa, and tea with which Francine was cosseting his malady, wedged under his cap, or so I assumed, from the amount that Francine was now buying.

"I know, I know," said Francine wearily, when I finally remonstrated with her (she was getting her second large tin of cocoa in a week). "I know he still gives to that woman, but what can I do? He suffers so, he has such pain. He says warm drinks help him. What can I do? *Your* medicine doesn't help the pain and *you* won't let him have aspirin all the time," she said, turning on me and fluffing out her feathers like a broody hen. She snatched the cocoa off the table and clucked out of the shop, back to her cockerel at last beneath her wing.

After Jean had been sick for three weeks with a very bad pain that changed location a little and was always worse at night, so that Jean only got to sleep in the mornings and therefore only felt well enough to get up in the afternoons, we decided to confine him to bed to await a boat to Mahé.

He seemed quite a lot better by the time a boat came, but we assured him that it was best not to take any chances. "I don't know what your pain is," I told him, "and I can't take the responsibility of assuming you are now really better."

Rather reluctantly, Jean went. Francine he told to stay here and await him, but he took all his belongings with him except his double water bottle, made from the shell of a *coco-de-mer*, which had a crack in one side.

Two months later he wrote to Francine to say that he was still sick and could she send him forty-five rupees to pay the doctor because he had not been able to work? Francine sent it to him, through us. Three weeks passed, another boat stopped by (we had quite a rush of shipping that spring) with a second letter for Francine. He needed just fifteen rupees more. The mail, which comes to us for distribution, also brought a letter addressed to Léonie in the same handwriting. Francine said she was going back to Mahé, but we talked her into staying a little longer; she was one of our best workers now that her emotions were no longer kept raw by Jean, which had given her so many headaches and kidney aches and toothaches and other troubles that we had very nearly given up on her too. All right, said Francine. "I descended with Carmen. I will return to Mahé when Carmen goes. I am *bien contente,* Madame—it's not that —but it is difficult to be alone here without a *bonhomme* to get my *bouillon.*"

I was chagrinned. I had never thought of that. Now that I did, I remembered having seen Francine out on the beach with a hook and some string, jigging for rockfish. I spoke to Mark, and he spoke to the fishermen, and from then on, Francine always got a fish free, supplemented by salt fish when Mark and the others were away.

XXV

UNFRUITFUL AS LÉONIE had found the Esparon-Alex-Liliane triangle for actual gossip, it was to Mark and me an interesting social experiment. Mark, who had himself been shared between two sisters amicably enough in the Marquesas, used to say to me, "You see, Wendy, it's only Europeans who are so jealous about sex," while I would counter with the rareness of polyandry in the world, and the opinion that in any case the situation would inevitably blow up. "The Seychellois *are* European," I'd add, "even if they don't waste much time on moral fortitude. And you know how jealous they are."

"True," said Mark, "but they don't think about sex quite the way we do. I think the men would share if it seemed the best solution. Either Esparon or Liliane's bound to get some benefit out of it."

"Cloth, I suppose. Or soap. Oh yes, and those bras Esparon ordered last time you went to Mahé; Alex actually paid for them. On the other hand, I know Liliane does all the cooking and washing and ironing, and does embroidery for Alex as well, which Alex sends back to Mahé . . ."

"Well, you'll probably find out at the end of the month. You say they are planning to buy their rations together. See if Esparon pays for two shares, or if they divide the cost of Liliane between them."

"Liliane *and* Little Maxime. We'll see. Even so, it won't go on forever. One of them is bound to get less, or more. And Alex doesn't look to me the type to take any orders from Esparon just because Liliane was Esparon's first."

"That is certainly true," laughed Mark.

But the more we saw of the workings of the *ménage,* the more it seemed (as might have been predictable) to be Esparon who was taking the orders, or at least doing all the heavy work, while Alex led a royal existence, whenever he was not out fishing. Esparon, belying his reputation for laziness, would be up early and off to collect coconuts for the pigs' food. When he came back, he would throw the sack on the ground. Since he had already husked them *dans bois,* the noise the sack made was like the clatter of small rocks dropped from a bulldozer's shovel. This was the signal for Liliane to emerge (to make breakfast, I think), but Alex never appeared until nine. And from then on he did not lift a finger. While Esparon and Liliane grated the nuts, Alex sat with them, back propped against the veranda posts, talking. While Liliane cooked, Alex apparently slept. And when they fed the pigs in the evening, Alex would saunter up to the pens, not to help but to watch the generous amount of thigh displayed by Liliane flitting from pen to pen and bending over the gates.

I was watching too, but for different reasons. The pigs were not doing well, so that I was obliged to check each day on the number of coconuts grated and on the amount of grated meats that arrived at the pens; and there was constant friction between myself and Liliane on the subject of the size of the grass packets, and between myself and Esparon on cleaning out the pens. All this "snooping" made me particularly unpopular with Liliane, and with Liliane to think was to speak. Whatever criticism I made, however politely couched, her reaction was an outpouring of self-justifying jabber, so I usually waited until I could speak to Esparon alone. At least he was polite and amenable to orders, even though he usually did nothing about them.

Things finally became so desperate that I told Felix I would have to ask him for Small George, his assistant, and with Small George's help do the pigs myself. Esparon and Liliane I told to collect coconuts until Monsieur returned.

At this Liliane flounced off, trailing Esparon behind her. I called him back. "No work, no credit in the shop," I reminded him, and stalked off myself. Little victories had become necessary—especially in view of what Liliane was thinking: that I had a secret yen toward pink Maxime the elder myself. Nothing is too much for a Seychellois to imagine if sex is involved. Why else would I try to talk to Esparon alone? Why else would I be so critical of Liliane's work, if I were not jealous of her? Liliane had grown used to arousing this emotion in other female breasts, I suppose; and being the official mistress of a *blanc* removed any respect she might have felt due my color, while her upbringing had evidently not included the teaching of manners.

I suppose, also, that Mark and I had been putting up with a number of cheeky responses from her and from Alex, ignored for the sake of getting on with the work. This was a grave mistake. In the end, Alex and Liliane taught us a good lesson: if you go on employing people who are even guardedly insolent and who make difficulty over work, it is your own fault if you finish up with an undignified scene after which you *have* to get rid of them. You should have got rid of them long ago.

What we believed at that time, however, was that we were above worrying about such petty matters when other people we might hire to replace them would very likely be worse. All young Seychellois are insolent and restive these days, we'd say to each other, and at least Esparon himself is polite enough . . . look at the trouble we had with Servina's Marguerite, and those awful Boys. One can't keep on weeding out. It's too expensive.

How wrong! How wrong!

On a small island, shut up with your employees and they with you, there is nothing so disturbing as bad labor relations. I suppose the very likely possibility of having bad relations with some of the laborers some of the time is a great point in favor of having a manager, which puts these relations at the remove. But Gappy had soured us completely on managers—or me, anyway. I suppose, too, that getting to know one's labor well—not as equals but well—might lay one open to an abuse of this certain degree of allowed familiarity. Had I acted like a "typical American" and not kept my distance enough? Yes, perhaps I had; given Liliane's character, any "amelioration" would probably be taken as an invitation to walk all over one. We should certainly have got rid of them all, under the circumstances, and that quickly.

But the days when the Esparons were still here were the days when the *France* was still not ready, and even though a number of boats did call that spring, they were never willing or able to arrange for room to take four passengers. Thus things slid along.

Shortly after I had "fired" Maxime and Liliane from the pigs, Mark returned from a fishing trip and we spent the evening thinking out what we would do. "All right," he said finally, "I'll tell you what: we'll put the lot of them on African Banks. I've always wanted to exploit the Banks for fish better than I can from here, yet I've never had people to spare. If they refuse, then we really will have to get rid of them and find others."

They did not refuse, although Alex looked sour enough. Mark worked out the prices he was willing to pay for salt fish, shark, *bêche-de-mer*, turtle, young turtle hatched from eggs they would look after, tortoise shell, *calipée*, mother-of-pearl shell—in fact, all the produce he was himself collecting. He gave them salt,

Anchoring at South Islet, African Banks

and their equipment, and the materials to make over the house on South African Banks, and I saw that they had enough rations to last two months, one month's food always in reserve in case for some reason the *Bouilloir* could not call there at the end of each month, as we planned. Correspondingly, we had to allow them to buy enough of the necessities not on ration (milk, tea, soap, matches, curry powder), even though this made them even more in debt. I noticed, however, that Esparon paid for Liliane and his son.

In the way of boats, we let them take one of the whalers, and a small pirogue to keep in reserve.

When all was ready Mark told Tristan to tow them across the thirteen miles, and as the little *Bouilloir* disappeared, with the whaler loaded with iron roofing bobbing in the stern, we let out a great sigh of peace. Until they had gone, neither of us had realized what an unpleasant aura of "trouble" had emanated from the house so close to ours.

XXVI

IN FACT, the departure of Liliane and Company lightened the whole island; we all seemed to float several inches higher out of the water. But no one forgot them; on the contrary, we wondered almost daily how they would make out. Theirs was the real desert island, not Remire. After two weeks or so, Mark said, "Why don't you go over in the *Bouilloir* and see how things are?"

"Oh no," I said, "you'd better. You haven't had the trouble with Liliane that I have. I don't want to go to see them."

"You don't have to spend long on the south island. Stop there then go on to the north island and find out if the terns are laying yet. They should be starting. It would be a break for you—you haven't been off Remire since we came. I'll stay home and mind things for once. Go along."

So I did.

Anyone approaching African Banks must think he is seeing coral islands newly risen from the sea; they are so bare and lie so flat upon the water, seemingly mere mounds of sand more visible from the white line of breakers along their reefs than from any feature of their own. But as one draws closer, features do appear: the low coral overhangs along the shore of North Islet, and the two stunted palms which barely pierce the skyline, near a mound of guano; and on South Islet, the squareness of a hut surrounded by low bushes. This time the bushes were green, thanks to the rain, but no one thought about that. We had eyes only for North Islet, which lay in dark shadow, under a moving cloud as big as the island of soaring, diving, wheeling, screaming terns—the sooties and noddies were indeed starting to nest. The men on *Bouilloir* gave a great cheer. From now on, the terns' eggs would be awaited greedily by every living thing in the vicinity, from the skink lizards of North Islet itself to each human being on Remire. Birds' egg season at last!

• • •

I've had a word to say on the importance of coconuts and fish in the Seychelles; by comparison, birds' eggs form a very minor item in the local diet. But not so in mind. During the season, which runs from whenever the birds start to lay (usually by the end of May) to the closing date in July, every Seychellois living on or near a bird's egg island counts on making a pig of himself, while in Mahé *grand blanc, grand noir,* and *petit noir* await the arrival of the egg-laden schooners with equal eagerness. It's the only time of the year when eggs are both cheap and relatively plentiful, and the Seychellois can eat an astonishing quantity of them. Probably the favorite way is plain hard-boiled with pepper and salt and chilies, but they are also made into huge omelets, richly filled with onion, or cakes and cookies, or mayonnaises, sauces, and custards; or whipped raw into milky tea; or added to curries and salads. No one coming from a country where eggs are so cheap they can be thrown at public speakers or opera singers can imagine how much an egg can be valued. The world of students armed with eggs or clowns with custard pies might be on another planet to a Seychellois; even we, raising our own chickens, never use an egg without debating several either/ors. Except in birds' egg season. Except then.

But no mere European can outdo a Seychellois in egg eating when he has a chance. An adult has no difficulty with twenty or thirty eggs at a sitting, and a child will consume at least five straight away by picking a hole in it and sucking the raw contents down his gullet, to say nothing of the number he can eat cooked. A hundred a day is just enough for a family—but for the poor, such bliss is only possible on the outer islands; in Mahé the competition is too fierce.

On the nesting sites the eggs are collected by the boat crews, by the resident labor of a nearby island, by children, by women, by anyone, everyone who can get onto an island at the time the terns are laying. It is, I'd venture to say, the one sort of manual work no one will refuse. Admittedly, the women and children don't get much chance, since the birds' egg islands are not for the most part regularly inhabited, but the women of Bird Island, where the terns actually lay on a part of the island, don't hesitate, and children go mad.

The grownups go mad too, and in a way bound to grieve anyone looking on from the vantage point of a fuller stomach and more refined sensibility—or even only from the point of view of making the most efficient use of nature's bounty. The tern is a feather-light, delicate-looking bird that can live twenty years or more, has a long needle-sharp beak, and produces eggs that weigh one fifth of her own body weight. She lays one egg at a time but can lay again if this egg is lost or stolen or strayed, and often again. It is the characteristic that has squared the exploitation of terns' eggs with the conservationists, and quite rightly so; no one objects to the idea of a reasonable cropping of the eggs, but only to the wasteful manner in which it is done. To look at the question from a strictly practical point of view, potential layers and relayers should never be harmed, and the eggs themselves should be packed and transported more carefully—increases thus gained being of benefit to lessee of island, shipper, and consumer alike. More birds laying means more eggs per acre and greater ease of collection; more eggs arriving in edible condition in Mahé means better sales and more sales, as well as better contracts for the year's crop. But so far, the number of birds and eggs that survive the egg collection (adjusted for each island on a quota basis) always seem to produce the same profusion the next year, and so in spite of flurries of talk, no one does anything to make the operation more efficient.

Consider, for a start, the way the eggs are collected. First, the island is systematically cleared of all the eggs already there —who knows how long they've been sat on? These, except the ones eaten on the spot (raw), are shoveled into a pile under a bush. Then, the next day, collecting starts. The terns lay usually in the early afternoon, so about three or four o'clock the boat noses up to the beach, the men jump off, and chaos reigns until dark. Open boxes are placed at intervals, and a little bit of seaweed is put in the bottom. Then the men go up the beach, yelling and shouting to scare the birds from their nests. If a bird hasn't got off the ground by the time a man wants to pick up his or her egg (terns take turns), the bird is either kicked aside or lifted up by one trailing wing and hurled into the air. I think this is because the Seychellois, male or female, is afraid of being pecked—true even of poultry keepers here—though the contest of bird versus man looks a very unequal one to me. In fact, when I have collected eggs, I have often taken from a bird hovering nearby, on the ground, and he or she seems paralyzed with fright, making little movements with the head and hopping a bit, but nothing more; so without being in the least sentimental about it (which would be easy because the birds are pretty), I cannot see that all the shouting, stick waving, and rough treatment is necessary. On the other hand, it is often a kindness to launch a bird obviously trying to get away but, in its panic, getting bound up in a bush instead, and since the only way to launch it is to lift it by a wing with enough momentum to get it airborne, I may be misjudging some of the collectors' efforts. Some, but not all.

Take Rogile, for instance, one of the gogglers. Rogile is very tall, very well muscled—the one with the big pigeon-toed feet. In comparison with a sooty tern he is like Antaeus beside a pygmy. But far from being gentle, he always makes the most noise, yelling *"Ai-yo-yo-o-o"* furiously as he wades into the nesting area, twirling with his stick like a dervish until the area is clear of anything alive, whereupon he judges it safe to remove his big straw hat and gather the eggs.

That's the second thing: the collecting receptacles. Birds' egg collection in the Seychelles has been going on since there were people to do it, and commercial exploitation certainly since the twenties, but the eggs are still collected in shirt fronts, hats, *coco-de-mer* scoops, wobbly old beer cartons, anything handy. From these containers they are *poured* into the—again unsuitable—Tiger Beer crates. No layer-of-seaweed, layer-of-egg system is used, nor are the eggs placed by hand in the crates, nor are the crates picked up or set down carefully. Suggestions on these lines cause the suggestor to be stared at pityingly. Egg boxes with molded sections? One person just to pack the eggs? Properly arranged stowage on board? Care in loading and unloading? All is regarded as so much foolishness and put aside as totally irrelevant to the economics of the industry (if one may call it that), even though—*even* though the tern's egg has one of the most fragile shell casings I have ever touched. I am by no means ham-fisted, but I have often broken an egg just picking it up.

When the broken and unbroken eggs have spent sometime together in a crate, the gluey nature of albumen and yolk when exposed to air insures that the shell of one will invariably stick to the shell of the other, so breaking more. That any arrive in salable condition at all in Mahé is a result of their weight and inertia once in the crates (a Tiger Beer crate holds seven hundred eggs) rather than care, and under these conditions the annual wastage of eggs is terrible.

I suppose that if feeling as we do, we stuck by our principles, we would either personally supervise all egg collecting from our particular fief or forbid it altogether. In fact, we vacillate. We do not disturb ourselves to go with every boat trip, but neither do we sell the eggs in Mahé, which means systematic daily depredations of the type described. And while we are enraged by laborers bringing back the stunned or suffocated bodies of sooties and noddies in a sack as well as the eggs, we don't really do anything except get mad. What can we do? We give the men only a limited number of boxes so that we will not take more eggs than we can use before they spoil, but we use Tiger Beer boxes too. As we don't go in for the egg collecting commerically, why should *we* import molded egg trays? It wouldn't be financially worthwhile. So much for principles. It's sad, but there it is. We are really no better than the others.

The only thing these wraithlike regrets do accomplish is to make the men sigh if we announce we are going along, and us sigh when we get there and have—short of rushing around like anti-blood-sporters at a hunt—to watch. The best way to avoid spoiling the day for everyone is just to ignore what the others are doing and fill our own hats. Or, better still, to time the expedition to coincide with a low tide and spend the day out on the reef, a good half mile from all the screaming birds and yelling human beings, peacefully collecting shells.

On this visit there were hardly any eggs on the ground, however, so the men restrained themselves. We made a rough estimate of the number of terns, collected a few bowlfuls of coquina clams from the sandbanks below high water, and returned to anchor at South Islet. As it was low tide, we all jumped overboard and half swam, half waded ashore through the clear green water, leaving Payet on board. We could see a very pink Esparon gamely trying to launch the pirogue from the beach; the anchored whaler, judging from the amount of freeboard left above water, was obviously full of turtles. Alex and Liliane and Petit Maxime did not seem to be around.

Esparon was, as usual, full of complaints. The water was bad, Alex used too much, the well wasn't any good—all clogged with guano and feathers (this wasn't surprising, as it hadn't been used for years; Mark had told Esparon and Alex to clean it out on arrival but he knew they wouldn't, not while they had barrels of fresh water from Remire). Had we brought more sugar, more water, tobacco, and flour? Sweets for little Maxime? Little Maxime was poorly, we were told. Where was he? Oh, out with Liliane and Alex, collecting shells, said Esparon vaguely, gesturing behind him where the sand stretched out in a long thin curve of white toward the northwest.

But we were more interested in the progress of the fishing, as evidenced by the *farfars*. Some shark, quite a lot of oily cod the men shook their heads over, too much of the usual oversalted *lascar,* some moray skins—that must be Alex—a few ray tails and salted ray flesh. But not a great deal of anything. I demurred, only to be told about strong currents, a leak in the boat, losing an oar. But what about the turtles? "We have three turtles!" said Esparon brightly. "Monsieur will be pleased with that."

"Naturally," I said. "But try to do better. Why is Alex collecting shells in perfectly good fishing time?"

This was unanswerable, so he returned to the subject of the turtles. "I have buried the eggs of the female, as you told me,

Madame. The others are males harpooned by Alex on the reef. They are fat, fat. You will get a good price in Mahé..."

Eventually I was able to wander off myself to look for shells, while the men began to prepare for the night we were to spend there by ferrying in Esparon's supplies and my small tent as soon as the tide was high enough, gathering firewood, and poling off in the pirogue to catch a few fresh fish for dinner. Ahmed put on the clams and the rice pot, singing lustily as he did so, then strode over to help me with the tent. He was in a seeing-to-everything mood, as in the old days in Arabia, an impression reinforced by the sand and the sea and the campfire and the miles of nothing on the horizon. The sun was low, night fell and it grew colder. Alex and Liliane and the little boy had returned without undue banter from the men, to find dinner already cooked, so we all ate early and settled down—in the men's case, for an evening's talking and laughing and sharing the jug of toddy Mark had sent with us. I commandeered a cup of it and lay back to watch the stars.

I wondered what had happened to the Chinaman's grave since Mark had been on North Islet last. The men and I had had a good look for it, on Mark's instructions. In taking over the lease, we had inherited the obligation to keep reburying his bones higher up the beach, for he had been interred by the British Navy on a side of the island that was gradually disappearing into the sea. No one (including us) thought to move him altogether. It didn't seem right. Besides, one apparently could never tell exactly where North Islet was going to shrink or gain from season to season. The coral outcrops with their stunted bits of vegetation remained firm, but sandbank became island and island bank easily enough, and the poor man was probably minus half his earthly remains already. I wondered why the frigate had taken such trouble to bury their servant on land instead of at sea, since it had meant anchoring in shoal waters and losing easily a day's sailing time; and having done so, why they hadn't buried him properly in the islet's center, where his femurs and ulnas wouldn't keep floating off. Perhaps we should move him, after all. If he wasn't gone already.

The Great Bear marched on, much nearer the horizon than—than it should be. Three years south of the equator had not accustomed me to seeing so many constellations from a different angle. The polestar was out of sight.

When had the Chinaman been buried? I couldn't remember the date. Possibly the frigate he was on was doing a survey? But the most recent admiralty surveys of the Amirantes were in 1882 and 1891. Too long ago. I thought about the passage on African Banks in the *South Indian Ocean Pilot* (1958 is the edition we have) which cautions sailors about the heavy seas and currents off the northern end of the banks. It goes on to say that the islets are very dangerous to make for when bearing more than a hundred eighty degrees (anything west of south) because while in the daytime they can be seen about eight miles away, at night, and here I remembered the *Pilot*'s words: "a vessel might be on the eastern reef without seeing them." "From the observation post, on a clear dark night," the *Pilot* continues, drumming the lesson in, "the breakers could not be seen three cables distant, neither could the islet be seen from the vessel eight cables distant under similar circumstances." The islet referred to was the northern one, off which the survey ship the *Alert* anchored in 1882. Since these cautions had been handed down through generations of *Pilot* books to our modern one, Mark and I suspected they had originally been written with the wreck of *H.M.S. Fire* in mind. The words made these tiny banks loom so large with danger—while about potentially more dangerous places in the Indian Ocean the *Pilot* had nothing to say.

An older edition of the *Pilot* had revealed the *Fire*'s story, and we read it avidly, though it left us with many unanswered questions, as pilot book information is apt to do. (For the full tale, or as much of it as we could piece together, see Appendix B.) But that a ship had been wrecked on African Banks was no particular surprise to us. Even nowadays, no local captain willingly gets onto the Amirante bank at night, but sails to the east or the west of it and makes his landfall in daylight, and big ships are at pains to avoid it altogether. But the African Islets being the northernmost of the Amirantes and close to the edge of the bank, a navigator might well calculate his course to miss the bank with all its loathsome shoals and currents, yet still come a cropper near its northern edge, as the *Fire* did.

The whole business about the *Fire* led us to wonder why the northernmost of the Amirantes were called the African Islets when they are so far from Africa. Who could have mistaken them for islands off the African coast? Or were they simply signposts on one of the old routes from Africa to India? Signposts to keep away from, one would suppose, except that in the fifteenth-century system of navigation the importance of having a landfall to make for was enormous, and even today the pilot of the seaplane serving the American satellite-tracking station in Mahé has told us that Remire and the African Islets are the first landmarks he picks up in the wilderness of the Indian Ocean between Mahé and Mombasa. And we have noticed that—with all the navigational aids he must have—he often banks slightly, to change his direction, after sighting us through the usual high cumulus clouds.

And as if the origins of names weren't tantalizing enough, it is not as though anyone in those days bothered very much about spelling. Not only did people rarely bother to get names exactly right, but they went about changing them constantly as well. Each vessel's captain sailing these waters seems to have assumed himself first on the spot, perhaps understandably, and the practice of liberally scattering names on islands already called something else continued late into the eighteenth century. And even in the twentieth, names have been arbitrarily changed (people have such a blind fondness for their own language, or their own heroes). Amongst the Seychelles, name changes are positively dizzying, and it's only the more out-of-the-way islands that have been left moderately unrebaptized.

Which brings us back to Remire. Remire is an odd name. We toyed with the idea that it might share a root word with Amirante, but it didn't get us anywhere. Nor does it appear to be either the name of a person or a boat that had anything to do with the Seychelles. Duc de Remire? Not mentioned in dispatches. The famous French admiral A. de St. Remire, known as L'Aiglon for short because his small body contained an intrepid fighting nature? Oh well, it was a thought anyway, just to tie in with Ile d'Aigle, Remire's other name. The Seychellois always pronouce "Remire" as though it were spelled "Remi." Did this offer a clue? There is St. Remi, archbishop of Reims, who accepted in the cathedral there Clovis the First's decision for God, but this was in 496 A.D.; we are clearly getting too far afield. It seems most likely that whatever the name may mean (and according to Larousse, neither it nor anything like it means, in French, anything at all), it was probably bestowed on the island during the Chevalier du Roslan's voyages among these islands in 1770 and 1771. Horsburgh does mention that the French *La Marie* happened to pass African Banks on the seventeenth of September, 1694, but the credit of the Amirantes' true exploration seems to go to du Roslan and his romantically named vessels, *L'Heure du Berger* and *L'Etoile du Matin,* and the islands' naming to their captains, who named them after themselves, or their saints' days, or the saint's day on which they were "discovered." Though by an odd coincidence, a certain Charles Casulo, an Englishman and captain of the ship *Eagle,* or *L'Aigle* (it might have been a prize), is also said to have passed our island in 1771 and to have called it Ile d'Aigle after his ship. Coincidences like this probably occurred elsewhere; quite a lot of shipping was by then trafficking back and forth between Europe and India. Remire is only exceptional in that having received two names in a single year, she has retained both of them.

About her second name giver, Charles Casulo, there hangs a vague air of disrepute. That he was wandering around the Amirantes at all is odd: he was employed by the British merchants of Surat to come to Praslin and Curieuse Island to "collect" (read steal) boatloads of the marvelous double coconut, indigenous to the Seychelles, which these merchants were selling at high prices in India. *Nux medica,* they were called, highly praised as an aphrodisiac. (Homeopathic medicine: the husked nut resembles closely the pelvic area of a naked woman.

When the shell is cleaned and polished, as it still is for the tourist, there is an area between the "thighs" very difficult to scrape; now the local workmen no longer try, since a certain amount of pubic "hair" gives an even greater similitude.) In 1771 the trade in these nuts, uninhibited by government restrictions, was still booming.

But Casulo did not stick to filching French land produce. He is also supposed to have spent some time in Praslin, defacing the Stone of Possession there by removing the coat of arms of France and substituting his own name and that of his ship, like a naughty schoolboy; and not only this: his ship's crew is blamed for setting fire to the whole of Curieuse Island as well —accidentally, we hope. Or was he acting on instructions from Surat to cut down on the *coco-de-mer* acreage to keep the prices high? Only the year before, the French entrepreneur Brayer du Barre is supposed to have burned *coco-de-mer* groves in Praslin after sending off *his* shipload of the precious nuts.

Whatever the case, Casulo was soon dismissed his command and is reported in 1773 to have settled on Mahé; if the fire was accidental, it might have been this that cost him his job.

But it is not through any snobbish desire to dissociate ourselves from this roguish character that we call the island Remire. Remire persists as this island's name locally, and the fact that Casulo's is the name chosen as the official one, to be seen on charts and in government files in tidy English as Eagle Island (as befits a British colony), impresses no one here with any need to stop using the name of Remire.

XXVII

WE SAILED BACK to Remire the next noon, the men having taken the *Bouilloir* along the reefs in the morning in the hope of harpooning another turtle, but without success. It was a cloudy day, and the water was ruffled with the beginnings of a wind. I sat in the bows, watching the patches of green sand and purple coral heads gradually give way to deep blue, then suddenly become green again as we passed over the many shoals and deeps between African Banks and Remire. One turtle surfaced briefly, but too far off to chase.

At the anchorage, we picked up *Bouilloir*'s moorings from the small pirogue, transferred ourselves to the pirogue, and rowed ashore. Felix was coming quickly down the beach as we approached, and some of the women were standing among the corner pillars of the new house, so Berley, from the stern, mimed "No eggs yet" with his free hand to relieve their suspense. But Felix was making gestures toward our house, and the minute I had stepped on shore, he said, "At the house, Madame! Monsieur wants you quickly at the house!"

My heart jumped. The children! I flew along the *allée* and up the steps. Inside I found Mark in the children's room, but it was not one of our children in bed; it was the Barbé's four-year-old girl, breathing shallowly, eyes shut, her dark skin yellowish and cold. I lifted her eyelids, felt for her pulse, felt her feet colder than her hands. The breathing was becoming fainter. Léonie sat crying at the foot of the bed, while Barbé watched from the doorway.

"Oh, Léonie, how long has she *been* like this?" I asked, and Mark answered that they'd brought her to him in the morning. Under the blankets, her legs were like ice. "Brandy, Mark? Do we have some?" Propping her up, we tried to get a little down her throat, but her tongue seemed to fill all the space in her mouth, and when we opened her mouth wider the liquor ran out the sides. The pulse was getting weaker. In desperation —just to do something—I tried mouth-to-mouth respiration, which we'd only read about. After five or six times, there seemed to be some response . . . did I imagine it? Yes, the pulse was stronger. But then the breathing became audible, horribly so, and stayed that way until her tongue protruded slowly from between her cold set lips and she died. We were shocked at the suddenness, but Léonie did not seem surprised. She said she

Liliane and Léonie—Feline Disturbance / 231

knew, and Barbé said they had realized three days ago "they didn't have a little girl any more, she lay on her bed so quiet and said such funny things."

They had, however, said nothing to us. Perhaps they were right; by that time, it was too late. But my thoughts were frantic. Why hadn't I seen? This thin potbellied child, so like all the others except for her terribly whining nature, must have been dying for a long time. It was always she who had the most worms, was most anemic, and had such a bewildering variety of malfunctions of her system; she who always threw up the medicines, or let them drool; she who used to wander along the paths after her mother, uttering the same high-pitched wail until she was caught up or sent home; she who was so ugly. If only I had had more experience! I should have—oh, I felt as though I had killed her willfully by not having had the prescience to send her back to Mahé in time. And the worst was that when Léonie had stopped bringing her for medicine I had happily assumed she was cured.

There was nothing to say. In silence, Barbé picked up the small body and went out, leaving Léonie to collect the few things they had brought with them. At the door, she turned and said "Thank you" to us, without rancor.

They held the wake in Lenclume's house—the "best" house —generously vacated by Francine, the feud forgotten. And it was Francine who trotted busily between our house and hers with the many requests from the parents, and from the chief mortician, Berley. For a rough fisherman, Berley was very gentle with his hands. First he washed the body, while the women combed the hair and cleaned the nails; then Francine was sent for cotton to plug the orifices, and gauze bandage to keep the jaw in shape; then for a new dress, never worn (luckily I had one for Ming), and a handkerchief to cover the face. Again Francine presented herself. "Cloth, madame, from the shop. White poplin," she stated firmly. "And candles."

I took the keys and a lamp; it was getting dark. The cloth was for the winding sheet, candles for the vigil ("If we have candles," I had often been told, "we are not afraid to die"). Frankly, our shop is always well stocked with candles because I used them to make floor polish, but I was glad that at least in death we had not been found wanting.

Back at the house, Berley had another request. "A bed," he said. "Francine is afraid to lend her bed." So I got out the camp bed on which (I couldn't help reflecting) little Wendy had so recently been born. He took the rubber sheet too. He seemed very proficient about death.

Finally all was ready. In the last of the daylight, Ahmed and Rogile were still out at the cemetery, digging, and Felix could be heard planing wood across the yard. But everyone else had changed and stood at the edge of the moat of light that surrounded the house.

The vigil is kept by the nearest relatives rather than the parents; in this case, it should have fallen to Maxime and Liliane had they been there, but they weren't. After some talk the Payets were selected because Felix, the obvious choice, was busy with the coffin, and Mrs. Felix would never have managed to last out. The Payets were the sort of people one would select: imperturbable, stolid. Through the long night they sat one each side, adjusting the handkerchief, changing the candles, talking to visitors, dozing a little. Payet was used to nights at the wheel.

In the morning, as soon as the coffin was finished, the procession to the cemetery formed, with Felix in charge. It wound out through the coconut palms, past the pigsties, along the edge of the washing pool, and through the long grass to the eastern dunes. The new hole gaped, and the fresh coffin with its brass screws was lowered into it while Felix sang the service. Léonie shed a few tears with great dignity (I had expected a scene), and we all trouped back.

At least I thought we all did. I learned later that Léonie and Barbé had stayed behind, waiting until we were out of sight to drive a series of six-inch iron nails into the fresh earth above the coffin to prevent the restless spirit from wandering from her unblessed grave. White people are known to be rather uncompromising about such important and necessary measures, and it is always best to say nothing. In fact, we only realized the nails were there when we had built the little girl a small cement horizontal gravestone, on which I carved her name and the date of her death. When I finished, the mason smoothed the last of its edges, but by the next morning the cement was all cracked and broken around the holes of more great nails hammered in amongst the letters. And so it remains, Mark having vowed that he would not spend the time or money to fix up the grave again.

Yet even these double nailings did not seem to be very effective while the people's memories of the child were fresh. True or not, nearly everyone claimed to hear her at night, and said that she kept the babies awake by tickling them, and wanting to play with them, and calling out to them in her whining voice as she did when she was alive. The one house she apparently never bothered was her own. Barbé insisted that he could not understand people complaining about her, for she never came near them "after the first few days." But then, Barbé was not—mercifully perhaps—overgifted with imagination.

XXVIII

AFTER ANOTHER TWO WEEKS had gone by, Mark again sent the *Bouilloir* over to African Banks with orders to inspect the progress on South Islet and to bring back some terns' eggs for Remire. Ahmed reported that they didn't seem to have done very much work but that they did have some shark, *cordonnier* (a variety of fish easy to dry and much appreciated locally for its flavor, since it is one of the few the Seychellois do not over-salt), and more salted ray. Mark himself was preparing to go to Mahé again to see to the *France*, so he said, "Well, leave them there a bit longer. Give them a chance." Then he was gone on the next boat that called.

A week later, I was hanging out some clothes when I heard a polite *"Bon soir, Madame."* It was Esparon, followed by Alex, just coming around the corner of the house. A wretched feeling of *oh no!* came over me, and I barely managed to give them a civil greeting before I hotly asked why they were here.

"Oh," said Esparon, "I was sick. I was very sick, excreting all the day and all the night. I could do no work. I could not stay on that place."

"But what about the medicine I gave you just for that? Didn't you take it?"

"It did me no good. Oh, Madame"—rolling his eyes and stroking his chest as he always did—"you cannot imagine how sick I was!"

"I am still sick," he added. "My bowels are grinding and leaving me no peace."

"But what have you brought with you? Just nothing? What about the shark and fish? Turtles? What's Alex doing here? Couldn't you and Liliane have sailed back and left Alex to look after the things?" In my mind was the fact that fishing boats from Mahé often called at African Banks, which made an ideal starting point, as it was uninhabited, for their illegal depredations in the Amirantes. "The wind is perfect!"

"Oh, no, Madame," said Alex sleepily. "I would not stay there by myself."

"So all your catch may be stolen and you don't care? You stand to lose too, you know," I retorted, "not just Monsieur."

Alex shrugged and half turned away, as usual.

"I will prepare some more medicine for you," I said to Esparon coldly. "It is the same medicine, which is all I have here for that sort of ailment. Go to your house. I will send it down."

The minute they had gone, I went to the camp to see Tristan and Ahmed. On my way I noted with even more displeasure that they had sailed back in the pirogue, leaving even the valuable whaler over on the Banks. We stood to lose a good deal, it seemed.

"So," I said to Tristan, "I suppose we will have to take the *Bouilloir* immediately and get everything there. Obviously, they will not go back."

"No," laughed Ahmed. "Esparon says you can —— African Banks for all he cares." Ahmed was speaking in créole, which he picked up quickly and indiscriminately. In Arabic he would never have said such things in front of me.

"So I supposed," I replied. "When will you be ready to leave, Tristan?"

"We can go tomorrow if you like, Madame."

"Good. Do you know exactly what they left there, besides the boat and equipment?"

"There are two male turtles on their backs in the whaler, Alex says."

"In the whaler! In all that sun? They'll be dead!"

I went back to our house, mixed the kaolin and tincture of opium, started toward Esparon's, then thought better of it. Why have to listen to Liliane? I called Rory and asked him to tell Esparon to "arrive" at the House as soon as possible. When he came, I gave him his medicine. "The *Bouilloir* will be leaving tomorrow. Will you be well enough to go to collect your catch, or will just Alex do?"

"Oh, I am far too sick, Madame. Alex will go," muttered Esparon stubbornly, looking at the ground.

"I cannot understand you," I said. "Well, tell me what you have left there." I got a pencil and paper and wrote the things down. It was hardly worth the trip except to rescue our boat and gear, and except for the turtles, if they were still alive.

"Oh, we covered them well with palm leaves," said Esparon, suddenly more cheerful. He had thought of a lie to comfort me, and perhaps himself. There are no coconut palms on South Islet, and only two on North Islet. I could just see Esparon and Alex rowing four miles to get leaves. I glared at him.

"I can't think what Monsieur will do with you two when he gets back, but he is sure to be angry."

Later, I was even more annoyed to find Esparon and Alex turning up with the others for their free ration of toddy. "Toddy," I said stiffly, "is for those who work. And you, Esparon, are too sick to drink anyway."

Prig, I could see them thinking, but I did not care, though my hands shook from being so angry. I went to bed that night, wishing they'd all drowned instead of coming back while Mark was away. I was sure there was more in it than a case of diarrhea, but I was not prepared to be soft just because things "smelled like trouble." Let there *be* trouble, then, I thought defiantly. Things always happen while Mark's away.

The trip to the Banks was uneventful, and Tristan returned in two days. One of the turtles was dying, so I had it killed and salted. The fish I refused to weigh until it had been properly dried and cleaned of sand; the same with the *calipée*, shell, and other produce. But I immediately accepted fifty-one baby hawksbill turtles to be put into our rearing tanks, for which Mark had agreed to pay ten cents each.

When everything was unloaded, I consulted with Tristan and Ahmed again. What were they interested in doing with Alex and Esparon? Did they want to let them rejoin the fishermen, or what? I could not really force them to do so, but I certainly hoped they would. It was the only chance of getting any money back on those two so we could get rid of them on the next boat.

Ahmed and Tristan shrugged. "Let them come along as fishermen, if you want, Madame; when Monsieur returns we will see."

"Good," I said. "Make them work!"

Ahmed and Tristan shrugged again, as one man.

For a week things went calmly enough, then one day Alex did not go out with the boat. No explanation was offered, so I cut his toddy ration that evening. The next morning Felix reported hearing a crash some distance in back of his house, near the palm being tapped for toddy. By noon everyone knew Alex to be sick, suffering from a backache. No, he could not possibly clean *bêche-de-mer*; no, he could do nothing. He kept to his bed in Léonie's old half of Esparon's house and had Liliane fetch and carry for him. This situation prevailed for a week. There were murmurs from the fishermen about allowing Alex a share of their catch if he was not willing or able to work. But they did nothing about making it official: that is, they didn't come to me. Instead, they began to bedevil Esparon. "What's happened to your friend?" they asked. "Lucky you don't mind his staying here while you're away!" Or else, even more annoying, they would stop talking just as he approached. Cowards! With hindsight I can see they were all scared of Alex but knew Esparon to be safe game. Then one morning Esparon came up to the house and said, "I have told Alex to leave. He has gone. I have given him back his cooking pots. He owes me money for Liliane's doing his washing all these months, and for embroidery work, but never mind. I am satisfied to be rid of him. He will not enter my place again."

I said "All right," and off he went.

That was on a Sunday. Things seemed quiet enough. Monday, the fishermen were to go away for a few days, leaving about four in the morning. I gave them their rations Sunday night.

But daylight on Monday revealed Alex still on the property. The fishermen had left without him. According to Felix, Alex had hidden *dans bois* until they stopped calling him. I cursed myself for not having got up to see the boat leave. "They shouldn't have gone without him," I told Felix.

I went straight to the bachelor quarters. Alex was lounging on the steps. He smirked by way of a polite greeting. "Why have you not gone with the others?" I demanded.

He shrugged.

"You will have to work to eat, you know. If you will not work, you will get nothing in the shop." (Fishermen are not "on rations," and so have to buy their food.) "You can starve, for all I care."

He smiled his sleepy smile. "There are those who will feed me."

Then he added, "I would not go with the others because I

Suzy

will not share anything I catch with that pig Esparon. If you will mark everything I catch separately, and pay just me for it, I will go the next time."

"That's impossible. What about the diesel? The salt? The men who handle the boat while you are in the water?"

"Then give me the boy and a pirogue, and I will fish on my own."

"No." The boy could not be spared, as he was Mason's helper. "You must either fish with the others or work on shore, collecting coconuts. There is nothing else. Choose for yourself."

He shrugged again.

"Monsieur will be very angry," I said dourly. It was infuriating to know that Alex wouldn't be behaving like this had Mark been here, but there wasn't much I could do about that. I turned away and took the path from the camp to the pigpens to see to my current crop of baby ducklings and to visit awhile with the pigs. Our young sow Suzy had just had her first lot of piglets and was waiting impatiently for her ration of powdered milk. Then there was my friend Vespa, the boar, to scratch behind the ears, after which he always threw himself on his side to have his belly stroked. Whitish, another sow, had a form of prickly heat; I rubbed her daily with a mixture of coconut oil and sulfur powder. She loved this. Suzy had had the same affliction before farrowing down, and whenever she saw me coming, used to roll over on her back in hopes of the soothing oil rub. The only time she didn't do so was the day before she farrowed; then she stayed on her feet and made the short loud grunts expressive of discomfort, dislike, pain, or fear—and I was forewarned, so that she had plenty of dry leaves for bedding that night. In the morning there were six rotund piglets snoring among the leaves, and Suzy was waiting at the door as usual. All the other pigs merited a visit too, of course; six noses at each gate, twenty-four pairs of ears to scratch—grunts of rage, however, when Suzy got her milk and no one else got anything but affection.

The company of the pigs was soothing, and now that Little George was looking after them, I rarely left the pig park with anything to complain of. So I was in quite a good mood again by the time I reached the yard, on my way home. It was early yet. I could probably get in an hour and a half schooling for Rory before lunchtime. I paused, to see if he was on the swing or seesaw under the bell tree (so called because the property bell hangs from one of its branches). As I hesitated, a harsh high-pitched *"Madame! Madame! Veeni! Veeni!"* (Come! Come!) broke the stillness made up of Felix's quiet sawing noises and the whispering of a gentle wind through the palm trees. After a second's interval, the sawing noise went on. I looked around. The yard was empty. Nothing going on in Francine's house. Felix's house, quiet. So, I thought resignedly, it must be Esparon's. The call came again, more urgently, and I recognized Liliane's voice then. I came around the bushy corner where the *allée* enters the yard, and saw the depressing sight of Liliane and Alex tearing at each other and at some garments they were holding. Alex had just got a bra away but dropped at pair of panties within reach of Liliane. She paused to pick them up, saw me, and turned on her usual verbal torrent—she must have been fighting silently up to then for me not to have heard her.

In the jumble of words, I gathered that Alex was trying to take things that were hers by right since he had given them to her and she had *worn* them, in spite of Esparon and Alex having agreed the day before what was whose—all this given out while she and Alex circled each other as warily as two cats, each waiting for the opportunity of a fresh snatch. Alex said nothing. He was concentrating. Suddenly he reached out and grabbed Liliane by the skirt, spun her half around, caught her to him, clamped his bundle-holding arm tight against her shoulders, and with his free hand, neatly pried the rest of the clothes she was holding away from her. Let go, Liliane bounced to the back of the kitchen, picked up a half-rotten two-by-four beam she and Esparon had been cutting for firewood and swung it sharply at Alex's head. Alex veered away, but not in time to escape a long graze down the hand and arm he'd raised to defend himself, made by the rough end of wood as gravity brought it to earth. A brief smile appeared on Liliane's face.

"Liliane!" I said, somewhat shocked in spite of myself.

"Yes," said Alex grimly, not one to lose an advantage. "You see? I merely come for my things and she makes me bleed!"

"Your things!" exploded Liliane. *"Your* things! You come in here when Maxime told you never to set foot in this yard again and try to kiss me then tell me you will have your irons back only one is mine then try to press me on the bed there's Little Maxime as witness may God punish me if I lie then take our cooking pot when Maxime gave you yours yesterday after all the embroidery I did for you and washing and you never paid a cent for it all that work . . ." Liliane was crying well now, in jerky sobs. Little Maxime, witness, peered blankly from around the corner of the room where he had been hiding, but jerked back inside as he saw Alex coming. I had been suggesting with what I hoped was hypnotic calmness that they both surrender all articles in question to me, to be put in my house until Esparon's return, when we could settle things between both parties. But no one was listening. Alex had evidently thought of something else of his inside. Seeing him, Liliane let out a fierce yelp and went after him.

In a second or two Alex, followed by a battery of thrown mugs and plates, stormed grinning out of the room with the other of the pair of sad irons held high above his head. Lilaine screamed "Thief," and running after him bit him soundly on the scratched arm while he tried to fend her off with his hands full. The bite stopped his smile. Enraged, he swung his arm —now weighted with fourteen pounds of cast iron—straight at her chest. Liliane leaped sideways, but even so the blow sent her sprawling in the dirt.

"Alex!" I shouted. "Both of you! Stop this at once! Felix!" I called toward the yard. "Come here, please!" I should have called him before. I wish I didn't always think I could manage everything by myself. On the other hand, there hadn't been much time.

With this invitation people began to gather, those that were in earshot anyway. Alex turned away with his booty; Liliane picked herself up, nursing her shoulder and started to cry again.

"Alex, stay here, please. I wish you to give me those clothes now. There's been enough trouble about them."

"No."

"I will have to make a case against you then for entering another's house without permission, and against both of you for assault and disturbing the peace. It will be most unpleasant."

"Make it, then."

"Give over the clothes to me or Felix," I said. "That will at least show you willing to discuss the matter."

"Take them, then, if you want them." He smiled grimly, and reaching to the back waistband of his shorts, drew out his knife.

"Alex! Don't be a fool! You know that's a serious offense!"

Alex continued to hold the knife ready to use, having by now transferred the clothes and irons to the other arm.

"Felix," I said. "There is nothing else for it. He must be shut in the cell until Monsieur comes back."

"There is a hole over the door, and it is full of coconuts," said Felix.

"Fix it," I said. "Now, take him there, all of you." So saying, I gestured to Servina, Felix, and Barbé and grabbed the knife arm myself, knowing he wouldn't dare harm me for fear of real trouble with the police. I had no illusions that I would be able to hold him, but I expected to disarm him long enough for the others to hold him without danger to themselves. I was mistaken. The moment passed. Alex threw me off, inadvertently grazing me slightly with the blade, laughed rudely, and turned away. I turned around, and there were Servina, Felix, and Barbé, standing rooted to the spot. "What's the matter with you all?" I raged. "Can't you do anything to help me? Why are you just standing there?"

"He has a knife, Madame," said Felix with finality, while the others nodded their heads. "Who are we to lay hands on a man with a knife?"

I looked at them with loathing. I despised them. I hated them. You useless bloody bastards, I thought.

Liliane broke in tearfully. "If you can't make Alex go in the cell, put me in there. I'm not safe outside! I would *like* to go in the cell until Maxime comes back. Put me in!"

At this, everyone except me breathed a sigh of relief. "I think that would be wise, Madame," said Felix. I looked at him hard, then at the others, and decided that under the circumstances it was the best I could do. Good old Liliane, I thought—idiotically it did make me feel better to be able to put someone in the cell. I got the keys out from my pocket, and Liliane stalked ahead of us to the cell door. I unlocked it, and she turned around and called Little Maxime.

"Oh, I'll look after him," I said. "Don't worry."

"He is coming in here with me," said Liliane.

"But Liliane," Felix began.

"P'tit Max-*zime!*" reiterated Liliane, cutting through our objections. Obediently the small figure detached itself from the doorway of their house and came to the cell. They both went inside, and I shut the door. "Stay here a minute, Felix, please —I'm going to get some dry gunnysacks for them to sit on. Then get your tools and put some boards over that hole above the door."

This was done, and I went home to prepare the lunch. Rory and Ming had, happily, been playing in the house, pretending their beds were ships and the floor the sea, out of which dolls and toy animals had to be pulled and rescued. Perilous trips for the smaller dolls were also made between the beds along a length of dippy string. I wiped the blood off my arm without their seeing it and left them to play, telling them only enough to explain Liliane's presence in the cell and why I was cooking her lunch as well as our own. Pleased with this novel entertainment, they helped me carry the food, and when I unlocked the door they gave Liliane and Maxime their water while I handed in the plates. Liliane said nothing and did not look at any of us. My children stared quietly in at the pair, then I shut the door again.

In the afternoon, we at last got around to schooling, but not for long. About three o'clock, Felix came running up to the house and announced Alex to be inside the cell with Liliane, whose screams had alerted him.

"But how?" I demanded on our way down the *allée*.

"There is a hole over the storeroom door too," Felix said. (The storeroom was right next to the cell.)

"Yes, but—"

"Unfortunately, we forgot the gap between the wall and the ceiling. It is not very big, but—big enough."

"Oh, my God, so we did." We hurried to open the door, much as I was tempted to board up the storeroom door and leave them both in there to cool off.

"What do you think you're doing now?" I demanded of Alex.

"It's this dress," wailed Liliane. "He says this dress is his too and I must take it off and give it to him at once or he will knife me in the stomach! See! There he has that knife in his hand again!"

As far as I could see, it wasn't, but it probably had been. I noticed her lunch had not been touched, though Little Maxime had eaten all of his. Felix spoke up. "Let her return to her house and take off the dress while I fix up the door of the other side. Then she can come back in."

It was the only thing to do. We could neither lock Alex in

nor keep him out at this rate. I think I hated as much as Liliane to give him that bright yellow dress with orange and red roses all over it and loathed my inability to enforce law and order until my mouth was as bitter with the taste of it as it had been before lunch, but I still assented. We all trooped back to Liliane's house, waited interminably while she changed, and then led her again to the cell, which was now safe. Alex went off with the dress. At that point, I felt a great bond with Liliane.

After the door had shut behind her and that poor little child she would not release to us, Felix said, "You are quite right, Madame, to keep Liliane in there. It is she who has caused all this trouble by telling Alex to come to her while Esparon is not here, then fighting with him to get you on her side. You will see, when Esparon returns, if this is not so."

"Oh. Indeed? But you must agree that threatening us all with a knife is going too far!"

"Yes, Madame, that is true. You should have a *commandeur* here. A *commandeur's* job is to take risks for the sake of the *propriété*. No one of us, family men, will do so unless it is our job."

And so, like a child, I was learning again about "matters of form." Hardly surprising no one would back me if I was not only exposing them to danger but fighting on the—to them—wrong side as well. Oh, they had it in for Liliane, all right, the beasts! You are a self-righteous little man, I thought at Felix, but said only, "Of course I did not know she asked him to come. They both appear to be at fault, in that case. Would that I could lock them both up." Felix's agreeing that that would be a good idea established some harmony once again. After all, even in a minority of one I had to continue to run the property somehow.

The late afternoon brought the half-hoped-for, half-expected return of the *Bouilloir*. Esparon had not succeeded in preventing them from going without Alex, but the fishermen are never averse to returning to dry comfort at night if any excuse offers itself, and did not oppose Esparon when he suggested coming

Liliane and Léonie—Feline Disturbance / 245

back to Remire. His unease, and mine, had proved to be well founded.

I saw him strutting—pink and angry—up the path to our house, and went out with the keys in my hand to unlock Liliane, while he stood beside me, breathing heavily, the very picture of outrage. He had started to berate me for locking up his darling instead of the Beast, but this was quickly quashed. Then, having collected Alex, Felix, and the other witnesses, I held an impromptu court hearing. It was now that Liliane chose to state categorically that Alex had had intercourse with her, after forcing her backwards into her room and onto the bed ("pressing" was the expression used before, which can mean almost anything up to and including intercourse), and again she called on Little Maxime as witness; undoubtedly he had been: privacy is always a luxury amongst the poor, and even more so in the tropics.

As she said this I glanced at Esparon. His expression did not change, nor had Liliane paused for emphasis on this unstartling news. She went straight on to what one felt were her real grievances, the removal of her clothes and irons. About this she was the usual voluble Liliane, and we finally cut her short. Esparon then launched a heavy balloon of oratory about what the division of spoils had been when he had kicked Alex out, and he too would have gone on forever had we let him. I turned to Alex. "We must hear the other side."

Alex continued to sit at his ease. "The clothes were mine. I bought them," he said with an air of finality. To give Alex due credit, he never overexercised his tongue.

Sputters from Esparon and Liliane.

I said I had understood that everything had been divided the previous Saturday. He had had all Sunday to complain if he wanted to. Why wait until Esparon had gone on Monday and then take extra things—perhaps his, perhaps not his—by force?

"I was sick," he said quickly. Then he thought better of it. "I had expectations."

"What do you mean?"

"Lilaine was going to go with me. Leave Esparon and go with me. So I didn't bother about all my clothes because they would be coming anyway."

"Yes," said Esparon, getting still pinker. "Liliane said Alex had been trying to get her to go with him—even on African Banks he started this, so I had to kick him out—after I took him in my home and we were good friends, this is how he repays me!"

I started to ask why, if it had begun on African Banks, he hadn't kicked Alex out as soon as they got here, but realized I would get emeshed in lies to no good purpose.

"So why did you decide you had to have these clothes today all of a sudden?" I asked Alex.

"I didn't."

"Well, that's certainly what I saw you doing, taking clothes, and so did everyone else here!"

"I didn't go to Esparon's house to take clothes."

"Esparon told you not to go to his house again. Yet you went. If it was not to take clothes, why were you taking them when I saw you if you went just to—to press Liliane," I finished a little lamely.

"Liliane asked me to come."

"That still does not answer my question," I said firmly amongst the objections of Esparon and Liliane. "We saw you taking clothes, and when I wanted to take all clothes in question to my house you brought out your knife to prevent me. As far as I am concerned, you are twice at fault, or three times: entering another's house without permission, removing property in that house, and threatening people with a knife. So answer these charges!"

Alex looked dreamily away, and my temper rose. Then he said, "I was out by the *saline* to wash myself and I saw Liliane just leaving, carrying her washtub and things away on the other path, and she gave me a sign."

"I did not!" said Liliane hotly.

"She did not," said Esparon, who couldn't know.

"She gave me a sign, like this." He mimed lifting a tub off

his head and jerking his head in the direction of Esparon's house. He did it very well; everyone smiled.

"I clearly forbade Liliane to talk to you or even see you again after Saturday night," said Esparon. "She would not make you signs."

Alex ignored this. "I followed. A woman makes a sign, I follow. Why not?"

"So you follow. Then what?"

Alex looked at me with lifted eyebrows. "I press her, that's what."

I flushed. "I mean about the *clothes*, of course. What about the *clothes*?" I did not care to look around for any reactions to the supposed rape this time. "Why the fuss about the clothes?"

The murmurs stopped. "So I was there," Alex said, "and all of a sudden she picks up a stick, starts hitting me with it and making a big noise and starts calling you and says I forced my way into the house when she never wanted to see me again. I say 'Good, give me back the rest of the clothes, then,' and she just goes on yelling and hitting me with this stick."

"I didn't hear any yelling. I heard someone call 'Madame, Madame,' that's all."

"You were up at the pig park. 'Madame, Madame' was when she saw you. So while she's looking at you I open the suitcase and take my clothes, all except the dress she was wearing and my irons, and push her aside to get out the door."

"He pushed me!" shrilled Liliane. "He hit me here on my face with his fist and Little Maxime picked up his little stick and hit Alex on the legs with it and the brute pushed Little Maxime away so hard he fell then he hit me again so I fell in the doorway and he—"

"Liliane! You'll have your chance. Let Alex finish!"

"That's all," said Alex. "I took what belonged to me."

"And the knife? I suppose you felt quite right to threaten people with a knife? You know it is against the law."

"I was defending my person."

"What?"

"You wanted to put me in that cell. I was defending my

person. I had only taken what was mine and I was not going in that cell."

"You were defending the clothes," I said. "There are plenty of witnesses to when you pulled out your knife."

"The clothes and my person, then," said Alex grudgingly, and turned away. He had finished. For form's sake, Liliane was allowed to speak, then Esparon, then Alex again if he wished, but he just shrugged his shoulders. It was true that nothing new had been added. Everyone waited for me to give judgment.

"There are no witnesses except possibly that small child to say whose story is true," I said carefully. "It is possible Liliane signed Alex to come, and possible she did not. I can only judge by what I saw." I listed again what I had seen. "It would seem both parties are guilty of assault, and one of threatening with a knife." I paused for inspiration. "If you wish to avoid trouble with the police, you had better settle who owns what clothes right now, in front of everyone, and swear not to break the peace again."

Silence. "There is also the matter of some money you owe Esparon for Liliane's washing for you," I added, addressing Alex. "It would seem to me that if you take back the clothes you gave her, then you must pay some cash." This was a trial compromise on my part.

"I bought soap and food," said Alex sulkily.

The soap was for your clothes, and she cooked your food. Besides, you *gave* her the clothes and she has worn most of them by now. How can you take them back unless you pay her money instead?"

"She was to come with me. Now I don't want her, but the clothes are mine. Let her stay with that white pig—"

Esparon raised his fists and bounced back and forth until someone restrained him. Felix barked at Alex something about respecting the court.

"If you refuse to compromise, then a case will have to be made against both of you, but I will emphasize that Alex is the more guilty because of the knife. There are many witnesses to the fight, and so no difficulty in proving it. And if there is more fighting—and that goes for all of you—it will be still more of a case. Esparon, are you willing to compromise as I suggested?"

Esparon spoke briefly to Liliane, who flushed with anger and turned away. "Yes," he said, "we are willing."

"Alex?"

He looked off into the palms, frowned, then sneered; finally, with the corners of his mouth still downturned, he said, "I will pay her what Esparon says I owe them. Take it off my wages."

I turned to Esparon. "Agreed?"

Lilaine's enforced restraint gave way. "Let him keep his filthy clothes and his dirty money! I will bring a case of rape against him as soon as I get back to Mahé and as soon as we get off this island Esparon will push his face in!"

Alex smiled evilly and opened his mouth for some rejoinder, but I managed to get there first. "Do so, by all means, do anything you like as long as you're off this island, but you'll have to work to pay your debts first. I'm not going to listen to any more. The subject is closed, so, finish. Let's go, Felix. And if there's more fighting I'll bring the gun down."

Behind my back Alex laughed rudely, which made my hands shake as usual. Alex was quite without fear of my daring to wound him, and I felt correspondingly futile. I had no legal power, and they knew it. When "good relations" broke down there was no one to enforce law and order. I should be the Peace Officer, not Mark, who was away half the time.

In a few days, Mark came back and the gloom lifted. He went straight to Alex, after he had heard my tale of woe, and told him, "I'll bloody well kill you if you make any more trouble." A little to my surprise, this was effective, and in due course we were able to pack off the lot of them on a passing schooner. It only remained to get rid of Léonie and we would have finished with troublemakers on the island. I said as much to Mark as we were standing together on the beach, watching the last load of copra and dried fish go off on the whaler, with Esparon, pale child, and the fair Liliane perched on top of the bales, and Mark was just agreeing, when a horrid noise from the beach down by the camp impinged on our ears. We looked. There, coming along like something out of Hogarth, all tatters and gin, was Léonie—screaming and yelling at the top of her lungs, evidently in high glee. She was carrying a long pole, which she waved from side to side, then pointed jabbingly at the retreating form of Liliane. At the end of it danced the red and orange roses of the bright yellow dress.

XXIX

BUT LÉONIE could not be got rid of immediately. Not only was she heavily pregnant, but she and Barbé were still very much in debt as well. And Barbé himself was just the sort of man we liked to keep: quiet, self-sufficient, a patient if not brilliant fisherman, and a good collector of coconuts. This quality certainly set him apart from the younger fishermen. Soon after Liliane and Maxime left, the southeast trades had started to blow in earnest, and Mark had put all the fishermen onto collecting nuts. It made sense to use our labor force this way, on a summer/winter basis, but the young ones barely tolerated the arrangement. Knowing that the price paid for one turtle would equal two weeks of nut collecting, they spent most of their first week on shore discussing whether it was or was not calm enough to go out, and only resigned themselves to nuts when the weather was obviously foul. Even then they kept their fishing hours, late to bed and late to rise, and did their collecting characteristically in spurts, dashing through the woods with loud shouts to each other for two hectic days, then spending the third shored up against the walls of their verandas, sleeping or playing cards. Not so Barbé. Barbé was a man of regular habits. Out by six, home by eleven, out at twelve again, and in

The new boathouse

The new boathouse

the number of nuts garnered each week by steady application, no one could beat him; that is, Payet and Berley were good too, but they could not match Barbé for speed. Our copra-making really depended on these three, and on a new man Mark had brought back from Mahé, so we finally put the young fishermen, with Ahmed as leader, onto collecting rocks. It seemed to be our solution to most problems, and it certainly made the building progress. The walls of our house crept slowly upwards on the days when Armand was not finishing off the turtle-pound wall; Felix began the doors and windows. Then, by the time all the piles of coral near our house had given out (we could get no more from Grand Brisant in the southeast), Mark was able to start the new calorifier up at the pigsties, for which the gogglers had been breaking *pavé* on La Plaine. He also began a slipway and new boathouse on a part of the beach flagged with sandstone slabs and opposite a natural channel through the reef: another dream—to be able to draw our boats out of the water easily and as easily launch them again—and a hedge against the days when we would no longer be employing so many people. "Once get the building done and the plantation's in good heart, we could probably do with half the number," Mark said, frowning over the end-of-the-month accounts.

Thus our winter set in. The island got a windblown look, and the vegetables suffered, but the wind also blew away the flies and mosquitoes and made us cool.

And because in the southeast boats rarely leave Mahé, we received no visits from passing fishermen, so no one was distracted by messages. With our own boats drawn up on shore, the island turned inwards and concentrated on itself: the men on their work, us on our plans. This sort of isolation was good in that it forced our people to pull together. But we knew that to the fishermen it was only a "for the duration" mood, one that would change with the wind, so we were careful to make the most of it, and when September came, careful to use the carry-over period of togetherness to make them collect the last loads of coral for our house before thinking of starting to fish again. It

Coming in on the southeast side

was an expensive time—no money coming in and much going out—but a satisfying one. We had got on with things.

In September, in the quiet time of the change of winds, Léonie's baby was born. She had assured me and everyone else that the child was due in November, but September it was, and a fine full-term infant came into my hands, a boy, who luckily did not resemble anyone in particular. While in labor Léonie had made a few last-minute attempts to worry officially about having a *pre*mature baby, but she said no more about it when she saw her son; and Barbé, far from being suspicious, looked as shy and as pleased as if the child were their first-born male—they had had rather a lot of girls. That evening Mark gave out some extra toddy by way of celebration, but even with loosened tongues no man mentioned Nioz: one would have to have a cruel nature indeed to be mean to Barbé.

I was especially relieved that Léonie's confinement had gone off well, both socially and physically; socially because we wanted no fights within our newly cohesive labor force, and physically because the health of all the Barbés except Maxime himself was always a source of anxiety. One death was enough, and childbirth, though a lot simpler than modern European women like to think it, can't help but increase risks. When Léonie walked home with her number eight, I felt delivered myself.

Next on the list was Carmen, but she had several months to go. About Carmen, who was both healthy and clean, I didn't have to start worrying now.

As our first year on the island ended, therefore, we found we had settled in in every way, and were looking forward to enjoying the second as we had not been able to enjoy the first. Our labor troubles seemed virtually over, and even though we did not yet have our own schooner, it was nearing completion; it would only require, Mark thought, his making two more trips back to Mahé before the final trip to collect her, and in this he proved correct. How we looked forward to the day when she would sail into view, ours to command! The little *Bouilloir* was all very well, but only the schooner could do the fishing Mark planned, and yet carry enough stores and people to make the trip worthwhile. The *Bouilloir*—strong, trusty twenty-five-foot stopgap though she was—was too small to go far enough for either purpose. Oh, the luxury of not being surprised by a boat any longer, of being able to plan. And for us personally, no long waits for Mark in Mahé, and the worry all this entailed. With the *France*, if we felt like it, we could both go, or at least I would know when to expect Mark back.

So it was with a sense of purpose that Mark returned to Mahé in the beginning of our second October, and with a sense that these long partings would soon be over that I saw him off. Our own schooner. That was worth a great deal. And he had promised that no matter what happened, he would be back before Rory's birthday at the end of the month.

On the morning of the eighteenth a sail was sighted. It was first seen out by the turtle pound, where some of the men were clearing away seaweed, and I heard, with that lift of the heart it always brings when Mark is away, their faint "Sail-O" carry across the island.

Liliane and Léonie—Feline Disturbance / 255

The boat, when she was close enough to be seen through the glasses, did not appear to be any of the Mahé schooners. Still, we could never know if Mark had found some new means of transport, so I assembled the men to stand by to push the big whaler into the water; Mark was expected to bring six months' rations, as well as all the Christmas supplies and mail for our employees, who miss Mahé more keenly at this time of year than any other. By Christmas supplies, I mean toys for the children and cheap wine for the adults. We had kept a little beer hidden in the shop from a trip earlier in the year, just in case, but from the laborers' point of view it does not go as far or make one as drunk as wine. It is loved—any drink is loved—but respect is accorded a drink in strict proportion to the alcohol content obtainable for a given price. Christmas means wine, and all hands were soon in the shade of the boathouse, carefully watching the approach.

I went back to our house to have another look through the glasses, for she was still far out. Her single mast was very tall—a yacht? She was headed straight on for the anchorage, so that it was difficult to judge her size. Then she turned, and I laughed ruefully. A small blue yacht. I went down to the yard again. To my surprise, Felix, in spite of his seasickness, had already gone out to her, and soon he was back with the news. An old, old man, said Felix. Yes, an Englishman, but with no tea, no water, no milk, no sugar, only a little diesel, no food—and, laughed Felix, no idea where he was! This struck everyone as very funny. Imagine an old man like that, all alone, sailing around with no food, and no tea even. Must be crazy. (He was too polite to say stupid, which is an insult in *créole,* but the implication was clear.) Felix added, disapprovingly, that he had told him the Master was away, and that only Madame was here, quite as though he thought any polite person would have pulled up anchor and come again another day.

I looked out toward the boat, but there was no apparent activity. "Did he say he was coming ashore?" I asked.

"Yes," said Felix.

I shrugged my shoulders. Everyone seemed to be waiting for

something to happen, but I told them they might as well go back to work. I could see that the boat carried its own dinghy. Regretfully, they all sauntered off, and I returned to the house to get on with my work. I had got so in the habit of being alone that the arrival of a yacht with some desperate old man on board did not even seem very interesting.

Still, it was a little difficult to concentrate.

Two hours later, the man climbed into his dinghy and started to row. By this time the tide was dead low, and the passage through the coral heads evidently not clear to the rower. Finally he turned around and rowed forwards. I went down to the water's edge with the children to greet him.

"Hello," I said.

"Hello," he replied. He negotiated the last few feet, beached the boat, and together we began to pull it up the long stretch of sand. I examined him. He was a small man, thin, with a cordy neck, square shoulders, uncoordinated. When we were halfway up the beach with the dinghy, he said, "Let me know if this is too much for you," but it was he who was breathing hard. He was not old, though—about forty-five, I thought—but his eyes were as rheumy as an old man's, the whites blurred and the pupils cloudy. Not at all a keen, seafaring sailor's eyes. Only his hands seemed to match his life: work-calloused, square and strong, with a generous portion of black engine grease under each nail. His hair stood up in a shock, stiff with salt and dirt, so dulled a brown that it might have been gray, which was probably, with the eyes, what had given Felix his impression of extreme age.

"Our carpenter says you have no idea of where you are," I said. "It's Remire, or Eagle Island on the charts, in the Amirantes."

"Yes, he told me. Hard to tell. I've only the big chart from Delagoa Bay to Guardafui with me."

I was astonished. This chart covers the eastern coast of Africa from the Horn of Africa down to Mozambique, but just barely included the Amirantes. It stops short of the main islands of the Seychelles. Where had he been going? I said nothing however, except "You were lucky to come across us, then," and he said, "Yes, bless you, for I'm out of milk and sugar and just about all my water. I was just going to set up my little still this morning, when I saw this island. I have a Primus, see, and a kettle with a bit of hose pipe . . ."

He described this primitive affair in lugubrious detail, until I broke in. "But what can we do for you? We can let you have some food, and diesel and water, but come up to the house first. I am sure you would like a cool drink and something to eat, and of course, if you don't have to hurry off"—I became aware that I had not been very hospitable—"and you are planning on staying the night, I should think . . ."

We had by this time got as far as the corner of the shop. "Oh yes," he said. "I won't be leaving here for a while. Certainly not before November. I need a long rest after all I've been through!"

"Oh," I said. "Well, that's fine." I tried to put some heart into it, but my spirits sank. Still, I recalled my duty. He was tired and dirty. He would probably like a bath and a shave. "Lets go up to the house," I said again. He had stopped, and I started to walk on up the path, gesturing toward the house at the same time. "Do you like palm toddy?" I asked, to keep the conversation going. "That's what we drink here—fresh, sweet toddy, or perhaps an orange squash—"

He had stopped again. "Don't you have a beer? Oh, I'd give my soul for a beer!"

"Well," I said slowly, "we do have a little saved for Christmas. We've locked it up in the shop though, and Mark gave strict instructions not to open it until he came back . . . the laborers like it so much, you know, that it would be unfair to—"

"Oh, just one beer. I'd give anything for a beer. I've been dreaming about a cold beer for days."

Beer saved since June! He was asking for gold. "Well, we must do that for you, anyway," I said as graciously as I could, and I told Rory to run home and get the keys to the shop. Rory ran off, well pleased with the errand. There were sweets in the shop. "It won't be cold, though," I added as an afterthought, but he didn't either hear me or notice.

"I think," I said, "that we might introduce ourselves. I'm Wendy Veevers-Carter, and you?"

"Oh, Sandy. Just call me Sandy. Everyone calls me Sandy, even my son."

"But, well, Sandy what?"

"It doesn't matter. Just Sandy. Mmm. Anderson. But everyone calls me Sandy."

"Where have you come from?"

"I've been a month at sea, just a little over a month. All alone! From Tanganyika. I was going to Aden. But off Guardafui—you know Guardafui?" I nodded. "Just off Guardafui, I met strong winds, and the sea was all roughed up. I lasted just a day of this, and then I thought I'd better turn around and head south, so I decided to make for the Seychelles. Yesterday I must have been off Mahé—anyway, a big island with a mountain. Thought it was a cloud, but it was an island all right. Off it the night before last, hove to until morning, but by morning it had disappeared."

"That might have been Silhouette," I ventured. "You were to the west of it?"

"Uh, yes, must have been. But in the morning it had disappeared. Then I drifted about all day and night, then this morning I woke up and I looked around and more of those clouds. I didn't notice this island right away because you were in the rising sun, and when I did see you I thought it was a cloud. But it was an island, all right. Never so glad to see anything. Must have been eleven miles off. Just the tops of the trees showing.

"Yes, that's right," I said. "You can see this island ten or eleven miles away on a clear day."

There was another pause. I couldn't seem to think of anything to say, not being helped by my opinion of his vague navigation and ill-preparedness.

When Rory arrived with the keys, we went into the shop. "Oh, you have a real shop here," he said. I opened the carton of beer and got out ten cans. "Is there anything else you'd like while we're here?"

"Fags," he said. "I'm right out. Was saving my last for today."

"I'm sorry, but we just have tobacco and cigarette papers, not proper cigarettes—"

"That'll do." I gave him a piece and he looked at it dubiously. "We roll it the navy way," I explained. "That's a segment. We'll cut it up at the house on a board."

"Oh, yes, I was in the navy." He pocketed the tobacco and papers and picked up some of the beer. I picked up the rest, and we went out. By then, fortunately, it was lunchtime and there was no one around, though I imagined I could feel covetous unseen eyes on the beer.

"What branch of the navy?"

"The navy, you know."

"I mean, the merchant service, the Royal Navy, or what?"

"Oh, the R.N."

"What were you doing in Tanganyika?"

"Government. I was in government there."

"In the administration?"

"No. Mines."

"You've just left the service?"

"Yes."

"You got Africanized?"

"Yes."

The conversation languished again. We entered the house. "Ah, this is nice," he said.

"Yes," I replied. "The thatch keeps it very cool. An oasis on a hot day." I sent to the sideboard and rooted around for an opener, long disused. I had forgotten to look for one in the carton. I found it in the back of the drawer eventually, and carefully opened the warm can and filled his glass. I then got myself and the children an orange squash each, but by this time, with a "Bless you, that was good," he had emptied the can, so I opened another. Before we had finished our squashes, he had downed that one too, and Rory, an observant child, brought him another can and the opener. "Bless you," he said, to Rory this time.

I banished bad thoughts at this most precious liquid quenching so voracious a thirst. After all, a stranger wouldn't realize we aren't supplied by a vessel weekly from Mahé, or that the life we lead is generally frugal and abstemious. Naturally, the *France* and improving the island had eaten a lot of our capital. But how would he know all this? I must seem awfully mean. If he noticed. Besides, he came from Tanganyika, and I had not spent nine months there on safari without consuming a goodly amount of "Tusker" beer myself. Still, I thought I would tactfully bring him around to palm toddy, so I began by asking if he had ever tried it.

He said no, beer was what he wanted, bless me.

But I persisted. His obtuseness was beginning to be interesting. Toddy is very like beer, I told him; then added that it was the effervescing fermented liquid tapped from the inflorescence of the coconut palm, knowing no more exact way of putting it, pompous though it sounded. Presently, he allowed that when he had passed through the Comoro Islands, some of the natives had brought a jug of "coconut beer" on board, and they'd had a bit of a party, and they'd left a bottle behind, and the next morning he'd spent a hell of a lot of time looking for a leak in the boat because of this steady *hisssssssss* noise, until he found the bottle . . . I laughed, and said yes, that would be it. I then excused myself and went to get the lunch ready and sent Rory back to the house with a glass of toddy for him. When I came in to set the table, I asked him how he found it.

"A bit weak," he said. "I think in the Comoros they put in a lot of sugar and keep it around awhile. At least, it gets a hell of a head on it and pretty strong—"

"Oh, they do that here too, but we prefer it straight from the tree."

I went out to bring in the lunch. He had, meanwhile, been turning the matter over. "I tell you what," he said when I got back, with an air of solving all, "let's get a big jug of this stuff and try putting a lot of sugar in it and tonight we can have a *big* tonk-up!"

Four hours later he was still sitting in the living room, nursing his last beer, when we heard another "Sail-O," and it was like a miracle. Sails do not pass twice in a month, let alone in a day, and this one, no matter who it was, promised relief. He had refused to go around the island, no he did not want to see the newly finished turtle pound or the pigsties; he didn't much like walking around in the middle of the day . . . I had therefore made my rounds alone, leaving Rory to look after him, and had returned to fix the tea. I had offered him a bath, a place to nap if he wanted, but these had not interested him either. What I was going to do with him all evening I had no idea, but it was certainly not going to be a "tonk-up." Just being polite was becoming a strain. I began to feel a sort of panic. It had been so peaceful alone; I hated him for coming here. The more I tried to look at things from his point of view as a poor, tired, worn-out, sea-weary sailor, the less sympathetic I felt. Knowing how selfish my feelings were did not help change my attitude, and the discovery that he knew of my old haunts and camping grounds in Tanganyika, and even the man I had been going to marry before I met Mark, *and* the paintings I had left behind, decorating the round *choo* in Banagi ("Bless you, did you do those? I could hug you!" was his enthusiastic comment), did not move me. I had become so solitary that it was not only hard to adjust to the presence of a guest intending a long stay—I didn't even want to. Besides, I thought with self-justification, he's not making any effort to be a good guest. No hint had any result, no lead made him do anything but what he wanted to do, which was drink. Didn't even want to drink what there was to drink! I thought crossly. He could no more solve the puzzle of why beer was not flowing the way it had in good old Tanganyika than he could superimpose the image of this rather cold serious woman on that of the author of the paintings in Banagi. Poor little man, with your rheumy eyes and your thirst! We should never have been able to talk if you had stayed a thousand years.

"Sail-O" came again, cool on the wind. Rory rushed out, and I was not slow to follow, leaving Anderson no choice (the last can was empty) but to come along.

It was, as I had hoped, Mark back from Mahé.

During the next few days I made attempts to return to my writing, but since in our old house the rooms lay unceilinged under a single roof, and Sandy was always in the house, it was impossible. In any case, I found I had to spend increasing amounts of time in the kitchen—for our sort of meal did not suit our guest; I saw that after the first day. I dearly love to cook, but what with Rory's schooling, my island duties, and the time I steal for writing or drawing, there never seems to be much time left for executing anything lengthy in the kitchen. Furthermore, the kitchen can be very hot. We do not, therefore, go in for formal three-course meals, but depend a great deal on fish, or casseroles, or cold meats roasted on bread-baking day, slices of bread and butter, pickles, and a salad. As for deserts, never; at least, not with the meal. The children get custards and jellies with their light supper at night, but our own supper is always a snack: pizza, or sandwiches, or soup.

Sandy, however, faced with a one-course meal, would eat a little, talk and drink a lot, and wait and wait for the next round. He would watch Mark and me and the children wade through a second helping with his murky eyes, and ask if we minded if he smoked. Then when we all got up (after pressing more on him, naturally) he would look first startled, then resigned. Pretty soon he began asking what sort of things we stocked in the shop. Sardines? He was very fond of sardines. Bully beef? Nothing like good old bully beef. He was getting "kind o' hungry."

I finally fell back on curry. Knowing the former habitat of the animal, I was sure this would appeal, and I was right. The day it came on the table, he looked up in surprise from his first mouthful and said, "This is quite good!" Which would have been funny, if it had not had the prospect of going on forever.

Mark, as always, was a social brick. He likes to talk, you see, which I don't particularly, and he doesn't seem to care so much if he's not listened to, though even he found Sandy's extreme inattention annoying. The fellow never seemed to take anything in. There they both sat, Mark unable to get anything out of Sandy, and Sandy uninterested in anything Mark said. Mark, despite his patience, soon showed the strain too. I noticed that the island began to demand a great deal of his attention outside. At least some of the time, however, he dragged our guest with him, and so we spelled each other.

It was the evenings we minded the most. All through the day we have separate things to see to, and meal times are busy with food and children; it is only in the evenings that we have a chance to talk. Ritually, we have our few glasses of toddy, listen to the news on the B.B.C. or the Voice of America, play some music, plan the next day, put our feet up, relax. None of this seemed possible with the pinched figure of Sandy between us, and after he had been around for three days, we laughingly found ourselves going into the kitchen, just to have some place to be alone. We couldn't adjust to the constant presence of a third person, this dull stranger who must have thought us as mad as we did him. However, I passed my boredom and resentment off in activity, and Mark did the same. At least we had the nights to ourselves: the incubus left us about ten or eleven and went back to his boat, not returning until after breakfast the next morning.

But after a week the weather did one of its abrupt shifts, and the wind blew from the north, hard, to great effect. It poured with rain, a good deal of it through the ancient thatch of our roof, and we were suddenly really imprisoned together much more effectively than before. Sandy did not stir from the house at all in the daytime, and at night it was far too wet for him to return to his boat.

The second day of the storm, Mark explained to Sandy that he was going to move the *Bouilloir* around to anchor her in the lee of the island; if he wanted to, Sandy could follow and anchor where she did. Of course, it was up to him, but the bad weather looked as though it would last for a few days. Sandy hesitated, then said all right, then said he needed some diesel. Mark said "Certainly," and in a break in the rain, took him down to the yard, opened the store, and filled his jerry cans while Sandy waited behind him impatiently, not offering to help. But when Mark had finished, he looked up to find Sandy gone. He picked up the jerry cans and went down to the beach. There was the little dinghy, abandoned on the shore, and in the water, Sandy's head bobbing about. He had, without a word, obviously decided to swim out to his precious boat, which he had ignored for two days—to save her? Had he thought her anchor was dragging?

Our own men were just boarding the *Bouilloir,* so Mark signaled Tristan to pass by the yacht to see if she wanted a tow. But when the *Bouilloir* approached her, Sandy frantically waved her away, screaming "F— off, f— off," so Tristan brought the *Bouilloir* up to the beach to collect Mark. Mark met with the same reception, replied in kind, and departed for the other side of the island, leaving Sandy to raise anchor and follow as best he could.

"The man is mad," Mark said, when he came back, soaked to the skin. "But we won't be seeing anything of him for a while. His dinghy's ashore, and he won't swim from where he's anchored. Boat's jumping around like a cork too," he added with evident amusement. "Didn't go far enough 'round. *Bouilloir*'s nice and quiet where she is."

I was instantly filled with remorse. "Oh, Mark, don't you think we should do something?"

"No, he'll be all right. Besides, it'll be good for him to cool his heels for a while. The man can't even be sensible, raving like a maniac and very rude. Let him simmer down, I can't think what got into him, swimming out to his boat like that and not taking his diesel or anything. Fellow's obviously mental."

After two days the weather cleared a little. Mark and I were having some coffee when we heard the stamp-stamp of bare feet on the steps, and Sandy came in, wet and disheveled.

"Hello," we said guiltily.

He wasted no time replying, but stood at the door and said peremptorily to Mark, "Look, can you let me have some diesel now before the boat goes on the rocks or something? I'm on my last legs. I'm all in." With which he staggered back down the path to the yard. Mark lifted his eyebrows at me, and followed, passing Rory, who rushed in a minute later.

"Do you know," said Rory, "what Mr. Sandy did? He kicked Little George! He said to go get my water and go put my dinghy in the sea, and kicked him! And Little George said 'E-ou' and ran away!"

"Kicked him?" I asked.

"Yes, like this," said Rory, kicking, "and Little George did this"—Rory shook his fist—"and said 'E-ou,' and ran and ran. And do you know what Ming said? She said you will be cross!"

I was. But as Mark said, the man must be crazy, so what could one expect?

Meanwhile, Mark was persuading Sandy to stay on shore. He had ascertained that the boat had two anchors out and so assured him she'd be perfectly all right where she was, with our own men to keep an eye on her. Besides, he'd feel more himself after a few good night's sleep. This idea was found acceptable, and he moved back in. The bad weather continued. He spent much of the time staring out to sea, complaining. Curiously, he seemed to hold the transformation of our quiet anchorage into choppy water fully exposed to the wind as our fault, or something we should have warned him about. He kept saying, in a hurt tone, "But the first few days were so quiet! I thought you had a good anchorage here . . ." It was no use explaining how rare our northerly blows were, so Mark passed the time telling him about Mahé and what he could expect to find there; a quiet anchorage was high on the list, and Sandy dreamed out loud of this daily. I wonder how he had survived a month at sea when two nights' rocking had so unnerved him.

On Rory's birthday we had a roast turkey, and Sandy was again able to look up in surprise and say "This is quite good," which this time I accepted gracefully as the compliment I supposed he intended.

After three more days of rain, the sun came out strongly and the wind dropped away. Sandy said he'd go out to look at his boat. He took more milk and sugar from the shop, and Mark had his dinghy brought around to the other side, with the diesel in it, and had one of the men row him out. This was accomplished without incident, and connection was once more established in an orderly fashion between man, yacht, and dinghy.

I went out to the kitchen to prepare lunch. By now, I was used to the preparation of proper meals and a little more regular in my habits myself.

Toward noon, however, just as we were beginning to wonder when Sandy would be coming ashore, we caught sight of the yacht about two miles to the north of Remire, off Grand Brisant. While we watched, up went the mainsail, and with the freshening breeze Sandy was soon out of sight.

He left behind quite a few of his belongings, the letters (crime of crimes) he had promised to mail for us in Mahé, and of course us and our island, we supposed, forever.

Felix made the final pronouncement. "I think," he said, "he is just sailing anywhere and does not care if he dies. He is sailing to be taken before his time."

At the moment this seemed a good explanation of Sandy's erratic behavior, but Mark's next visit to Mahé proved that he had managed to make that quiet anchorage, though he was very drunk and vaguer than ever. He didn't, in fact, recognize Mark on the street, which was a mercy, so his coming upon our island in the wilderness of the Indian Ocean could not have been as impressive to him as it was to us.

Or is this only wishful thinking? You see, there is something that worries me. The one fact he told me willingly about himself that afternoon before Mark arrived was that he too was writing a book. I remarked that it was hard work. He said he found it easy. The conversation languished again. But you never can tell what will get published these days. Perhaps as a punishment for my lack of charity only *his* will see print? A horrid thought: he might really have found it easy.

XXX

OUR NEXT VISITOR also arrived on a yacht, but a magnificently big one that came swooping down on the island late one afternoon while I was feeding the ducklings. Needless to say—I even hesitate to say it—Mark was not on the island but back in Mahé again, this time finally to collect the *France*. Naturally, the whole island had mistaken the yacht for the *France* at a distance, which had accounted for the definite excitement in the "Sail-O" and brought me running down from the pens—in time to change my clothes and climb into the pirogue just as the yacht was anchoring. Sandy's visit had given me food for thought: I realized that in the absence of Mark I had some civic duties to perform and couldn't treat a boat's arrival as just an unexpected nuisance, no matter what my thoughts.

Even Mark had complained that when he arrived, full of worry about how we were—broken limbs? appendicitis?—we never appeared on the beach. That we had rushed to the kitchen to make sure refreshments and a hot bath awaited the tired traveler before appearing didn't impress him. "The first thing I want to see when I anchor off Remire is you and the children standing on the beach where I can count you, and if you can bring yourself to wave, so much the better."

This sarcasm was justified. Mark was right. In the course of all his comings and goings I had got into the habit of relieving my worries by simply picking up the glasses, checking on his presence on board, and sighing with relief, not thinking how seeing only the men on the beach would affect *him*.

It's lucky my ways were mended. As we paddled closer, I saw a familiar shape at the rail—blond hair, sunglasses, espadrilles: my mother! In her Truro clothes come to the South Seas. My mind blanked and then filled with a rush. How? When? With horror I envisioned Mother stuck for weeks in Mahé, waiting for a boat to come down here—then scuttled quickly away from the thought. We were almost alongside. Mother and I smiled and nodded and mimed surprise at each other, while the yacht's owner anxiously rushed all the fenders from the other side of his white boat before we closed the distance.

Once we were seated in the yacht's lounge and Mother had introduced me to the owner and crew, she explained that a friend had talked her into going to Egypt; once there it seemed a pity not to fly to Salisbury and Beira and catch the B. I. liner to Mahé. She'd written me from Cairo—hadn't I got the letter?

(A note from Mark said that seeing the Cairo postmark and recognizing my mother's handwriting, he had—luckily—opened the letter, and been able to meet her, and when the *Flying Cloud* had stopped in Mahé, he had arranged for the yacht to bring Mother down. She was to return on the *Argo*, which would call in on its way back from Aldabra. This was luck indeed: usually passages to and from the islands are not so easy to arrange. He, he said, would be down as soon as he could—on the *France*.)

So. We looked at one another. I thought that she had changed very little in eight years, while my mind ran busily over whether or not Carmen had given the house a last-minute polishing (boat drill) and put on the kettle, and wishing it weren't Monday and washing day so that the children could have been put into fresh clothes—it was only chance I'd had a clean pair of shorts in my drawer—and wondering what on earth she was going to think of the place. I could see her eyeing my arm. Our two male dogs had taken to fighting at intervals, and just that morning had had an argument over a rat. "It's nothing," I said. "Only we're out of adhesive tape; the bandage makes it look big . . ."

When we had finished our drinks, we went on deck and loaded ourselves into the pirogue. It was wet on the bottom, of course—there never has been a pirogue that isn't, like any canoe —so the *Flying Cloud*'s owner said he'd bring Mother's bags ashore when he came in his dinghy. Funny. Since the first day we'd landed on the island, I'd never thought about the pirogue being such a wet boat.

"What news of the *France*, Mother? Did you see her? Do you think she'll be finished soon?"

Mother's replies were vague. She was busy balancing, holding her dressing case on her knee and trying to turn around to see the island at the same time.

"That's the new house, there along the beach. On the right are the bedrooms, then that big room with the arches is the living room," I explained brightly, wishing to God we were in it. What was she going to think of the old tattered gray barn with the sheets of aluminum roofing propped up against the thatch inside where the worst leaks were? Where was she going to sleep? Children's room. Put up the tent. When was the silver last polished? Sheets, yes. Should have changed the carpet around to hide the faded place. Hope Carmen did the dishes early.

We arrived on shore without incident. The sea was like a millpond. I kept her talking about the new house while we approached the old one. How awful it suddenly looked, and I had loved it so well.

I will say for Mother that considering that she dislikes the tropics from atmospheric conditions to zoological specimens and furthermore is both an excellent (if slightly obsessive) housekeeper and exquisitely delicate cook, she bore up very well. She was game, from the start, and kept it up, with only a few breakdowns, right to the end of the visit. That it was hard on her was obvious—in a moment of passion she said she'd seen Georgia sharecroppers live better than we did—but she did her best. And the children made the visit go. They, who had never seen their only grandmother (Mark's mother had died before they were born), were delighted, and she was equally so. She took them for swims and they took her for walks, and Rory must have told her more about the island less self-consciously than I ever could have done. And toward the end of her three weeks

Ming, age three and a half—January, 1965

with us, Mark sailed in on the *France*. In our common joy at this event friction was forgotten. *France*, the beauty—well, rough beauty; she is a fishing boat after all—here at last, with the rakish Arab slant to her masts and her long slim lines. "In Mahé, they call her 'the big pirogue,'" Mark told us. And she is fast because of her likeness to one. Fifty-six feet long, eleven-foot beam, and every inch of it ours.

I think that at the time of Mother's visit, in March of our second year, we had reached both the lowest ebb of our finances and the height of our chauvinism of do-it-ourselves and thrift, one obviously being dependent on the other. We weren't spending a cent we didn't have to, and were making as much out of the property and the fishing as we possibly could. Any slight

Rory, age five—February, 1965

surplus was eaten up by Mark's trips to Mahé to finish off the *France;* there was nothing to spare. We lived more simply than ever. The new house, though it was well along on its September glut of rock, was at a temporary standstill. In good weather, were we likely to take fishermen off fishing to go to collect rocks? Copra-makers off copra to make charcoal for me to cook on? Eat lots of fresh pork and turkeys and ducks when we could sell them so well in Mahé and there was plenty of fish in the sea?

Water was short too. The dry (perfect) weather meant the wells were dryish, but was I to sanction the use of reservoir water to wash in? I certainly knew enough not to trust the weather by now. Last March we had been soaked and stormed at weeks at a time. Now look at it. Our first October had been a drought, but during Sandy's visit had we not had squalls? The present dryness might easily turn into a drought, and I wasn't allowing any waste of reservoir water, big reservoir though it was.

So the sheets were yellow with the guano-colored water they were washed in, and we wore only our oldest clothes; and though the children had some "Mahé clothes" put away, they had outgrown them and I didn't make more. We weren't going anywhere, so why bother? Besides, I did my work as fast as I could to steal as much time as possible to write. If I could sell the book, what a help that would be! But I was very slow at it, with all the interruptions that running things meant, to say nothing of Rory's schooling, which with his fifth birthday had become official.

One part of the kitchen was black with the wood fires I now cooked on, and as all the well water we could draw was six buckets a day, baths were sponge baths after washing in the sea. Our hair looked a bit dry; Rory's tan (and Ming's freckles) had deepened; my nose stayed rosy. And the old house—should we mend it now that the new one was so close to being finished? We protected the Victorian furniture from the worst leaks, moved the beds, and put up our bits of aluminum where necessary. Nor was I so fussy a housekeeper as I had been; even had I taken the time, I could not have kept the place clean all the day under the steady rain of tiny bits of dried coconut leaf from the roof. Carmen, pregnant as she was, swept and dusted twice a day and twice a day cleaned and scrubbed the fire-blackened pots in not quite enough water. I couldn't ask her to do more. Dust collected in corners; the silver in the glass-fronted cabinets no longer glowed; the brass on the Arab chests caught the light only when I could run down Ahmed on Sunday and get him to apply Brasso with his strength.

In fact, Carmen was nearly eight months' pregnant when Mother arrived; after Mother had been there a week, Carmen came to me and asked to leave a bit earlier than she had planned. Her veins hurt, she said, and she was sorry, but she'd have to go. I agreed, of course—and took Francine off property work to replace her.

I picked Francine because we got along well, and because she was docile and did what she was told. I was used to her by that time, and knew that even if she had never worked inside before —and I think she had, for a Chinese family in Mahé—she could still be made into an adequate servant. But when Francine sailed in for her first morning's work I saw her anew—with my mother's eyes. One thing at a time. On her head: the oldest straw hat ever seen still in one piece; her hair in ten plaits tied with gray rags; her blouse a loose patchwork of elderly threadbare pink satin which showed a lot of Francine whenever she bent over; and her skirt magnificently understudied by something in faded black lace. Pieces of Francine's clothing had clearly come down in the world. Her splayed feet were protected by the end bits of Japanese rubber sandals—the rest had disintegrated. These she left at the door, the better to polish the floor.

But there was hope. When she saw how half-heartedly the floor had been polished by the vein-troubled Carmen, she tut-tutted and set to work. *Swish-swish, swish-swish.* The petticoat swung and the coconut-husk polishing brush thumped back and forth; the house shook on its piles of rock. But the floor gleamed afterwards, and the gleam was reflected in my mother's eye. There was hope.

So we persevered through broken glasses, a dropped pressure lamp, beds made with the sheets on catty-cornered, cut fingers acquired through Francine's habit of putting knives back facing the wrong way, and some other minor troubles I can't remember now. I was glad to have her. And by the time Mother left, Francine really began to feel secure in her position: amiably she bossed the water boy around; she even informed Mark when he was measuring the evening's toddy that he should remember to pour over the gunnysack or he would make a mess of her floor. Her ego was definitely not suffering. And Madame Payet, a dragon herself, complained to me that she couldn't get Francine to bring the empty buckets when she came back to the yard in the evenings for the chickens' grated coconut; *she* had to fetch them. "That one," she announced. "Her head is finished swollen." And I suppose it was true. I know I often seemed to have to do her shopping for her.

"Madame," Francine said one day, "when you are in the shop tonight" (the shop was opened every evening at five, which was when Francine swept the house again and washed the luncheon dishes) "you must reserve for me one eighth of pepper, one eighth of curry powder, two boxes of matches, and one soap." I looked at her. I was tired, on my way to feed the ducklings and still in the clouds from writing all afternoon.

"I'll try to remember," I promised, and left.

When I got back, Francine quizzed me. (The actual goods had been sent to her house with any child I saw hanging about.) Pepper? Yes. Curry? Yes. Soap? Yes. Matches? Oh no.

"M*adame,*" says Francine. "What am I to do?"

"Take a box from here," I told her (I had only one box left myself, so could not give her two). "I will get some more tomorrow."

But when I saw Francine the next day, she said she had brought the box back. "Oh?" I said, wondering if it had something the matter with it, or what, while I looked for the bread knife. Francine handed me the knife, then explained.

"It's all right, Madame, I didn't need matches after all. *It* had brought some," she said shyly, "and I didn't know it would."

I pretended not to notice, remarked "Oh, that's all right," and started to cut the bread. This was the first time Francine had ever referred in my hearing to her new man. After this, she became bolder.

"Madame," said Francine one day, "you will have to tell that new 'goggling' not to bother me any more. On Saturday he threw stones at my window and It nearly got into a fight!" Suddenly, she started to cry. "Oh, I was so alone here for so long these men think they can do what they like with me, but now I am used to *him* and I am afraid there will be a fight and trouble and Monsieur will be angry! Oh, it is so difficult to be alone, one must have someone!" She paused, sniffing. "After all, Madame, I am still young, I."

"Of course, Francine," I said soothingly. "It's quite all right with us, you know. Very good idea. And I will tell Monsieur about the one who makes trouble, don't worry."

Then I said casually, because I had been wanting to know (she often had menstrual troubles and I thought she might be nearing menopause), "How old are you, Francine?"

There was a silence. I looked around at her, but she was looking up in the air with the soap in one hand and a dish in the other, thinking. Finally, she said timidly, "About—*nine*, I think, Madame."

Francine's new *bonhomme* is none other than Bo's'n Berley. A regular Barnacle Bill, ensnared at last, I thought, until suddenly I remembered that way back in the old days these two had also once shared a house, before the Barbés moved in.

XXXI

DR. BRADLEY, until recently the Seychelles' only historian, remarks in his book, *The History of Seychelles*,* that in visiting the Amirante Islands "we go [back] a century in civilization; these islands cut off from headquarters have only periodical visits every three months or so from passing sailing boats." This is certainly as true today, give or take a marine engine in the boats, as it was when his book was published; and if, as he says, we go back a century and realize we are not going back to any European 1840 standards but to those of the always backward Seychelles, life on an outer island hardly appears to have changed from the time there were Europeans around to be interested in using them.

We tend to think that this probably wasn't very many at any time. Even now not all of the islands are permanently inhabited.

* John T. Bradley, *The History of Seychelles*, Clarion Press, Victoria (Mahé), 1940.

The island may not offer a living, or its lease may have expired and not have been retaken. That Campbell found someone on African Banks in 1801 is made the more remarkable to us because we ourselves do not keep the islets staffed all the year 'round; nor is Desnoeufs* permanently inhabited; nor would Remire be, we suppose, if it weren't for the upkeep needed and shelter created by our small coconut plantation. And if living on the outer islands seems an isolated, remote sort of life to us today, think how much wilder, more lonely, more deserted the islands must have appeared to the would-be settler a century or two ago.

Just the reverse is the truth. When one examines the records, there is evidence enough to suggest that by Dr. Bradley's 1840 the islands had reached not a "high" of development, at which they have since stuck, but a low.

The inhibitory factor in their discovery, in their getting to be talked of as good places to go, was their lack of water—water in wells, that is, or running over the ground in rivers, the way it does in Mahé. But the islands do normally enjoy quite a reasonable amount of rainfall (we, with our new reservoir, do not run short), and the pioneer settlers of the Seychelles must have noticed this. Once over the water barrier, it was perhaps an easier step for them than for us to set sail for an island, there to make their home. For what were they leaving? Schools? Roads? Cars? A crowded social life? Modern medical care? The care and solace of the Church? Hardly. Living in Mahé may have meant seeing a little more of the world in passing ships, but aside from a charity school which shut down after three years' operation in 1842, and various church schools opened after 1850, all of which aimed at the education of "the descendants of slaves," European Seychellois had to send their children to Mauritius or Europe, or employ a tutor—a fact that living far from Mahé did not change. And while the earliest funds for a road were collected in 1849, one gathers that little prog-

* Christened Ile de Neuf, the ninth island, by du Roslan, who seems to have run out of names by then, but its status as the colony's largest birds'-egg-producing island within practical striking distance from Mahé has been too much for its original name.

ress was made: the first horse carriage was not imported until 1895. People moved around slowly on horseback, or in litters, or by pirogue. As for doctors, by 1837 there was a "Medical Office" in Mahé, but in 1838 and in 1842, visitors report no doctor being available at the port.* There was no priest until 1852.

No, the more we think about it, the more obvious it is that the outer islands have already had a boom time, and that further, when it come to pioneering, the early Seychellois were just as good at it as any other adventurous Europeans (including the English). And since there was at this time no "manager" class but only Europeans and slaves, the Europeans could not run islands from Mahé the way they do now.

Still, there must have been a reason to leave, for the early Seychellois, Mahé's lusher shores—and it was, we think, the introduction and success of cotton as a crop. The Poivre† Islands, forty miles to the southeast of us, still have much wild cotton growing, as do Marie-Louise, Cosmoledo, Astove, and Farquhar, farther south.

The north island of Poivre must, in fact, be one of the longest inhabited islands outside of the Mahé group. One can still see there the old slave quarters, with a door so low that the slave had to stoop to pass through, thus preventing a rush on the guard, and high stone bell tower that bespeak the age of the settlement. No one bothers to build such things nowadays. Poivre was at one time the center of farming operations for the whole of the Amirantes, and probably became so in the first year of the nineteenth century if not before. For this there is an interesting bit of evidence.

Late in 1803 a frigate sailed from France directly for Poivre, carrying on board a nineteen-year-old boy and his guardian, a M. Aimé. The boy was called Pierre Louis Poiret. The frigate stayed at anchor off Poivre for five or six months—at

* When the *Sibylle* sank *La Chiffonne* (see Appendix B), *La Chiffonne*'s doctor swam ashore, married a local lady, and set up practice for a while. From A. T. Webb, *The Story of Seychelles*.

† Presumably named after M. Poivre, the first Intendant of Ile de France, now Mauritius. The outer islands do not grow pepper—too low a rainfall.

Poivre, whose anchorage is far from the shore and exposed to every sea! Then, leaving Poiret, Aimé sailed for Mahé. Of course, those were more leisurely times, but still the length of the stay is remarkable.

Still more so is the possible identity of Poiret. From all accounts he dropped hints during his long lifetime, but it is only on his deathbed that Poiret revealed himself to have been the young dauphin of France, escaping incognito. Of course his family believed him, but there has never been any concrete evidence produced. There are a few pieces of crested silverware, but for the most part the family believes in their descent from royalty as an article of faith.

Whatever the case, the youth was quite uneducated. He was put to train in the cotton-ginning factory on Poivre, married a girl he found there named—a nickname?—Marie Dauphine; had two children by her, and stayed on the island eighteen years, leaving Poivre for Mahé in 1822. Once settled there, he proceeded to have seven more children by a certain Marie Edresse. All his girls he named Marie something (one Marie Antoinette); his boys equally were Louis. He died in 1856, a respected and popular local mystery.

Nor was Poivre alone in being settled early. Coëtivy was exporting coconut oil by 1811; the corsair Houdoul had a fishing camp on Aldabra before he died in 1835 (Aldabra is six hundred miles from Mahé); and on Juan de Nova, an island which retained the name of the Portuguese explorer right up until 1932 (when it was rechristened Farquhar), a French family was living, with their slaves, in the early 1830s.

But today we are, or were, the only Europeans living on an outer island—"were" because recently Poivre has been bought by another English couple. Two white lairds in the Amirantes is startling everybody, including us, and it will probably be some time before we (suspiciously: what can *they* be like?) get around to exchanging visits. The fact that we are both regarded as insane by the tame "colons" of modern Mahé gets under one's skin until even we think we're queer—an attitude that a little reading of history puts in perspective.

Liliane and Léonie—Feline Disturbance / 279

All of which does not make Bradley's point any the less true. Our life is lived remote from modern standards; except for things I can count on my fingers (things like battery radios, pressure lamps, petroleum products, modern forms of roofing and electricity if we wanted them, and such imported luxuries as beer and wines), our life here must be very like life was in Mahé when life in Mahé began.

The only effect of this fact on us is to make us wish we were vintage a hundred years too. Sometimes I think it will be another twenty years at least before we shall have succeeded in accumulating the experience and mastering the simple skills that every (undeveloped) European took for granted a century ago. Then we might be truly proficient in our "backward" life.

Especially do I worry about my deficient modernity when it comes to midwifing. Let me say right away that Carmen had a delightfully easy (from the midwife's point of view, at least) time producing a daughter for Ahmed; nothing went wrong. The midwife was not so butterfingered as before, and more at ease mentally. But still, early-nineteenth-century housewives must have been more used to these things than I could ever be—or perhaps more accepting of the chances of failure.

And no sooner had Carmen returned to her house with little Noor Ahmeda than Felix shyly took me aside and began talking about September in such elliptical terms that I at first did not understand. But yes, it was true. A fifth Amelie had been conceived in the cavernous depths of the asthmatic Mrs. Felix. The news spread like wildfire, and Felix, his face puckered with prudish delight, was the butt of male humor until the novelty was past.

Mrs. Felix, pregnant. Well, that was a worry. All that fat! And suppose she got one of her attacks while in labor? I wrote to Mahé for more ephedrine and settled in to watch and wait.

Now that I think about it, the Amelie family provided most of my early doctoring practice: an asthma-ridden wife, four children who need iron, or vitamins, or cough mixtures, or worming—to say nothing of Felix himself, who seems to be accident-prone and whose wounds always seem to "go septic." They are not by any means as unhealthy a family as the Barbés, since they are better off financially and far cleaner by nature or upbringing, but they have been here longer and so must claim first place.

Ahmed was indirectly responsible for Felix's first injury, which was certainly a painful one and nearly made Felix think of returning to Mahé after only three weeks on the island. Ahmed, in good Arab fashion, believes hair to be hot. So even though he is most unhairy physically, he always shaves head, armpits, and groin in hot weather as a matter of course. Our first southern spring here was certainly hot, and Felix was suffering badly from prickly heat. "Shave," said Ahmed, always ready with advice, and Felix did. But he was careless and cut the skin of his scrotum. The cut went septic; Felix went to bed in great pain, and after receiving a certain number of mysterious excuses for not appearing at work, I was finally called in "professionally." I tried two days of fomentations and sulfur pills; when these had no effect I started penicillin injections, which did. But for two weeks, both Felix and I had to suffer the necessary indignities of dressing his wound, and during his convalescence, keeping the bandage in place became quite difficult. We finally devised a sort of little bag, with strings attached to an elastic worn around the waist, into which the tender parts could be placed, bandage and all, so they wouldn't bang around, and which left his natural bodily functions less inconvenienced than before.

All this happened just after Mark returned to Mahé for the first time, while Gappy was still in control, and I have often wondered if perhaps the intimacy made necessary by his wound bound Felix closer to us (making him less susceptible to the blandishments of Gappy) than had the odd jobs he did for us while still in Mahé. If so, the injury served some useful purpose besides making him more careful with a razor—for, as must be apparent, Felix has been a great help in many ways.

He is a quiet man, and gentle, tall but slightly built, spare

Liliane and Léonie—Feline Disturbance / 281

of frame, and spare of humor. He has sensibilities instead. He seems to derive his joy in life from a strict and proper attendance to duty, on doing the proper thing at the proper time in the proper way. He is also gently, nicely avaricious, as a result of his philosophy of frugality. But with Felix, all these could-be-faults are really almost-virtues because of his moral code and —for the Seychelles—high standard of self-discipline. Sometimes this is a little wearying to live with; I am sure his wife finds it so, though she is three times as irritating in her own right. We call her "the pillow." Like many people with a bad allergy, she seems prone to get other ailments. Over the years Felix, being a good man, has spoiled her, so she now does nothing after an attack, because she is tired, and nothing in between attacks in case unwarranted activity might bring on another—as well as, quite naturally, nothing during an attack but lie plumply on her bed, moaning.

Usually Felix makes no comment about this, but come Saturday, when Mark gives out a grog to each employee, Felix will, thus fortified, say to the other men, "Oh, I will get rid of this one. I am sick of her." And to Mark he confided one day that Mrs. Felix was "the cross God sent him to bear." But Sundays see him dutiful again. And besides, in the eyes of God she is his wife forever.

Felix is very religious. When Gappy left and we put Felix in Gappy's house, allowing him to retain some of Gappy's privileges in the line of extra furniture, free water buckets, a lantern, pencils and paper simply because the house "came with," he took it upon himself in return to bring out the altarpiece and Book on Sundays, to ring the bell for church, and once those interested assembled, to intone some sort of service as well. I thought this both enterprising and commendable— whom would we have found to conduct the church service had Felix not volunteered?—but it turned out on questioning that he thought something dreadful would happen if formal praise of God was not carried out every Sunday. So quite as many bells seem to ring then as on other days, and Felix really has no day of rest. For his other Sunday duties are to chop the week's firewood, to sweep the house and polish the floors, and to cook, if there is anything he would like to eat other than the rice and *bouillion* Mrs. Felix does consent to throw on the fire when she is not actually ill.

Felix undoubtedly leads a hard life, but in recompense he thinks correspondingly well of himself. If our opinion of him is high, his is higher, yet held without vanity, which would be a sin. Felix thinks Felix is wonderful because this is his honest opinion, and to think otherwise would be a perversion of the truth. Socially, he also thinks well of himself. He is an educated man. He can read, write, speak some English. And, we found out the other day, he believes he is white, just as Gappy believed he was.

Looking back, we think that when Gappy left, Felix probably entertained ideas of being made manager in his turn. He has never actually said anything—he wouldn't—but there have been several moves in this direction, in which the reading of the church service (a duty of island managers) can probably be included, under a secondary heading as it were. The first "property" duty he took over, quietly, was the coconuts. Coconuts have to be handed out every morning for grating and they have to be counted after they have been gathered and brought in. In stock they are kept under lock and key (even though hundreds are always lying around on the ground) because this is the Seychelles. And besides, when one pays to have them collected and husked it seems natural to lock them up. Felix noted that Mark and I were slow at counting the nuts and often not around when a laborer wanted them counted, or when the women wanted the nuts for grating, or some such. So he asked for, and got, the key.

The next thing was the water. Drinking water is also kept under lock and key. This is not because we pay to have it collected by anyone, except in that we must build and maintain the reservoirs which do so, but because left open it would be consumed or dirtied within a week. Rain water is precious, and not a matter that can be put in the hands of the laborers. Felix noted again that it was a bother for us to supervise bucket

Liliane and Léonie—Feline Disturbance / 283

after bucketful for a line of waiting people, and took this over too, with its key.

He was now the church, and a two-key man. He was certainly saving much daily time and trouble, for me particularly, and I did not want to inquire closely into his motives. If it made him feel important, it also turned him into a kind of "trusty," on the side of property versus labor, though he has never become a mackerel like old Marcel. To get information out of Felix, one has to present a hypothetical situation to which a hypothetical answer is received, and this either Mark or I have to worry over to crack its kernel of truth or good guess or rumor, like any oracle. Mark, having found that Felix's information is not very accurate, rarely bothers with this rigmarole, but when Mark is away, I find it useful from time to time. Felix likes to feel needed, and he is.

The next thing Felix took over did not come with a key but it is a key duty, and one which none but the *propriétaire,* or the manager, or the *commandeur* ever does: he announces the orders in the mornings. Every morning at what is called "roll call," the labor force straggles into the main yard to be given their jobs for the day. After Gappy left, it was I who had to get up at five forty-five in order to be down in the yard by six. I believed it a good thing, for a while. The orders could not be misunderstood, I thought, and I could see for myself which laborers were cheating—like Sopha, for instance, with his habit of turning up at quarter to seven and saying he was sick, or not turning up at all and then saying he had been sick, or pretending, when visited at his job near the eleven-thirty bell that he had been given far too heavy a task; look how long it had taken him! However, there were certainly mornings I was late myself, having overslept, and many that I would have preferred to spend over a quiet cup of tea than standing about in the half-lit yard, waiting. And eventually Felix suggested that I could tell him the various orders in the evening for him to transmit in the morning. When I realized this would not either trouble him or take up too much of his (our) time, since nearly all his work was done in the yard anyway, I agreed. As for the cheating—well, I thought, it would really be more effective just to make nasty little spot checks during the day. Once established, this idea has remained firmly in force, even when Mark is here. Mark is much worse than I about getting up in the mornings because he likes to sit up late at night, when it is quiet and peaceful, to Think.

The fourth move, if any of these favors could be looked at in this way, came after what was probably a long mulling-over in Felix's brain. There are, clearly, many things we do that a Seychellois does not, and some of our ways must be peculiar, if not downright embarrassing, to a man of sensibility, though we gather that Felix has schooled himself to bear with us for the sake of his job—and perhaps we are, after all, quite easy to work for. But there was one matter about which he eventually felt constrained to speak, and when he did, it came from the heart.

It was Saturday, the eleven-thirty bell had rung and the men were sitting outside the shop, under the trees, waiting for their week's rations. Felix was first, as always—not that anyone holds back to give him preference; he is just more efficient at getting his bags, tins, bottles, and boxes ready as soon as he has rung the bell, which hangs outside his house.

This Saturday he got his rations in orderly fashion and bought his flour, coffee, tea, cigarette papers, tobacco, and matches (Felix's purchases never vary, and every penny is budgeted); then instead of ducking out the door and making off with his usual busy stride, he paused and said, "Excuse me, Madame, but there is something . . . there is a matter about which I must speak to you and Monsieur. The women, and all of us here on the Property, do not think it right that the fishermen should walk about all day long in—just bathing suits. And when they come into the shop they still have nothing on but bathing suits, not even shirts! We Seychellois"—I can always tell when we have gone too far; Felix uses this excluding expression—"we Seychellois do not do this. We never go to the bazaar in Town without a shirt and proper shorts and shoes," he added primly, but inaccurately.

I started to say, knowing full well what Mark would think of this nonsense, that I would tell Monsieur, but Felix interrupted—most unusual this, and another evidence of strong feeling.

"All you have to do," said Felix, "is to put up a notice on the shop door, and I will see that everyone understands. It is just not proper that things should continue in this way when there are ladies present."

I opened my mouth, then shut it.

He continued. "I have written the notice for you. Here it is, Madame." He handed me a very small piece of paper. I said again, suppressing a smile, that I would tell Monsieur, and put it on the table. The next person was already impatiently at the door, so Felix picked up his bags and left. I think he very much wanted the notice to be put up then and there, but didn't see how he could manage it.

Mark came in soon after, and we read the *avis* together. It was written in *créole*, which—not being a written language—is spelled according to the individual writer's grasp of phonetics. It said, in Felix's ornate and spidery hand, that men should dress properly and undertake never to enter the shop *"son chemize."* Mark laughed and said he thought a polite *bonjour* covered a man better than a shirt, and that shirts seemed to make people feel self-important anyway. We had had quite enough of the shirt-wearing types, other than Felix, to last us quite a long while. Mark's comments on the "ladies" I will not include.

So the fishermen's chosen form of dress continues to be offensive to the women, I suppose, and it's still only Felix who habitually wears a shirt. Poor Felix. For our own sakes he tries to improve us, to no avail. But he has made no further attempts at the role of fashion arbiter, and apparently his growth into the role of manager has with this setback been permanently stunted.

The last thing we want on Remire is another manager.

We are not so ungrateful as we sound, though, for the many services Felix now performs, and his salary has increased accordingly. What worries us is what we will do when he leaves, and he will. He is intent on doing the proper thing by his children, which is to send them to school, and now I fear he counts the months until next year when he has said he must go.

Where in Mahé will we ever find a man so honest and upright again?

At least it turned out that our house would be completed long before Felix's departure; in fact, from May through August, Felix worked exceptionally well, the reason being that pregnancy had given his wife nine months of blessedly asthma-free existence. It was remarkable. Her whole personality changed, and that she was fatter and heavier did not seem to bother her at all. Everyone marveled, and I'm sure Felix was pleased.

And to cap matters nicely, her confinement coincided with the pork-eating celebrations of putting-on-the-roof.

She bore up yell in labor, too, which surprised me. Her muscles looked so slack. But things were going smoothly and I was even more calm than with Carmen. I sat beside her, waiting. (Felix, unlike the others, had made her move up to the house sensibly early in the day—also a help to the midwife's peace of mind.) Then I noticed her looking at me expectantly, looking away, then looking back again. Something was worrying her.

"Is anything wrong?" I asked.

"No, Madame . . ." There was a pause while she had what the unfeeling medical profession calls a good long contraction. "But, Madame"—she panted—"aren't you going to measure my little hole?"

Firmly, I said it was not necessary. That there was no one waiting for the delivery room and that I was not a busy nurse calculating the time before I'd be needed made no difference to her, however. A ritual of the hospital care had been omitted. But I didn't change my mind. The more handling, the more chance of infection. Besides, it was soon too late to argue about it. In a few minutes a heavy boy was born, well packed in grease like his ma and squalling lustily.

They called him Remire, Remire Joseph Amelie, and he is the fourth child to be born on the island since we've been here.

FOUR

Our Third Christmas: Reflecting

XXXII

OUR THIRD CHRISTMAS, the third Christmas since we came to Remire, we spent in Mahé. We left the island in Felix's care and made the voyage not in any spirit of "let's go somewhere for Christmas" but only for the reason that our third child arrived in the middle of November. He was late, as all my children have been, and what with one thing and another, we decided we might as well return to the island after Christmas as before. But we had to make do with Hong Kong's idea of Christmas colors (orange and pink) rather than our own decorations, which my mother sends us, and disliked missing the celebrating of our first Christmas in the new house, gleaming white and rainproof.

But spending Christmas in Mahé was fine with Rory. One thing Rory clearly is, and Ming is not, is acquisitive. Remire

The new house, ready at last

is poor in shiny things one can buy. Also (Rory's second passion), we never *go* anywhere. Out is just Remire. *Dans bois* is not very far away to him now (age seven). And (third passion) we never go anywhere on Remire by *car*. His bicycle is no substitute for the wonders of riding while a metal engine does all the work, and he felt it keenly when, just before coming to Remire, we sold our Land Rover. This time in Mahé, we decided we would have to invest in another car to avoid taxi bills, and he was delighted. His eye lit on the local Jaguar, on a Rover, on the fleet of little Spitfires the tracking-station personnel are so fond of. But we bought a Mini-Minor. A secondhand Mini-Minor pickup, if you please, with only two front seats and an open back, in which he and Ming were expected to ride on a small wooden bench. Explaining the economics and the practicality of having an open back when we had two large dogs to carry satisfied him only intellectually. He could see why, but his heart was with the Jag.

Any car, however, was better than no car at all, and Rory in Mahé was in a state of transport (literally) that was bliss. "Where are we going today?" at six in the morning became "What about going to see so-and-so?" by afternoon. He'd think up anyone, dredged from an acute memory of all our casual conversations. And if I said I was going to the clinic, where he and Ming would have to wait outside, he'd promptly suggest leaving them at the club; he "could talk to Joseph, prob'bly." And if we weren't going anywhere, he'd immediately counter with "Who's coming for lunch? Isn't anyone coming for lunch?" (Or tea, or drinks, or dinner.) A day wasn't counted as complete without either a voyage in the car or a social engagement—Rory's fourth love is other people.

It was only Ming who shared our feelings about Mahé. The whole time we were there Ming asked us regularly when we were going back to the island, so that she could "find some more shells."

Ming has developed into a dreamy self-sufficient child of five, with firm ideas on how she wishes to spend the day. One never finds her hanging around at loose ends, the way Rory did at her

Ming on the eastern shore

age; conversely, she is less inquisitively involved in new sights and subjects. She sees, all right, but whatever her thoughts she communes mostly with herself; while for Rory, life couldn't be lived without talking—managing, organizing, being organized, going somewhere, out, in-question-question-out again. Rory's days are full of doing, while Ming's activities are in general more passive. Oh, they are both physically active, but Ming's approach to a new object is to watch it, stare at it, register its salient features, saying little; while Rory immediately bursts with the news of newness. Anyone handy is dragged over to see, or he rushes back to the house to get me; he describes it at lunch, repeats at dinner, is full of questions about it just before going to sleep. And he often, he says (aged seven), wakes up in the night to think about it and once awake he has trouble going back to sleep. But Ming sleeps and sleeps and sleeps, deep, far away, in another world, and if she wakes up often does not know where she is.

It would be difficult to say which one is actually the more observant. Is Ming when "in a dream" blind to the world around her? It is easy to suppose so, but frequently we will be talking about something with Rory—Rory in the room means talking with Rory—and will have asked him more about what he is describing, when Ming will suddenly lift her head and come out with an observation on it that is both true and essential.

On the other hand, I notice that Ming is by no means so silent with our laborers' children. Among the Seychellois, talking is a positive disease, a congenital, incurable habit of verbal noisemaking started at sixteen to eighteen months and never stopped until they are too weakly dying to spare the breath. With them Ming chatters away, but in her home, while being by no means shy or inhibited, she mostly turns the radio off. An odd mixture, and it will be interesting to see how she turns out.

Some of the contrasts in their character and in their attitudes toward the island may be accounted for by the difference in the ages at which they came here. Ming, at two, was just the right age to make of Remire her real home mentally as well as physically, while Rory had already known three different homes in Mahé. Even so, I think the island will become "theirs" in a way it can never be ours; our memories prevent it. What we see a little of in Rory is this having known well too many other places.

But they are both fully part of island life and that life part of them. Rory, like Ahmed, may like the *fantasía* of Mahé—the dressing up, the car trips, the shops, social engagements, movies, and so on—but nothing could have been greater than his air of importance the day he caught his first fish off the turtle-pound wall, and in Mahé he was quite superior to the English children he played with, who knew so few practical things—how to husk a coconut, make brushes and thatch houses—and nothing at all about pigs. Here on the island, Rory is busy every moment left over from school, collecting seeds for his garden or coconuts for his pocket money, making coconut-frond houses to play in or more of his towers or palaces or abstract geometric figures carefully constructed out of pieces of *zik* (the stiff part of a coconut leaf) stuck into ripe *bois blanc* seeds (*Hernandia peltata*); this while Ming adds to her ever-expanding collection of the minutest shells our beaches offer, or sits absorbedly, drawing sketches of the people around her: Felix's little girl, Jenny, with her six pigtails; Ahmed with his mouth open, laughing; Mark

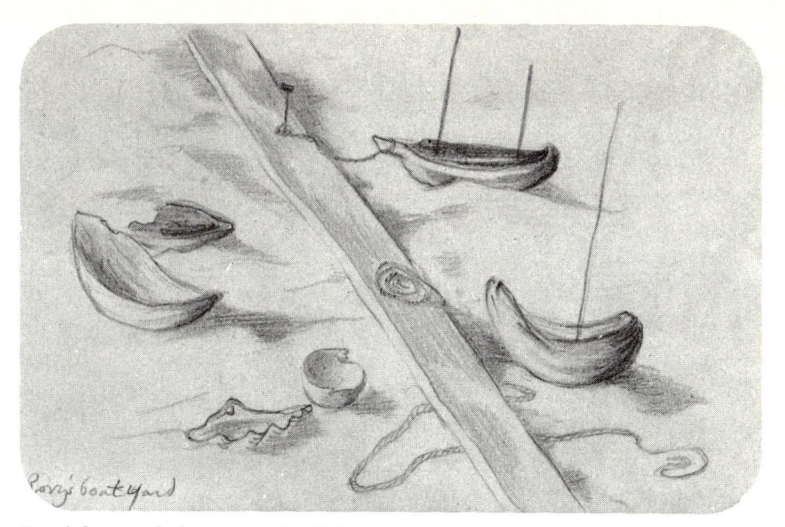

Rory's boatyard: the coconut husk fleet

out walking with his inseparable long stick in his hand; me with my hair on top of my head, holding the baby; Rory with his fishing line a mass of wicked hooks.

And it has been interesting to watch them expand, take in the island. A tiny child's impression of his environment is so myopic. A tree here. A large root there. Tall steps up and up into his tall room with the roof so far away one can't be sure it's really there, except the sun doesn't show through. His landmarks are all so close; a trip to the privy is a voyage to the end of the world for which the corner of the kitchen and the landward side of the chicken pen are vital navigational aids. But then the points of recognition begin to accumulate, spread out—one hundred yards, two hundred, three hundred—and soon their adventuresomeness is limited only by how far they will go *dans bois* without one of us. At first they were very hesitant even to go from our house to the yard by themselves; then Rory would consent to do errands if Ming came with him: hand in hand, they would pad softly down the path; then come running back, their mission accomplished and a story to tell of a chicken in its nest, or Little Felix getting thrashed again. But soon, they went almost too far the other way. There was a stage when we hardly saw them and had to develop a bell system for meals, baths, swims, pick-up-toys-it's-sweep-the-house time, and so on. Mark and I began to worry that they were being much too independent. They, in our island life, were always certain of finding one of us when they wanted to, but we often had to go looking for them.

The arrival of School made home more important again. I had been teaching Rory bits and pieces—the alphabet, how to count, reading the numbers—while we waited to hear if the correspondence school to which I had written would consider accepting such an out-of-the-way family. It might be months before I would receive their answer, as I explained to them. Did they think they could send me lessons a year ahead?

After three months an answer was brought by a passing fishing boat. (Fishermen had started, cautiously, calling at the island again. They no longer expected chickens and pigs free, but Mark was generous with the toddy.) Yes, the Parent's National Education Union, which runs the Parents' Union Schools, would be happy to enroll Rory in their preparatory class; please send five guineas for membership, five guineas for school fees, et cetera. And with the letter came their program for the year.

I was amazed. I had expected hesitation on their part. Still, they sounded very competent. They even ordered the first books I would need so there wouldn't be any unnecessary delay. Obviously, they were used to this sort of thing. My letters from the States might come redirected from Rhodesia or with "Indian Ocean?" written in red ink over the address, but the possession and running of an empire had made the acceptance of us on our tiny island as easy to this sturdily British Victorian school as it is to the British Post Office. No trouble there.

Rather, it was I who was slightly worried when I read over the entrance form I would have to fill in for Rory and, later, for Ming. All the questions seemed ordinary and sensible and leading, in that one was encouraged to tell them properly about the child's personality, except for one aberration: they wanted to know the shape of the child's head and fingernails! The first

Our Third Christmas: Reflecting / 295

conjured up visions of phrenology or of little black boxes into which they possibly feed this information, getting God knows what valuable insight in return. A drawing of his hand had to be sent too. It was on this that the shape of the fingernails was supposed to be "indicated." I drew them in. But what about mothers who can't draw? And the shape of the head. With my training in anthropology I had no doubt of being able to give them an answer that would not be ambiguous. But what about mothers who weren't anthropologists? The answers must be pretty subjective, I thought. And anyway, most children's heads are round. Now if they had asked about the proportions of head to body, there might be something in it: they might want to know early about enrolling a mongoloid, for instance.

Oh well, I sighed to Mark, we shall see. The other questions are good, and they really sound as if they take a special interest in each child. Mark then noticed that their directors all seemed to be titled creatures of the British Establishment; perhaps one should pin one's faith on that, he suggested.

We sat down to read the pamphlets and the book on home education written by the founder, Charlotte Mason (untitled). They were all full of the most inspiring goals and techniques—ideas that in spite of their Victorian ring are still solid enough now—so we were again encouraged to be hopeful. Besides, I had heard from an old Aden friend, a teacher herself, that their results were good. We decided to subscribe.

We are very glad we did. About any problem on which one cares to write them, they are helpful—even if the correspondence is, unavoidably, so slow. And the more we experience of their methods, the more we begin to hope that it will not be necessary for us to send the children away to school at all, until they are ready for college. I know this is exceedingly hopeful, but in our travels we have seen so many of the results of sending children Home to be Educated. Families working in the old Indian Civil Service or in Africa accepted it as a matter of course that young Nigel, or whatever, would embark at the age of six or seven for the lonely voyage to England with some female stranger who just happened to be going at the same time, there to enter a strange school full of strangers, from which, at Christmas and Easter, he was picked up by a strange unknown uncle or aunt or a Friend of the Family to spend the holidays. And all this with his parents miles, thousands of miles, and a month or two by mail (like us) away. It couldn't be right. And to judge from so many of the results, it wasn't. As people, they weren't secure; as sons and daughters, they were strangers to their parents; and as products of one or another of the Public Schools, they were Public School Snobs, with none of the leavening that their homes might have given them and none of the insight into other people's ways of life that, for instance, is the heritage of those who were kept at home or, rather, I mean abroad, with their parents. What novels we might have missed, had all the English children been sent away from India! Or the West Indies, or Guiana, or Nigeria, or Kenya. Mark and I both feel so strongly that a child's place is in a *home* with his mother and his father "on tap" as much as possible, that we believe we must be doing the right thing for them by keeping them here. Gaps we are too inefficient or too ignorant to fill can surely be filled later.

Of course, what kind of childhood one had oneself certainly forms the ideals one keeps in mind for one's children. Mark's love of lonely lakes and of the miles of salt marsh he used to explore as a boy in Poole harbor has made him want the same free surroundings for Rory and Ming, and the part of my childhood spent in Truro, reinforced by the contrast of New York, affects me the same way.

At least we can count on giving our children a childhood filled with good health. Mahé's being so much damper and more populous meant that colds went the rounds with irritating regularity—and Rory, when I took him to the hospital for his triple-antigen inoculation, came away with, I later discovered, measles. Here on the island we have no infectious diseases, except what might be brought by a passing boat,* no colds and, so far, no serious accidents despite Ming's proclivity for climbing. Broken

---

* Obviously boats pass often enough to spare us the medical danger of total isolation, and inoculations now take care of the risk of catching childhood diseases later in life.

bottles left around by the laborers, bits of tin, the pen knives both are allowed to carry, since they make so many things out of the coconut fronds and like to cut sugar cane for themselves to eat, and the coconuts which might fall on their heads—these could be classed as our natural hazards. These, and the sea. But children have a remarkably good sense of self-preservation, and ours have had early and rigorous training in water safety. Not only have they had to acquire this on board our boats, but living on a tiny island in the middle of a large ocean also gives one great respect for the sea and what it can do, what it could do. A child going too far out here is not made unwary by miles of visible land; on the contrary, young as they are, ours seem very aware that landfall is this island or nothing.

They are also well aware of the facts of life, of birth, of death. They see the pregnant bellies grow amongst both people and pigs; they see the ducks mating, and the geese and the chickens, and our laborers' conversations (the children are completely bilingual) are nothing if not explicit. They see a variety of animals butchered too, for the table; they can watch with unsqueamish interest a turtle's head being hacked off and Felix rushing with his cup to catch the blood that gushes from its severed neck, then the cutting-off of the belly carapace, which exposes the eggs floating in a pool of blood and huge intestines while the heart continues to pump and pump, a process that ends with the still spasmodically twitching meat sitting in a bucket by our kitchen table, waiting for me to cut into roasts, steaks, "pastrami" morsels, or grind for sausages and "turtle-burgers," all to be stored in the freezer. As I watch I think back to the first turtle we ever killed, at night on the beach near Mukalla. It was very gory; the transport officer and the military adviser both went off behind a dune and were sick. (I was not.) But I also remember the day in Truro when my mother took me along to buy a chicken from a neighbor. The woman caught the chicken, laid its head on a chopping block, and chopped. Then she let the chicken go, and it ran around headless, spattering blood. I retired to the car and refused either to say good-by or to eat the bird.

Considering the contrast between our children's behavior and mine at their age, I do sometimes wonder if they are not a little too hardened. But then I see Ming tenderly returning baby chicks to their mothers, or Rory fiercely protective of the cat (acquired to deal with the rats that soon began to plague us after Mark had denuded the island of wild cats, which ate chickens— the old balance of nature again) when Simon, one of the Labradors and champion wild-cat chaser, sits in front of it, drooling. And I know that their hearts are in the right place. I also think it is a good idea to spare them much senseless sentimentality. How I used to cry over *The Fireside Book of Dog Stories* or agonize over each stray bird I found broken-winged upon the beach. With a few exceptions, like the baby rats they insisted on keeping in a glove for two days, we usually manage to persuade our children to believe it kinder to end the life of the orphaned or injured rather than prolong it in captivity. And we clamp down hard on any signs of the careless cruelty of the Seychellois, who will keep young terns in small boxes deep in their own dung and living only on their own fat until they are ready to make a *bouillon* of them, or throw stones at animals, or play with the small owls that occasionally land here, exhausted by their flight from Madagascar or Africa, until the birds are dead of terror.

We do not, in fact, encourage the children to make pets of our domestic animals either; they must learn early that nice-looking as they may be, they are or will be food for us. The other day the sow Suzy was slaughtered, and I hated to do it. I don't think the children need to carry the extra burden this represents.

But in lifting our children out of the companionship of their own kind, such as they could have had in a limited way in Mahé, we did have our worries—particularly that being the children of the *propriétaire* would make them uppity with the children of the people who worked for us, or even with the laborers themselves. Both Mark and I had seen too much of little English sahibs and mem-sahibs abroad to want our brood to behave like

Our Third Christmas: Reflecting / 299

that. But we have had no trouble on this score—partly because of the children's characters, partly because we step on any show of favoritism and go out of our way to give, in an argument, both sides the benefit of the doubt. I think all children appreciate an adult's efforts to be fair. But most of all, we encourage them not to expect us to solve their arguments. If Rory is playing with Little Felix and it ends in a brawl in which Rory is hit, that's all right by us. They have to stand up for themeslves without pulling rank, and win their arguments, if they are to win, without pulling color. So much is just good sense.

But in leaving them to fend for themselves amongst the laborers, what sort of things might we be allowing them to learn? On the credit side, they would certainly learn early and at first hand that there is more than one way to live, and that some ways are better than others; that everyone has to work for a living, but some kinds of work are less drudgery; that using one's brain, applying the power of reasoning to a problem, generally results in making it easier; and so on. This they would understand by contrasting, I thought, our way of life with that of our wokers. But in moral values, the contrasts, while obvious to us, wouldn't be clear to a child—and, what's more important, might well confuse the child at a time when his own attitudes were still in flux. Our influence in this area would have to be strong.

Sure enough, we began to have some trouble with Rory and even more with Ming about telling the truth. Not in general— I mean they were not ever in the habit of lying about everything—but the truth is often a more troublesome concept that it is made out to be, especially as applied to personal relations. The best one can do is insist that the child tell you honestly what he thinks happened, or was said, or done. But the black Seychellois, the brown, and perhaps the white have no concept at all of an abstract uninfluenced truth. In a way, they are correct, though they carry it rather far. A perfectionist, a philosopher, would say that the truth in the very act of being spoken is no longer true; in being clothed with concrete symbols, it has been colored, transmuted, and that in any case, the thought was only true at the instant of its forming in the mind. But the Seychellois, in general, make no attempt even to form a true thought. They will say anything, anything at all, to suit their pleasure or what they see as the exigencies of the situation, and then protest that what they have said is the truth simply because they have said it.

This being so, it is easy to understand why as a people they are such easy prey to suggestion, auto- and otherwise, and why superstition has such a hold on all classes. Even their maxims are formed in this way, creating a sort of established body of untruths in which everyone believes, regardless of the evidence of their senses, until it suits them not to believe them. And this inconstant, inconsistent atmosphere carries over especially into the already murky field of personal relations. There is such a marked lack of loyalty (with certain rare exceptions) to anyone outside the immediate family that it makes, we think, our constant presence more necessary to the children than it might be in another part of the world; they can find at home a stability, a certain "always there, always the same attitude" sureness to come back to which is so evidently missing outside. We hope that—it being so rare—they will the better appreciate its value.

That school is at home is also a help. We have that much more chance to direct their thoughts. And school, we have discovered since we began it, gets more and more rewarding. Always knowing what they are learning gives endless opportunities for connected projects, or at least connected conversation; what they are learning in school is reinforced and made part of everyday life. When a child goes away to school, the demarcation line between school (learning things) and being at home (just living) is much too definite. School, ideally, is expanding the understanding and dispelling the ignorance of a child. Here, by the very nature of the life we lead, it is never confined to school hours.

Developing good habits of thought as well as action must be one of the greatest gifts the parent can give, and having to take the entire responsibility for this, unaided by any handing over to a schoolmaster, has impressed us profoundly. So much so, I sometimes wonder if "school" isn't doing us as much good as it is the children.

So while we are not at all blithe about our responsibilities, we are hopeful.

XXXIII

THE OTHER BAD HABIT of the poorer Seychellois, which I have enlarged on before, is stealing. Just as the truth is a foreign concept, so the idea of possessions being inviolably thine or mine cannot be grasped. Or rather, it can be grasped only in the face of strong-minded insistence on the part of the owner. Reiterated insistence backed up by a watchful all-seeingness that would do credit (no disrespect intended) to God Himself.

Unlike the matter of telling the truth, however, on the rights of ownership carried over into our household, we have not met with doubts. I think it must be a very warped child who takes to stealing; children have such a well-developed sense of their own property that it is only a short step for them to respect that of others.

We also (and I must be superstitious enough to make some sign—touch wood) have had hardly any trouble with stealing by the people who have worked in the house. Again, the fact that valuable material things can neither be enjoyed nor got rid of on a small island is a great help. Furthermore, they know that in a house (unlike the great outdoors) if anything serious is missing it is quickly noticed, and there's only one direction for the blame to head. This is, if one has one servant. Two are more difficult—it's always the other one. The Right of Monsieur to Search, however, is remembered. But for things of little value—

especially needles, spools of thread nearly finished, buttons, marbles, ribbons, Christmas decorations and other shiny objects —the property demarcation line is less finely observed. This may be because things of this sort are often left lying around in odd places. Do we value a needle if we leave it stuck in a book on the window sill? Obviously not. The fact that I habitually give away needles to anyone asking for one has no bearing; as with picking the green ordinary coconuts instead of asking for *coco l'eau*, it is easier just to take.

I like to think that our reputation may have something to do with the honest manner in which our household runs: we did, after all, fire Marguerite when I found a bra of mine, two small dolls, most of the marbles, and one or two of Ming's dresses missing and not just mislaid. We searched; there the things were in Marguerite's house in her suitcase, along with two unmatched socks and a photograph of Mark. (Female servants dote on photographs of Englishmen, which they then pass off as a "conquest" or an ancestor, depending on mood or occasion.) And what is more, we were as good as our word and did without a servant rather than have her. But we are not too "mean" about a little harmless filching. And now that the children are older, they are very useful in getting things back. Their alert little eyes spot things that half the time I don't even know are gone; they come to tell me, and I later ask "if by any chance" that particular person has "seen" the article. "You know how children are—they play with things and then leave them outside . . ."

"But yes, only the other day I picked up a shirt of Ming's under that bent old tree she climbs!" the questioned will reply enthusiastically. "I'll have a look."

The article usually turns up.

What I find curious—at least, it always surprises me—is not so much the lying or stealing, mostly petty, that surrounds us, but the fact that hardly anyone is ashamed if he or she is caught out. (I mean flagrantly caught with the goods on him. If the goods are not on him or if they are unmarked utensils or agricultural products, he will brazenly deny everything, no

Our Third Christmas: Reflecting / 303

matter who the witness or what the evidence. He will simply declare that he "came from home with" or, in the case of an outer-island worker, he "descended with.") But when I stop to consider this properly, it is obvious that he will not be ashamed because he has not been taught to be honest.

This being so, the tempting thought lurks in the back of my mind, unwanted but persistent, that here on the island—with seven, nine, ten children at any one time "in our power"—we do have the opportunity to influence them. Caught young enough, might they not change their attitude? It would be a social experiment well worth undertaking: a school in which moral standards could be so interwoven with what they are taught that . . .

But I get no further. It is a worthy ambition, but I so very much don't want it to be me doing it. Day in and day out? I haven't the devotion.

Still, it does stay obstinately in my mind. Look what Sylvia Ashton-Warner Henderson was able to do with her Maoris! I am no Mrs. Henderson, but I don't have a Maori *pa* to deal with, either. The Europeanness of the Seychelles should give one something of a head start. So I remain nagged by my conscience, dangerous though the path of "doing good to others" often is. Also, we keep losing workers like Felix who want to return to Mahé only so that their children can go to school.

And whenever we go to Mahé and talk to English people (our Seychellois friends, characteristically, never think of such a possibility), I am asked if I intend to teach all the rest of the children on the island as well as our own.

Any evangelical fervor I might have arrived with, however, soon evaporated under the demands of running the island. Then, as soon as that became more organized, I had to begin Rory's schooling in earnest. Now I have Ming as well. The day—what with the cooking (Ahmed still fishes) and writing and keeping up with the making and mending—already feels crowded enough. But finally I thought of a way out. Why not get a young girl, just out of school, to come down to teach?

She could do kindergarten level anyway, and I could impose the—ahem—force of my moral personality on the stories from which she would inculcate in the little ones better standards of behavior. Mark was enthusiastic, so we began to talk seriously. She would probably have to be "white" or nearly so, we agreed, to set her apart for respect's sake. And for the likelihood of her own moral character being reasonably good, she would have to come from such a family as, say, Felix's, who were (1) married, (2) father known to be strict, (3) children in the habit of working for what they earned. And she really would have to be as young as possible, keeping in mind the scholastic requirements, so that she would not be too worldly to want to come to those hick joints, the outer islands. Girls on Mahé, young girls, don't. And it only takes them two or three months after leaving school to make up their minds about this.

But every single one of these necessary qualifications contained a snag of difficulty. Married families with strict fathers wouldn't be likely to want a daughter to go to the outer islands, away from them, out of touch, and exposed to all those sex-starved "boys" or just plain lascivious ordinary men of the sort, lower-class and black, who habitually form the labor force of an outer island. And the whiter and younger she was, the less likely her parents would be to approve. If, on the other hand, we chose only on the basis of the girl's character, we would have to stay a long time in Mahé: ferreting, interviewing, and so on. We could not afford to bring someone down here "on spec" and then chop and change until we got the right one—meanwhile possibly having all sorts of disruptions of the type Liliane, for instance, caused. Island communities have to be handled carefully.

Nor, we thought sadly, did a girl's coming of a good family necessarily mean she might not "go off the rails" down here and get tied up with some fisherman, getting pregnant, having a black baby, and all that—which, while common enough, would be Our Fault, and who would give us their nicely brought-up daughters then?

Another point: she would very probably have to live with us. We'd never get a parent to allow his child to live alone down

Our Third Christmas: Reflecting / 305

here, nor would any young girl be independent enough; yet we couldn't get an older girl for the reasons already mentioned. Even an older girl would probably want to live with us and not be boarded with a laboring family. Unless she had a husband. But an educated girl's husband wouldn't work for us. The ideal solution would be to get a whole family and have them all work for us; the father as a shipwright (we imagined longingly); the mother to help me in the house; the oldest daughter teaching the other children on the island, her brothers and sisters included, who, when they grew up, would stay with us forever, being faithful diligent ethically fine honest workmen . . .

"Now," said Mark, "let's get back to the point. She must live with us. You know I've been wanting to get you some more help besides Carmen—you must have more help if this writing business is going to go on. Why not try out a girl just to 'help,' and you can see what she's like?"

"All right," I answered, sighing. This was at the time when I was pregnant with our third child; I knew I would need someone. I knew that. But—living *with* us? The nanny we'd had for the children in Mahé had lived with us, Ahmed had lived with us; the kitchen had always been decorated with this friend or that, being fed, talking loudly or screaming with laughter. Leaving Mahé I had shaken off all these hangers-on, put Ahmed under another roof, and was free at last. I love a house "to myself"—that is, only a husband, two dogs, a cat, two children, and myself—where one can wander around and be sure of not meeting anyone not part of one. But babies—well, I had to admit I didn't like looking after my babies twenty-four hours a day either. And I'd noticed that the laborers often brought down older children to care for their younger ones while they worked. Obviously this was a common practice, and I began to see that we might kill two birds by, as Mark said, seeing what the girl was like, as she baby sat for me.

"But let's put it off until a little nearer the time," I said, putting it off. Mark wrote to a good friend, however, who lives very much *la vie du* (hardworking) *seigneur* in a little-frequented (equals relatively unspoilt) part of Mahé. Surely among all Henri's friends and relations someone would know of a girl. This was in June.

At the end of August, a shy virgin of fourteen arrived with Mark on the *France,* bearing an enormous suitcase containing a pillow, one sheet, three dresses, some underthings, and the usual dried herbs. She stood, eyes firmly on the floor, in the doorway and refused to say anything but *"Oui, Madame"* in a tiny voice. So I called Ming and sent them off together on a tour of the island while I thought about what to do with her. Somehow I had not envisioned Henri and Mark producing a girl until we had actually moved into our new house; the old one was leaking so badly by this time that we and our furniture were squashed into the dry spots as it was. And what about her food? She appeared hardly capable of cutting bread. I sighed. To have another slightly bigger child to look after just now was a tiring thought. Heavily, I sat down. But just then Mark came back from "seeing the men," as he always does when he returns, and suggested the tent. He'd thought, he said, she could sleep with the children . . .

"In the same beds?" I asked, more tartly than I intended. "Find me one other place in there that doesn't leak!"

"Not even under the window?" Mark asked.

"Oh, you're way out of date! Even the rafter has split under the weight of that leak." (Wet thatch is very heavy.) "No, it'll have to be the tent. We can set it up just by the veranda. She'll be all right there."

So we got out the tent, a small external frame tent my mother had sent us, all very neat and easy for a child of five (or a pregnant woman) to erect, and Mark dragged the bedding down from the attic—the attic floor over the children's beds was the one dry spot where we now kept everything we weren't using. I made up the bed and found a mat for the tent's small floor, and then went to the kitchen to produce some sort of rice and *bouillon* to make her feel at home. It was, by this time, getting dark. Ming and Rory brought her back from the yard, where she had been introduced to the other children. They had supper.

Our Third Christmas: Reflecting / 307

I showed her the tent, gave her a lamp, and told her to be careful with it. I took her to the privy and the wash house. I gave her a towel, some toothpaste, a toothbrush. Then I got our own children to bed, and Mark and I sat down at last for our evening glass of toddy. It had been a tiring day, as "boat days" always are.

Then I heard Rory's voice calling me from his and Ming's small bedroom. I went in. "Mummy," he said, "Mitha's crying, over there."

"Where?" I asked.

"Over there, in the corner."

I looked, but the room was dark. I went closer. Wedged behind the children's little chest of drawers was Mitha, sniveling, with a cloth over her head. "What is the matter?" I demanded.

"Mon pas capave," came the small voice, with a loud sniff.

"Pas capave quoi?" (What can't you do?)

No answer.

Rory replied that he thought she didn't want to sleep in the tent.

"Oh? Mitha, are you crying because you don't want to sleep in the tent?" I asked in *créole*.

"Qui, Madame," came the muffled voice.

"But why?"

No answer.

"Why, Rory?"

"She says she can't sleep alone because she will see the shadows of angels passing."

"But there's nowhere in here for her," I protested. "Your beds take up the only dry space!" I went off, grumbling, to Mark. We discussed the matter and finally decided to put the tent in the part of the living room we had stopped using because it leaked. It would act as another room, and the tent was waterproof. It would do, for the time being. Mitha was apparently unafraid if she was under the same roof.

And there the tent stayed, until the new house was ready in October. Two sets of visitors came and went who laughed at the tent inside the house, but it was the only solution, mourn as

I might for the loss of Mark's and my evening privacy to the terror of passing angels.

Loss of privacy! I had a lot to learn. Once the shyness had worn off, we were taken over, completely. Then we went to Mahé for me to have the baby, the baby arrived, and I got another girl to do housework while Mitha looked after Digby. After that, we just gave up. The two girls were everywhere all the time; any efforts on my part to teach them their place, tactfully, were quite ignored. And to tell the truth, I have found that with the new baby it suits me to have them around to play games with Rory and Ming and hold the little boy. But as I try to write in the resulting turmoil, I look ahead to calmer days—though all the noise, like the imminence of death in battle, wonderfully concentrates the mind. Now, I think, we are indeed becoming Seychellois, for if our strange Anglo-Saxon desire to be alone at least part of the day is not overcome, it is at least in temporary abeyance.

But the question of making either of these girls into fine upstanding responsible teachers is in abeyance too. Paule, the younger one, has more verve and energy; Mitha is more serious and (slightly) more responsible. Paule is much better at playing games with the children than anything else, however—especially housework—and now that Mitha has tried to affiance herself to Rogile, the fisherman with the big feet (her mother had a fit and we had to send Rogile away back to Mahé or Mitha was not to stay on the island another *minute*. Mitha is herself one of a variegated brood of eleven. Her mother obviously knows what she is talking about), we think she will probably only last out Digby before she goes off and gets married. So we incline toward Paule (thirteen) as our possible schoolmarm.

She is quite a fierce girl, with a boisterous good nature not accounted for by how safe both of them feel now that there are two of them. Yes, we thought, definitely Paule. But—

One night the children (Rory, Ming, Mitha, and Paule) were playing in the hour before bedtime. Mark and I were

Our Third Christmas: Reflecting / 309

sitting out on our big veranda; I was giving Digby his milk. "Lie there," we heard Paule, always the organizer, say behind us, in the living room.

"Lie down. Sleep, my friend. What would you like, my friend? A beer? Some toddy? A whiskey? I get you whiskey, my friend?"

We looked around. Paule's arm was around Rory while he lay on the floor, a self-satisfied smirk on his face. His eyes were shut.

"Yes. My friend, that's good. You go to sleep now, yes?" As soon as she had allowed a few seconds to pass, she dropped his head, went to the "door," and called, *"A-nous, d'allant, a-nous! l' peu dormi!"* (Let's go, pal, let's go! He's sleeping!')

Then she rushed back in and began gathering up anything that was lying around—toys, a puzzle, a towel, Rory's pajama top, the cushions—while Mitha and Ming, who had been hiding in our bedroom, made off with one of the chairs, Mark's map case, several books, a boat model, and my button tin.

When they had escaped to the beach beyond the veranda with their loot, Rory, who must have been watching from under his eyelids, "woke up." He felt for his pajama top. It wasn't there. He jumped to his feet, looking wildly about him. When he saw how badly he had been "robbed" he let out a roar of rage, and arming himself with Mark's walking stick, rushed past Mark and me to the beach, where all the girls were waiting, giggling. Roaring again, he said gruffly in *créole,* "You there! Where are all my things! I've been robbed! I'll beat you up! What are you doing with my boat?"

"Your boat?" yelled Paule, who was holding it in her hand. "Your boat? I came from my house with this boat, just now!" With which Rory roared again and leaped on her and started to wrestle. Paule held him, struggling, and jerked her head at Mitha. Mitha and Ming, in fits of giggles, ran back into the house with all the stuff, then came outside and sauntered past Paule and Rory. Paule let Rory go.

"You!" yelled Rory at Mitha. "Where's my chair? You stole my chair!"

"Moi, m'sieur? Moi qui vole ou la saise? Pas moi, m'sieur. Allez guette dans ou la case si ou manque un la saise!" (Me? I who stole your chair? Go and look in your house and see if you are missing a chair!) *"Me,* indeed," she continued, flouncing down the "street" with Ming in tow.

By this time they were all laughing, so that game was voted over. Now it was Mitha's turn to lull the white man to sleep. She was much more seductive than Paule, fairly cooing at Rory. But when he slept, she picked up his toy gun and shot him, twice, and when he started to get up shot him again, pushing him down with her foot at the same time while Paule and Ming ran out with everything portable.

And we don't even have T.V.!

XXXIV

WE ARE JUST into our third southeast season on the island; the steady breeze has blown away all the mosquitoes and flies as though they had never existed, and cools our skins deliciously after excessively muggy weather still recent enough for us to remember it with hard words and bad tempers. But now we have our winter before us. In another month we will probably be complaining of the cold again, but at the moment the prospect is wonderful. We are in that pleasant transitional catch-up stage when the day appears suddenly to have more hours in it, and we so much more energy to fill them.

Also to our satisfaction, the island is beginning to show the care we have lavished upon it. A year ago we finally nerved ourselves to cut down every single palm, old or young, that was not bearing well and was too far gone in misery to be worth improving. The fact that we had to nerve ourselves shows how

Our Third Christmas: Reflecting / 311

coconut-conscious even we have become. But we made a clean sweep, and for weeks at a time—depending on the weather at sea, since Mark was using the fishermen as palm extractors—we lived on millionaire's salad (now that we have noticeably fewer people than before, any special gang work depends on the availability of the fisherman).

As we surmised at the beginning, the fishing more or less has to carry the island until the new palms come into bearing, so the property personnel has been allowed to dwindle to six: the aged Shokrah pottering around the garden; Small George looking after the pigs, a job that to our amazement and pleasure he still does as well as the day he started; Felix, Ahmed, and two new people (the brothers Rosa) who were brought to saw the timber for our house but have stayed on as coconut collectors. Barbé and Léonie have gone; we tried to persuade Barbé to stay, but he would not stay without his family, and on the whole I was not sorry. Maxime Finest, the coconut collector who came last year, and his wife have left too. Madame Finest, after she'd been on the island awhile, fell sick with a strange choking obstruction in her throat, moaning and keeping Maxime from his work until Mark finally took them both back on the *France,* in debt to us though they were. What the sickness was, I never knew. I alternated between Imaginary and Cancer of the Throat. She had no fever, nothing but something clawing at her gorge. Difficult.

"What *was* it?" I asked Mark the minute he'd set foot on shore. "Did you see the doctor?"

"Yes. I saw the doctor, but I don't think she did. Met Maxime in the street, complaining she was going off to work in Bahrein and could he come back to us. But he didn't owe enough to bother bringing him down here again, you know. Too lazy."

For carpentry work and to keep the pirogues mended when Felix goes, we have a small rough silent man called Charlie. I don't think anyone likes Charlie particularly except Berley, who recognizes a kindred spirit and likes to escape from too much domesticity with Francine. Charlie and Berley are often to be found in the boathouse, half a home-rolled hanging from

A well-planted young coconut seedling

their lips, quietly caulking and blacking whatever pirogue is up for repairs. At boat work, Charlie is very good; we will miss Felix, of course, but he is an awful shipwright.

With all the deciduous leaves blown off the trees and so many palms gone, the island appears sunnier, larger (if this can be said of sixty-two acres); yet at the same time there is lots of new fresh vegetation in the form of young palm fronds just beginning to show out of their mulched holes. We still wonder if we shouldn't have been braver and tried to plant, say, cashews instead, but familiarity with the island's stony surfaces made our final decision. So painfully little soil. It was simply not worth the risk. We have had to stay loyal to coconuts. And in spite of the difficult terrain, we also have continued the practice of planting in rows—trenching first, then mulching with husk and manure. It is time-consuming and laborious, but the mulching has to be done anyway (it protects against drought as well as nourishes) and seeing order brought out of chaos is aesthetically satisfying beyond all proportion to the actual necessity of having coconuts in rows—there is none. But rows, so axiomatic to normal farming, present a triumph over obdurate nature to us.

A less expensive triumph, and one we have really enjoyed, is the success of our bananas. They have spread and spread. After a year of bringing shoots from Mahé only to have them wither and die, we were able to move the pigs into their Remire Hilton quarters and took over the old piggery—the smelly, rich, sodden quagmire behind the yard—for the banana grove. It was a close race between various sorts of secondary crops to see which would win this valuable growing ground, but bananas came in a nose ahead of arrowroot and returns have been generous. And they look wonderfully luxuriant with their great long green leaves, and their fruit so heavy that the "trunks" must always be propped up with forked sticks. And once we have cut down the stem of fruit, we can cut out the parent plant, leave one shoot in the hole, and move the others to new territory; we follow a sort of aristocratic inheritance system: the oldest shoot gets the home acres, while the others go one into the church (behind Felix's house), another into the navy (behind Berley and Francine's which was Jean and Francine's, which was the house we built for old Lenclume), while yet a third (if there is one) gets sent out to the colonies, one of the sheltered protected new territories where goodish land and a chance to prosper can still be found by the hardy. Though, to stretch the parallel, we are hard put these days to find more colonial territory, and now almost find the fecundity of our bananas more worry than pleasure. Will the old pig-rich homeland become a slum, suffering the evils of overcrowding, the fierce competition for a place in the sun, for food, leading to the growth of degenerate stock, runty shoots from pinch-faced parents grubbing for a foothold in the old historic soil? Well, naturally, the answer is no—for bananas. We will keep the birth rate down by very old-fashioned tyrannical methods: throwing the males into the Nile, or exposing daughters to the devouring jaws of our caged pigs, or leaving the little dears to die, uprooted, of exposure to the hot sun, or, simply, "Off with their heads." What the bananas will think of all this—well, what does it matter? It's for their good and the good of the country. No more to be said.

Of course, we have also had setbacks. It has been easier to find out what will grow on these islands than to weigh up whether or not in terms of time and energy and manpower we can afford to grow it. And since we have not yet been able to afford any kind of pumped irrigation, we are as dependent on the vagaries of the weather as ever. Sugar cane needs too much fertilizing and watering to be worth the returns; maize we have virtually given up on because of the erratic rainfall and the rats. That taro is too gross a feeder for extensive planting we discovered by planting it extensively. Lots of this *vya* would save us on coconuts and harden the fat on the pigs, we reasoned, but it hasn't worked out. Nor has manioc been a success. Nor has pepper. We do not have enough rain for pepper, and have neither the staff nor the water to provide it artificially. A little to our surprise, however, our lines of vanilla are doing well, and have even survived being moved once. I did not think we had enough rain for vanilla, but then, the last two years we have been lucky with the rainfall. Being an air plant, vanilla is well suited to our rocky ground; let us hope it will flower successfully. And another hopeful is timber, which we dismissed as a main line, but which has done so well that it promises to be a valuable side one.

Our building efforts have created a greater sense of order too. Gone are the shacks for this and random shelters for that. Shop and store are all in under one roof, for example, divided internally only. All the coconut-processing is now done up at the calorifier/pigsty complex; this is the new depot now, not the yard. Fish-drying has been moved there as well, for ease in giving the entrails to the swine. Transporting the finished produce to the yard for shipment is no problem; Mark has a

New Dashes

small monotractor. The monotractor also saves us much time collecting the coconuts—with two men we are able to bring in more than six did before. But we are wary of mechanization as a principle for us to follow. Machines lead a hard life in the tropics, whirring through the heat and sand, never the right spare part within a hundred or even a thousand miles, and the mechanical services of just Mark or, much more terrifyingly, Ahmed (who fancies himself with engines, which is very dangerous to them and sometimes to himself, except that he is generally easier to repair).

As for moving the camp, we are glad we didn't. With the island better-ordered and the building finished, we need only a few houses—two new ones should do, one by the slipway and boathouse, and one by the pigsties, the third being our old kitchen, replastered. In relocating the laborers' houses to the various work areas, we will be moving them out of, as we have moved ourselves into, the yard. Long ago we realized that for control's sake, it is we who must live at the anchorage.

One of the houses at the camp I shall then take over as a place to work away from the family. There are times when that day cannot come too soon.

Mark's fishing is now more orderly as well, and much more pleasant for him (and for me) because he does not have to be away so much. The *France* has reduced the number of trips to Mahé, while at the same time being reliable enough and big enough to undertake long fishing voyages on which Mark does not always have to go. The fishermen no longer have the *Bouilloir*'s somewhat erratic engine, lack of sail area, and lack of space on board for the catch to use as excuses for popping back "into port" every few days. The *France* has plenty of hold space, and canvas, and a brand-new engine which has served us faithfully without a single breakdown so far (no one but Mark is allowed to touch it).

This year will be the turtle pound's second southeast to withstand, but we are not worried. It has given us little trouble while considerably increasing our earning power. Now that the market for *calipée* has inexplicably (to us) fallen so low, the difference in the price we can obtain for turtle alive and the price dead is enormous; the turtle pound has well paid its way by allowing us to keep the turtles alive until we are ready to ship them to Mahé.

And it has paid other dividends. Without having a source of turtle eggs at hand, Mark could never have taken up his hobby of turtle conservation. It may seem a contradiction that someone making most of his money out of the exploitation of the green turtle should also be so interested in conservation, but of course it is not. Only an enlightened policy on the part of the Seychelles government can now preserve the green turtle of this part of the world, and Mark contends that conservation should start at the egg stage—thus taking advantage of the turtle's proverbially impressive fertility—rather than by making prohibitive laws on the taking of adult turtles, which are in practice hard or impossible in these scattered islands to enforce.

Man has been the grown turtles' most assiduous and dangerous predator, but the decimation of adults by human agency is nothing compared to the decimation of young turtle by "natural" means. Starting from the time the eggs are laid, there is a gauntlet of survival to be run. Land crabs are good diggers and eat many eggs while puncturing others. Then, when the remainder hatch, they have to burrow upwards through at least two feet of sand in order to make their dash across the beach to the sea. If they are lucky, it is nighttime and high tide, but these conditions do not always prevail, and as they crawl energetically over the white sands, in their still-soft shells, they make tasty morsels for the patrolling sea birds. In the sea, the fish are waiting.

Quite how the baby turtles that have not become food for another species manage to feed themselves in the open sea, we do not know. For while young they are voracious eaters, both carnivorous and cannibalistic. Fish, shellfish, any sort of meat, they gobble with great snappings of their sharp little beaks, and if one of their number dies, they will try to eat him as well. But washed about in the open sea? Even if they manage to stay inshore on the turtle-grass-covered flats of the reefs, it is hard to see how they could winkle out enough crustacea. They are certainly unable to catch healthy fish.

What we do know we have gleaned by observing them in our turtle-rearing tanks. (All such previous projects in the Seychelles, conducted by interested planters, have resulted in a smelly mess of small dead reptiles, to the point where every Seychellois now says, "It can't be done. Won't live in captivity.") Mark was determined to succeed because it is obvious that if the initial survival tests can be avoided, an increase in the number of turtles reaching adult size must follow. But at what point should the turtle be released? This depends as much on the funds available for their upkeep as on the open question of at what age the hitherto "tame" turtles can best adapt themselves to life in the open sea. It is generally agreed that they become vegetarian feeders at about a year old; by this time their carapace should be nine inches long, enabling them to withstand most fish (though sharks continue to attack even grown turtles; we sometimes find whole flippers missing). If the turtles could be weaned gradually from meat to turtle grass by nine months to a year old, and then released to graze for themselves, the costs would be bearable—in the Seychelles, anyway, and particularly if their meat diet can be the by-product of a dried-fish and shelling venture, as it has with us.

But we have never been able to keep them that long. "I can't see our way to building large sea-water tanks just now," Mark mourns. "These tanks are all right for the first four months, but after that it's lack of space, depth, and coolness that would do them in." And the water must be continually circulating, or changed twice a day. Yet the natural seepage provided by the dry stone walling of the big pound won't do for the immature; as the tide recedes they are left on the ledges and in the cracks, and die of exposure before the next rise. "If only Remire had a lagoon like Aldabra's—or better still, the shallow one in the ring atoll of Astove. That would be ideal . . . La Plaine might once have been a lagoon, but to turn it back into one now would require a deep channel running out to sea, lots of blast-

Our Third Christmas: Reflecting / 319

ing and expensive walling, and pumps . . . I can't see us affording that!"

It makes, however, a fascinating hobby.

So even now—with much of the time-consuming (and challenging) breaking-in of the island, of ourselves to island life, and of the island life to us, behind—we both find plenty of occupations. What more could we want? A comfortable house, food for thought, good health (we hope), and clean living away from smog, riots, and car accidents; a year-long summer camp full of living natural history, sailing, and swimming for the children; a climate pleasant in spite of petty complaints, and which, while unhardy, certainly does not stunt growth; an unusual life of abiding interest. And the pleasurable thought of having a base and of being able to travel, later, when we are richer, for me and for the further education of our children; even though Mark so wants to be settled down, he surely won't mind a voyage now and then if we don't have to carry our home with us?

But Mark is safe for four or five years anyway, for this will have to wait until our third child, young Digby, is old enough, babies and toddlers being so much easier to look after when staying in one spot. And I don't know but that one does lose the urge to move on and see things. I'm not so very old or decrepit, but armchair traveling is beginning to appeal to me. And Rory and Ming's education is taking more time, making me busier than ever but in satisfying and worthwhile ways. And then I have my writing. No, sometimes I wonder if it isn't Mark who is the more restless. Will Remire always be enough for him? He thinks a lot about turtle projects; I have caught him looking calculatingly at the maps of other bigger islands, particularly those with lagoons. But Remire, if he waits, will reward him enough. When all our young palms come into bearing, we should be able to get twenty thousand good nuts a month, instead of five thousand poor ones, as it was when we came here. And since our rent cannot go up and most of our expensive building is completed, we cannot help but be richer.

Then, perhaps, his dream of large tanks or even a false lagoon can be realized. Why not?

And the island gets better and better for the children. Their knowledge of it increases daily, the more they look, the more they know, and to know one place deeply will give them a perspective on others. What they learn about our plants and wildlife, about the habits of the tides and the effect of weather on our lives, makes it easy for them to understand the ways in which every man is subject to nature. And they will, eventually, know practically everything about Remire there is to know—in a limited environment, every aspect must be pressed into service as a teaching tool, even if it is often used to illustrate an opposite. This close knowledge will give them roots, a firm base on which to build and from which to venture.

But I have noticed that using Remire as their starting point, while natural, has certainly resulted in their having what might be called an equatorial point of view. A little like the peoples of the ancient world, they believe they are in a central position on earth, and their reasons, while different, are no less reasonable: they draw their simple conclusions from the behavior of the sun. They know that the rest of the world is not filled with barbarians or monsters, but they also know that the sun, center of our universe, shines directly over *our* heads, winter and summer; that it is we who get most of its light and heat, while relatively, other people (except other equatorial peoples) are off in a corner. To them, brought up here, it is the queer cold folk who have snow in winter, heat in their houses, lights on in the daytime, and wear so many clothes that are the exotics. That Mark and I and all their books actually come from a "corner" lends a spice to what they learn—and we think they learn more avidly of cabbages and kings than we did because of it. We therefore do nothing to remove this reasonable idea. Why should we? Why indeed should they be brought up America- or Europe-centered? They must be aware of their cultural heritage, of course, and all this implies, but if we have chosen to make our life and theirs here, then they must be able to belong here as much as we once belonged "there."

Off through the woods

On the other hand, are they to become Seychellois mentally? It is a difficult question. We do not want to leave them in the limbo of personal statelessness, nor do we want to limit them. They will not want to spend all their lives on a tiny island.

What we would like to do—what we must do—is give them the freedom of the true cosmopolite, yet at the same time the security of firm beliefs: a code of honor by which to live, and by which they can live, anywhere. To do this, we are having to dredge ruthlessly in our own sets of attitudes, pretenses, prejudices, and beliefs. Such a lot of rubbish sticks to one, it would be a pity to pass it on when, in the nature of things, they will pick up quite enough of their own. If they are to resist a part of their environment, as they must, while getting the best out of the life we lead, they will have to be secure and strong.

It's a big job, and we can't make up our minds whether in our queer sort of isolation it is easier, or harder. But we do not intend to become too burdened by it. If living on a rented desert island seems to most people an odd, restricted sort of life rather than a dream, it suits us. And a memory of contentment surrounding them is no small thing to leave one's children as their heritage.

APPENDIX A

From Pirates to the Present

I SAID EARLIER the British are well enough established in the Seychelles to make a fellow-Britisher feel safe in settling too. The association of England and the Seychelles has been a long one, and the islands are, in fact, not much more foreign to the British than are the West Indies; and historically the connections between Britain and these once-French islands are very old, older than those of France. It was the British who next explored them after they had been mapped by the Portuguese —and where in the Indian Ocean were the Portuguese not first among Europeans?—the earliest recorded exploration being that of Alexander Sharpeigh. Sharpeigh (or Sharpey) was in command of the fourth voyage of the East India Company, and his brief was to establish trade between Aden and the new English foothold of Surat. He left England in 1608; by January of 1609 he was among the islands of the Seychelles (specifically, he thought, among the Amirantes). He counted nine islands, and though he found no water, he was able to get both coconuts and doves—the flocks of birds being so "tame that they could be captured by the dozen."* But he was more impressed with the Mahé group than with the corraline islands. Quite naturally, for on them he finds a wealth of water, virgin forests, and vast numbers of "tortels," "cokernuts," "allagartes," and fish. Even the boatswain was moved to note that "these islands seem to be an earthly paradise."†

Sharpeigh's exploration was not followed, however, by any British effort to claim the islands officially; rather, they seem to have been used as a convenient no man's land by ships needing water and food—particularly by the European pirates which by 1700 infested the Indian Ocean; to them these uninhabited islands, with their fine coves and bays, good careening

* Bradley, p. 442.
† Webb, p. 44.

beaches, water, meat, and timber were ideal. (The reason they never became a center of pirate trade like Madagascar, was that there was no one to trade with.)

But during the eighteenth century, competition between the French and the English for the wealth of India grew steadily, and fear that the English might take the islands and from them annoy French shipping eventually made the French think seriously about taking them themselves. The French had already occupied the island of Mauritius in 1715, and it was from the Ile de France that the first expedition to explore the Seychelles was sent, in 1742. French pirates, to be sure, like Oliver Le Vasseur, knew the islands well, but this expedition, under Lazare Picault, was official. In 1744 Picault again explored the main islands, and again returned enthusiastic, at least about the wildlife, though by this time, war had broken out between the French and the British in India, and nothing more was done for another twenty years.

It was 1756 that France first seriously claimed Mahé. The name of the islands was changed ceremonially from Iles de la Bourdonnais (Bertrand-François Mahé de Bourdonnais had been governor of Mauritius in 1742) to Iles de Séchelles, in honor of the Vicomte Moreau de Séchelles, Comptroller General of France. (This name the English only moderately Anglicized later by writing it with a *y*.) But if the islands were now "possessed," they remained uninhabited. Five years passed, then a Stone of Possession was placed on Praslin; another three, and an officer of one of the Chevalier du Roslan's vessels, *L'Heure du Berger,* took formal possession of La Digue by building a cairn of stones and placing in it "a sealed bottle with official papers . . . no *pierre de possession* was installed—probably due to the fact that the stock must have run out, as these stones were artistically carved in France and carried by French ships when sailing for unknown and uncharted seas."* Meanwhile, on Mahé, settlement tentatively started; settlers were recruited from Mauritius and Réunion, Frenchmen evacuated the sinking monarchy, and from India still others took refuge

---

* Bradley, pp. 432-433.

in the Seychelles. Understandably, they were all intent on making money or remaking their lost fortunes. But until 1788 nothing was done in the way of formal government, and no laws inhibited the unwise exploitation of natural resources or confirmed the colonists in any fixed possession of property. The islands in their virgin state may have looked lush, but Mahé, the largest, is only seventeen miles long by five at its widest point; and after thirty years of unregulated profiteering the wastage of the Seychelles' natural resources was noticeable even to contemporaries. Tortoises, which take eighty-one years to mature, *cocos-de-mer,* the Seychelles' famous double coconuts, which take twenty-five, are hard to replenish if cropped out or burned; the crocodiles were soon enough killed off as dangerous beasts, forests were felled, by ax or simply by fire, to clear the land for other crops (a fate in no way different from that which met the western United States, but in these small islands how much more quickly it showed).

Already the economic trend was downwards. But the little community of some forty settlers and their three hundred slaves soon received the stimulus of war—brief, yet profitable. In a state of war with France (the First Coalition) the advantages of the Seychelles as a watering and leg-stretching base were obvious to the British guarding the routes to India, and they calmly proceeded to use them, with little opposition from the French. That these "raids" also curtailed the activities of the French corsairs was an added bonus. The first capitulation of Mahé—whose Commandant, Chevalier Quéau de Quinssy, could do little else with the meager garrison at his disposal— to the superior strength of the British occurred in 1794, and the performance was repeated, with variations, seven times before the final formal surrender of Mauritius in 1810. But if this small correct aristocrat (once Gentleman of the Bedchamber to Monsieur) capitulated like a kept woman to an importunate lover, he also wangled generous concessions: in 1804, for instance, he suggested to the British that since the islands had surrendered, Seychellois shipping ought to be able to pass unmolested through the British blockades; charmed and apparently hypnotized, the British commander agreed. The ten years that followed were golden years, for slave traders, blockade runners, freebooters, corsairs; by 1811 there were one hundred houses and two billiard saloons in Port Royal township and a thriving shipbuilding industry.

But peace brought normality again. And although the beginning of the nineteenth century saw the introduction of cotton to the islands, a most valuable crop for a slave economy, even this boom did not last. The Americans were competing on better terms; by 1813 all trafficking in slaves had been prohibited, to be followed in 1835 by the liberation of slaves. Both these acts were forced upon the very unwilling Seychellois by, from the Seychellois point of view, their new overlords, those boors from across the Channel, and for the combination of events that caused their tenuous prosperity to dwindle away the islanders found in the British a handy scapegoat. It is an attitude they persist in, sometimes with justification, to this day.

I have heard it said that when the English finally became the rulers of these out-of-the-way islands (with the formal capitulation of Mauritius in 1810), they did a great disservice to their new colony by allowing the French language, the civil laws of the *Code Napoléon,* and even the French Commandant (de Quinssy) to remain in authority in them: all were, in the future, to be sources of trouble. There is certainly something to be said for this point of view. The French are no less determinedly French than the English English, or the Americans American. The concessions made to them by an England who even then liked to placate, keep the status quo, and avoid colonial "trouble" wherever posible only confirmed the islands in their Frenchness at a time when, it is arguable, Anglicization might not have been so painful as it is now. They had had only fifty years of being permanently inhabited and of officially belonging to one nation, and these were fifty years of rather distant rule, carried on from Mauritius; a rule which was troubled throughout by the French struggles with the British in India, and in all but the first twenty years by the violence of political affairs in metropolitan France. France was not really thinking about the Seychelles during this period, and settlers who came here were left very much to their own devices. The French did not even station a permanent garrison in the islands, or provide a priest or schools. The settlers and their slaves were "on their own." If the English, in 1810, had properly taken over the islands and made a strong stand of Englishness, half of the conflicts of the present day would never have had cause to develop.

But the British didn't really want the islands either. The Seychelles, beautiful as they were, and still are, were not rich even in their virgin state, and none of them were big. The Portuguese didn't bother with them. Nor did the Dutch. Pirates, freebooters, and privateers found them useful as hideouts but couldn't have cared less about their ownership. The English of the East India Company merely used them as watering stops, and the French, even after they owned them, hardly did more than profit in small ways from their resources of timber and giant tortoises (wood and meat for ships) and pass on. No, without making any value judgments on the relative merits of being French or English, I think the islands could have become English then, and the frustrated irredentist spirit that burns (a little dully, not being fueled by France) in the breast of many a *grand blanc* would have long since been extinguished.

What actually happened, however, is that the islands developed into a kind of bastard civilization—certainly nothing like the best of the French, hardly anything of the African, and very little of the English. The French themselves were expatriates or forcibly expatriated, the Negroes were slaves jerked out of context, and the English settlers, relatively recent arrivals, are all ex-something else too. Without exception, everyone looks abroad for fashion, manners, higher education, and careers; and no educated person, fundamentally, thinks of the Seychelles as Homeland, Fatherland, Ancient Birthright, and so on; while among the poor (of all colors, now) such thoughts are only beginning to seep in. People say *"Nous Seychellois"* in a casual, social way but without any real patriotic fervor, aware perhaps that the Seychelles always has (and probably always will be) considered "small fry," strategically unimportant except as an annoyance to shipping.*

When we arrived in Mahé, it seemed to be the sort of place no one could possibly take seriously, a kind of never-never land, where every Seychellois was agin-the-government, yet none wanted independence; where, as in any small place, everyone was so involved in his private squabbles that no one, as far as we could see, ever took the time to develop a world view, except in distorted glimpses; and where the bored middle-class British Experts and Administrators all floated around, like Polomoche, in a small green cloud that smelt, to the Seychellois, of third-grade apples, rotten at the core.

There wasn't, we thought, much to be said for either side. It is quite true that a tiny colony such as this could not hope to attract the best advisers, or pay them, except those for whom the islands are stepping stones on the way to somewhere better. It is also true that the British abroad are very insular and cliquey among themselves and are not generally given to linguistic bravery. But were the *grands blancs* more cultivated, more worldly, less insular? To an outsider, the old families would appear to have retained the worst characteristics of the French: a disdain of foreigners, especially of the English, an excessive pride in *la belle langue* (despite the fact that few speak it without *créole* words or usages, or at least a colonial accent), and a marked aversion to change. And though they are fickle enough and volatile enough for the most flighty image of Frenchness, they lack any light charm about it, being stiff and self-conscious socially rather than at ease. And while they are certainly given to elaborate meals, the food retains nothing of French éclat or delicacy; one rises from them sated with starch and sweet.

To add to one's own impressions, the English in the colony will also inform you that the *grand blanc* is inveterately lazy. Since not even the English can say the French are lazy, this

* To what extent the presence of the United States satellite-tracking station in Mahé or the British purchase of three Seychellois islands and one Mauritian group to form the British Indian Ocean Territories (a substitute for Aden) will affect the Seychellois' world view and the world's view of them, I don't know.

quality is supposed to come from living in the luxuriant tropics amongst slaves, or if not slaves, at least very poorly paid laborers, so that there are always lots of them and no one can afford to have everything done in an elegant manner.

And not only does the planter not want to work—there's hardly a planter in Mahé who does anything much about improving the looks or quality of his plantation—he doesn't want to give proper pay to the people who work for him; nor does he look after or even think about those he employs at such shocking rates, beyond wanting to keep them servile and "down."

You will also be told that the *grand blanc* is very snobbish (with the implication that he has nothing to be snobbish about), and very anti-British; and that furthermore, though he is nominally a devout, even rabid, Catholic, he is deplorably superstitious, rather lax in all but the ostentatious aspects of the Catholic religion, and has basically very little Moral Fiber, especially when it comes to practicing the *droit de seigneur* on any nubile dark-colored wench he can get his hands on.

Well, after we'd lived in Mahé for three years, all we could say was that there was some core of truth to each of these statements, but plenty of exceptions, which is the sort of conclusion one usually reaches after getting to know a place. Yes, they are insular and reserved and hard to know, and do have an initial prejudice against just another expensive expert who has been sent out to dictate to them on their way of life. Yes, they are vain about their use of the French language, and regard their homes as last bastions in the lapping sea of créole and English all around them. Their pride in French is the Frenchest thing about them. And if we see their lives as a little circumscribed, unstimulated, or dull, might not fickleness be called a desire for change, and volatility a leavening of sameness? As for their cooking, full of curries and roasts and the vegetable-fruits of the tropics simmered to candy in sugar or coconut cream, it is influenced both by what is available and by Indian cuisine. The planter, unlike the modern Englishman abroad, does not—cannot—live on imported food. And even butter, that staple of French cooking, is imported.

As for being lazy, the whites do—by busy New or Old England standards, anyway—an awful amount of sitting and talking; but whether one likes to or not, one has to make certain allowances for the climate. The Seychelles, graced most of the year by ocean zephyrs, has a balmy climate, but exertion at eighty degrees is correspondingly greater than at forty or fifty degrees; even the most conscience-bound physical-culture demon has to sit down during the day to let the sweat dry. Yet no one can beat the wiry Seychellois, visually a pale bag of bones, at steady mountain-traipsing through his property, and to oversee an estate efficiently requires a good deal more in the way of walking than most people realize. No, he does little physical work but he is "around," and by so being, succeeds in boosting the entire output of his labor force.

If he appears to do little for the appearance of his estate, it is as often as not because what manual labor he can afford he cannot expend on nonessentials; the accusation that he is a bad husbandman, on the other hand, is more serious. Yes, he is loath to cut out *Melittoma*-infested palms. Understandably. A sick palm bears something, but a young one nothing, for four long years. Yes, he is more inclined to burn rubbish than to pile it for composting. No defense there, except that palm leaf is slow-rotting, uncooperative composting material, quite unlike straw or grass, and needs good hot manure to make anything of it. A planter's livestock, which he does not really "go in for," is often not enclosed, so its manure is not conveniently in one place. Yes, he is conservative about trying anything new in the way of crops. All farmers are conservative. But his ancestors changed from field crops to coconuts because they require less labor and grow better on poor soil than anything else. Furthermore, the amount of forward-looking "new-products research" and help from the government in finding markets for them is almost nil. I am all against a welfare-state mentality, which is as bad as a slave mentality—or perhaps the same thing—but the Seychelles, stuck out in the middle of the Indian Ocean, the very opposite of a center of commerce or communications, surrounded by countries as poor as she is herself, *does* need help.

What she has been given has been underfinanced or applied with little knowledge of local conditions, and has not succeeded. And for those who try to help themselves, Mahé can be one of the most frustrating places on earth. One of the reasons we prefer the bedrock existence of the outer islands is that we know we can expect nothing to be on hand unless we make it or write for it; but in Mahé, full of agents of this and that as well as government departments, technical centers, and companies, one naturally expects basic things to be available; they are not. And the time wait for an order to be filled through an agent is an average six months—if he remembers to order it the first time you ask. Enough said about that though. Backwaters again: the other side of the quiet, peaceful, unbothered life.

Yes, the laborer's wages are low by present world standards, yet they compare favorably with those in preindustrial England, or with the wages of the sweatshops, which caused such hardship when the earner no longer lived in agricultural surroundings and nothing was free. But in the Seychelles many things are free or can be had by barter, and even in the town, Victoria, there are foods that can be bought for a cent. Besides, the manual laborer's needs are still so very few, while his ideas of what to do with extra money so (morally) deplorable. We had to agree with the planters that no laborer on high wages does better things with his money than the plantation worker on the minimum standard: food costs about the same (with the plantation worker faring better on "pickings"), and it is true that, bar the rare exception, all money surplus to his cheap food and low house rent is spent on booze (men) and new clothes (women). The lower-class Seychellois *is* improvident. God will provide. The government will provide. Or a relative, or a relative by marriage, or a former employer, or something; forethought, planning in any way for a time of sickness or old age is just not done. He lacks the concept of winter as naturally as nature omits it from the climate of his islands.

To the accusation that knowing this to be true, the planters do not sufficiently look after their employees, the *grands blancs* hotly reply that indeed they do as much as they can afford and if the present were like the old days, they could do far more. In the old days (when wages were really low and the planters were able to employ many more people) each employee housed his family on the planter's land, each had a little of that land for a vegetable patch, each a breadfruit tree, a few chickens, and a pig; in this way the planters looked after their labor by using the only currency they were rich in: land—not rich land, but tropical, easy-living land, where a palm-leaf shelter and a breadfruit tree could sustain life, and did. But now that they must employ fewer, fewer benefit.

The change to a predominately cash economy with all its spiraling prices is, I might add, quite as hard on the planters as on the descendants of the purchased or captured Africans.

About his Catholicism and his sex life, I do not think I care, or am in a position of sufficient utopian knowledge, to examine either minutely in public. It is enough to say once again that the accusations have a certain kernel of truth. Where on earth is man exempt from temptations off the straight-and-narrow path? And while superstitiousness can only very debatably be suggested as an African contribution to the culture of the Seychelles, African effect on the color of the inhabitants is certainly remarkable; as often happens in places with much racial mixing, some of the inhabitants are lovely examples of the random art of miscegenation.

On the question of color, nowadays a delicate matter, not a great deal is said by the English newcomer's English informants, so that one is left to collect impressions as they impress, and discard the ones that don't survive.

When the visitor steps ashore and sees the apparent amount of mixing of the races that does go on, and then if he stays long enough sees a fair sampling of obvious mixtures at all Important Parties as well, he will think that here at last is a haven from racial tension. He will, of course, be wrong. Intermarriage takes place sometimes, and intersex, if one may call it that, all the time, but the barrier of color is not ignored. Money now outweighs it (for the *grand blanc* planter is no part of the business world of Victoria, where Indians and Chinese are predominate), but it is there.

The *grand blanc* is undoubtedly a great snob about his color —about his ancestry in every way—and being so, is quite intolerant of legal unions with *les noirs*. Apart from its being socially unthinkable in the old days, a person legalizing his progeny foists them for all time on his family's name and bloodline. And because a mésalliance is so obvious (or was, before Mendelian laws had time to make the marriage of two seeming-whites so much more chancy), to the *grand blanc* of the old school, racial prejudice and pride in family amount to the same thing. Intolerance socially, where all the gentlefolk are white and all the poor black, is also easily taken for granted. But nowadays, things are more difficult. Even in a 1931 census it was impossible to classify the population according to color, and the interesting grouping— I hear a sigh of hard times were already upon us from the scions of old families that we know—was: (1) Europeans, European descent and Africans, (2) the Indian community, and (3) the Chinese community. Now neither (2) nor (3) bears any examination; it is just Seychellois.

As for racial discrimination, this is more difficult to judge. Every race discriminates, prefers its own. But in all situations where white has been equated with well-off and influential, light brown has naturally fared better than dark, and dark brown better than black, and so dilution of melanin becomes equated with a higher social class. Color snobbery then becomes upheld by the nonwhites just as strongly as the white. It couldn't be helped, and is no different in Mahé than in other parts of the world. Mahé is, however, unhampered by any discrimination in educational opportunity, thanks to the British; I do not think the planters like this mixed schooling at all, and are always complaining about low standards, use of *créole,* and funnily enough, discrimination against their children by predominantly darker teachers. It is true that fewer whites get the prizes than Indians or Chinese, but the reasons are fair enough— the clever soon make their way, whatever shade they are, and this is one of Mahé's saving graces. I would say that racial and linguistic groups do mix more freely here than any other place I have been to, and minorities who withhold their approval are forced—no matter what their private thoughts—to acquiesce in the realm of business and government.

That there has been no real *cultural* barrier along color lines is the most important factor in nipping discrimination in the bud. There are poor ways and rich ways, low ways and high, bad and good. But aside from the Indians and Chinese, who are as cliquey as the British, there are no African ways as opposed to European. The Africans soon slipped into the European ways of their European masters, from family organization, to language to religion; French culture was dominant, and rare is the recessive African chink that the anthropologist can find in this armor.

Those who search hard, for instance, may find suggestions of matriarchy, but is this not more likely to be the very natural attachment of "natural" children? Amongst the poorer classes, the father is as often as not simply not around.

And in vain does one seek for African origins in the *créole* language. I have yet to come across a single *créole* expression that cannot be accounted for either by a corruption of a French word, or French baby slang, or old slang words of former times. I may well be wrong, but most often the Africans seem to have taken one of the meanings of a French word quite arbitrarily, and then have used it to cover many situations and adjacent meanings in a way not French at all, and to twist the pronunciation into the bargain. This combination of mistakes that anyone can make in a foreign language has, in the Seychelles and in the French West Indies, almost developed into a language of its own. I say almost; there has been a great deal of argument about this. Champions of Seychellois *créole* say that it is a proper language in its own right and become heated in its defense. I do not see how this position is at all defensible. On the contrary, once one gets used to hearing and speaking *créole*, one is only startled by how French it is. Quite complicated words come through in pure form, as do words for specific objects the slave would have had no occasion to use in his homeland—which includes most items of material culture. In fact, I know of not one instance of the Seychellois using a word of African origin for anything, even in the practice of grigri.

That the blacks have managed to combine a very considerable amount of low-power magic, white magic, herbal lore, and vague superstitions into their already satisfyingly elaborate Catholicism is often cited as proof of their former beliefs showing through—showing through so strongly that it is the one area where they may be said to have influenced the Europeans themselves. But it is surprising how much the flavor of the superstitions is more rural European than African, and the few practices of black magic are all of types to be found in a little book called *Le Petit Albert,* written by a Frenchman (but unfortunately the last library copy was burned by a rabid librarian). Take the *vieux bonhomme,* for instance, used to frighten children into instant obedience; he is no more than a bogeyman. Or the prevalence of ghosts. A superstitious belief in ghosts is universal in some form or another, but Seychellois ghosts have strictly European haunting habits; that is, they stick to the places where they died, and don't float about animating things. There does occur the occasional dramatic evidence of witchcraft. A woman tied to a tree near a cave known to be haunted and no one able to untie her in the conviction that her bonds cannot be untied by human agency; a grave robbed, a child's body found dismembered—black magic seemed the obvious reason to the police. But these are exceptions. Minor soothsaying, prophesying, fortune-telling occurs all the time, and is believed by everyone, from important members of the government down to the poorest laborers. Women are always the practitioners of these arts: grigri women, they are called. "Grigri" is a word used by the French (and other countries have borrowed it as well) for, properly, a protective amulet or a person who pretends to some supernatural powers by the possession of such a fetish; the word is West African in origin, reaching France from her possessions there or her slaves in the West Indies, and brought to her Indian Ocean possessions by French settlers.

Another universal facet of "magic" is the quite respectable art of herbal doctoring; nor is it unusual to find this running in families: where healing is a source of cash (and where, alas, is it not?), the healer rightly regards his knowledge of herbs as a marketable commodity, as something to be handed down only when he is near death. But in a rural community many of the medical herbs will be common knowledge; can one blame the herbal doctor for dressing up his potion with a spell or two in order to earn his fee in his patient's eyes? It is here that the borderline area is reached: witchcraft is against the law, but herbal healing is not. When does the *sage femme* become the *bonne femme du bois*? The police, being Seychellois too, usually leave well enough alone. Magical practices seem to be tolerated as long as they are neither homicidal nor ostentatiously lucrative; their illegality lends the required titivation for the sophisticated and ensures that the number of practitioners is limited to the cleverer or more daring. In general, known "witches" are more respected than feared—by the whites, by the well educated. But the lower classes are as enthralled by the possibility of bad magic being performed on them as by the fear of God himself, and perhaps more so.

Still, it is all very minor-league nowadays. Though how people love the supernatural! Strangers coming to the Seychelles always hope for a visit to a witch or two, just as everyone who stops here hopes to find buried treasure.

Piracy-and-treasure. No tropic island is complete without them. There were pirates, yes, but where is the stuff that dreams are made of, the stuff that all pirates are supposed to have been too busy off pirating ever to sit down and enjoy spending? People manage to persuade themselves of its being practically everywhere, and no logical reasons enter in. The Seychellois are by no means alone in their belief in treasure. One Englishman of our acquaintance has, for instance, spent the last twelve years or so digging in the corner of an open bay. The spot he selected (for astrological reasons, mainly) has no anchorage, is heavily built up with coral for some distance from the beach, and is open to observation for miles. In spite

From Pirates to the Present / 339

of this, he has been supported in this way of life by all sorts of believers. People do believe in treasure, and certainly this treasure story has so many extraordinary elements that its existence has to be taken on faith. All the signs of faith are there: unshakable sureness in the face of factual discouragement, the scorn of the nonconvert (or pity, scorn in gentler form), the hot defense, the proselytizing, the sureness of the constant nearness of the millenium (the golden millenium of riches on earth, of course). And all of this faith extends to the person doing the digging: he has charisma, he is sanctified by his calling, he can do no wrong, appearances notwithstanding. Wonderful!

You would think that enough of such experiences on their own home ground would cure the Seychellois, at least, of any fervent faith in treasure not yet found. Not so. To him it is literally the stuff of dreams: to dream of treasure is to "know" where it is hidden. It may be that he does not have enough money to dig it out, or it might be under somebody's house, or his own, where digging would cause too much disruption, or perhaps he doesn't own the land where it is located. All sorts of factors can inhibit him, but he can "know" just the same. He dreamed it. Whitest to blackest, the belief is firm. The Chief Justice's wife dreams, and her son-in-law spends many hours supervising a giant hole. Nothing yet but an old teapot. She keeps this on her chest of drawers—to laugh at herself, she says. The hole is still being dug. A hotel owner has often dreamed. The treasure is under his sister's house in Praslin, but since he does not get along with his sister, he is waiting in silence for—for his opportunity. Of course, as is the way of treasure islands, just enough tidbits are uncovered to keep the dreams vivid. A piece of gold here, the odd little buried box, suitably old-looking, there; and always the plans, maps, old charts with mysterious markings, bits of precious paper worn by handling, papers whose ultimate source is of course one or another of the famous corsairs or pirates of this area: Houdoul, or the old Buzzard himself.

APPENDIX B

The Wreck of H.M.S. Fire *on African Banks*

THE WRECK OF THE FRIGATE H.M.S. *Fire* on the African Islands is, so far, our only documented wreck. With a Lieutenant Campbell in command, she ran aground on the reef on the twenty-first of August, 1801. On the twenty-seventh the *Pilot* records, Campbell obtained a canoe, and with four men set sail in it to get help from Mahé. By the twenty-ninth he had sighted the granitic island of Silhouette, west of Mahé and always our first landfall too. After stopping there for water and coconuts (did he neither ask for nor receive any more sustaining food?) he sailed again for Mahé, seventeen miles away. This leg of the journey took him a further two days, which seems, but is not, surprising. The southeast was blowing, pirogues make a lot of leeway (no keel), and to get from Silhouette around Mahé into Victoria harbor on Mahé's eastern side, he would have had to tack directly into the wind. It's only a wonder it didn't take him longer.

Once in Victoria—then Port Royal and still nominally French—Campbell had the good fortune to find *H.M.S. Sibylle* riding at anchor, and the next day he sailed with the *Sibylle*'s Captain Adams to rescue those he had left behind. Good fortune is not strong enough; the *Sibylle* had fought her way into the harbor on the twentieth of August—by calmly sailing past the shore batteries, which weren't very efficient, and opening up a broadside on the French *La Chiffonne,* lying at anchor in the roads "at pistol range. The effect was terrible: it killed or wounded 50 men and put 10 cannon out of action. The French Captain still fought on, but an English boarding party soon ended the struggle. *La Chiffonne* was taken as a prize . . ."* and two weeks later Campbell arrived in his canoe. Had Campbell and Adams perhaps had a rendezvous at Mahé, from which course

* A. T. Webb, *The Story of Seychelles.*

the *Fire* so fatally wandered? The closeness of the dates make one wonder. Adams must have been very sure of his fighting power to stay at anchor in Port Royal, furthermore, for two weeks. But there is more. When Adams and Campbell left for African Banks on the third of September, they were presumably unaware that the *Sibylle* was only just missing the chance both of being attacked by the French *La Flêche* and of aiding the English *Victor,* which followed *La Flêche* into harbor and, after a two-and-a-half-hour battle, demolished her, on the fifth of September. The Pas de Calais hardly enjoyed a busier schedule of engagements.

Campbell and Adams reached African Banks in an orderly fashion, perhaps with the *La Chiffonne,* the prize, under Campbell, but we don't know that. Nor do we have much comment by Adams on what he finds when he gets to the wreck, though he must have made an official report. All we have come across is a note in *Horsburgh's Directory* to the effect that when Adams of the *Sibylle* "visited" the Banks in 1801, he found the islands to be low, covered with bushes, almost submerged at high tide (surely an exaggeration: what about the bushes?), and lacking fresh water. He also reports, according to *Horsburgh's Directory,* that he saw there large quantities of sea birds and sea turtles. But there is no mention—recorded, anyway—of the human inhabitants who must have supplied Campbell with his canoe.

Of Campbell's story this is all we know, and how I wish we knew more. What was he doing during the six days before he left the Banks so bravely in his canoe? Were there wounded to care for? Was he wounded himself? And the canoe: were his ship's boats stove in beyond repair? He would have been unlikely to get sail in a canoe unless he had no boat of his own— or unless he took a crew from the island and left his own behind, in which case he would have been wise to choose the type of boat they were used to. On the other hand, the slaves or slave fishermen of those days must have been as used to a longboat as a canoe; the blacks were no native population—the Seychelles had no native population—but had come with their masters from Mauritius, or Réunion.

And what of these fishermen, as we assume them to be, that were able to supply him with transport to Mahé? If Campbell was lucky in reaching Port Royal on one of its "English days" (de Quinssy kept the Tricolor as ready as the Union Jack), think how much luckier he was to have found African Banks inhabited at all in the middle of the southeast trades. Presumably what he found was a party of turtle hunters, and it may be that there were so many turtles then, as Adams remarks, that they didn't need to worry if the sea was too rough for harpooning. Or it may have been that some specialized item of trade kept them there. Eggs? Late in the season. Bird skins? There used to be quite a trade in bird skins from the outer islands, but I know neither when it started nor what the skins were used for. Hats? Or powder puffs? For this one must have the chicks, which are cleaned by turning them inside out, tying off the appendages, then drying the skins fluff side out. But August would have been late for chicks too. Perhaps the boobies, who retain their beautiful eiderdown coats longer than the terns, were still nesting on the Banks in 1801? It is even likely they were still on Remire then: we found a partly calcified booby egg in a matrix of *pavé* only last year, when we were digging out an ex-guano pit.

EPILOGUE

Mark did become more restless and frustrated by the limits Remire imposed, not least on his turtle project, and in the end we did leave Remire for the larger island I mention at the end of Island Home. We turned in the lease of Remire and signed one for 99 years, subject to two review periods, for Astove, abandoning our new house and all our work to start again. Because Astove was so far from Mahé (500 miles instead of 120) we sold the France: it would be cheaper to use others' bottoms than to maintain and crew our own. Instead, we had a trimaran built cheaply in Hong Kong to use as a fast boat for emergencies

Rory was eight, Ming six and Digby just 11 months old when we boarded the vessel which would take us, our labourers and all their and our possessions and livestock to this distant island to the south, 100 miles from Aldabra and closer to Madagascar than to Mahé.

Were we crazy? Looking back, I suppose we were. But we were thoroughly hooked on island life and on the turtle project - and Astove was famous for its turtles. That it was also famous for its mosquitoes deterred us no more than the extra hundreds of miles. Its size (1200 acres instead of 62), its big lagoon, and its greater fertility far outweighed its disadvantages in our eyes; furthermore, a "government boat" - the Nordvaer - had begun to "service" the outer islands and would provide something like regular if infrequent communication, more reliable than the old sailing schooners.

We even overcame the first serious setback to our plans: a government moratorium on all catching of green turtles in Seychelles waters. Collecting eggs, raising hatchlings, freeing them over the reef - all this was also banned, in spite of the likely conservation benefits, as the government believed any such "management" would provide a loophole for illegal activity. Government control, of course, was light to non-existent in the outer islands but the law looked like progress on the statute books and international conservation organizations were complimentary. We went back to fishing, copra production and livestock. At least we had more room and better soil, in pockets: Astove had been a productive guano island and there was plenty left.

With the help of our secondhand tractor, landed gingerly over the reef with its wheels in two wobbly pirogues, we were able to collect coconuts husked dans bois by the trailer-full, and haul building stone (raised reef rock) from distant parts of the island so the mason could gradually replace the decrepit shacks we'd inherited. Meanwhile, the fishermen fished successfully in waters less exploited than the Amirantes.

We also had a bit of luck: a Kenya company wanting to offer an air connection to Mahé from East Africa looked at the map. Astove, 500 miles from both Mombasa and Mahé would make a good refueling stop for the small planes they used. Could we provide an airstrip? We could and did. A beacon was brought down and installed, and barrels of avgas supplied, and we were paid per landing. It was only as a stop-gap until the airport in Mahé was completed for large planes, and we weren't paid much. But the flights meant better communications; things seemed to be going pretty well.

This was also the time of Ian Smith's rebellion in Rhodesia, and the Royal Navy ships patrolling the Madagascar Channel used to call in occasionally for some R & R. The children watched their first Zodiacs negotiating the surf on our reef, not always successfully, and their first cricket matches. "Have you any old sports equipment we might have?" Mark asked, thinking he'd teach all us islanders to play. But he forgot the naval penchant for nicknames: one of the young officers, grinning broadly, brought ashore a huge tin full of condoms. Our nanny took advantage of this supply, we later discovered, in her affair with one of the married men.

The East African Marine and Fisheries Research vessel, the Manihine, also started visiting us, and the Lindblad Explorer on its way to or from Aldabra, and the ships of the Mombasa-based Bamburi Cement Company sometimes called in on their way from Mauritius in order to wait at Astove - no port charges - for the right tide in Mombasa. We began to feel we were definitely on the map as we had never been in Remire.

The visitors made it easy for Mark, when two teeth of his flared up and little Ming also had tooth trouble to declare that he'd hop the next boat for Mombasa and go to the dentist. He and Ming left on the Manihine one day in March of 1970, the boys and I waving cheerfully from the beach.

Ten days later, the Bamburi Cement boat stopped by and two

of its young German officers came ashore. They stood in front of me, stiffly. "We have bad news," they said, and stopped. "How bad?" I asked, thinking of my aging mother. "As bad as it can be," one of them said. "Your husband is dead."

One says some pretty idiotic things at such moments. "Will you have some tea?" I asked.

"We have come to take you to Mombasa. The British High Commissioner is looking after your little girl. You must come with us."

I thought, I can't just leave. The men's rations. How soon will I get back? We have no manager. Who can I leave in charge? And Mark - dead? "Why - how - how did he -" I asked.

"We believe, at the dentist," one of them said, and the other, "Yes, it was at the dentist."

"I need two hours. There is much to do."

"You must hurry. We must leave by six, for the tide."

Mark had had what it known as an anaesthetic accident in the dentist's chair. The death certificate read "cardiac arrest." By the time I reached Mombasa, he had already been buried. The first thing Ming asked me was "where is Fafa (as the children called him)?" and I had to say, "He is dead."

Ming seemed almost relieved. "I wondered and wondered, but no one would say anything. I thought he had just gone away and left me." Then she cried.

Adjustments are made very slowly. I kept expecting Mark to appear and explain the mistake.

Of course I had to return to the island. All our people were waiting there, and could not be abandoned. Everything we owned was on the island. In any case, after a death you cling to the life you led together. I was even determined to carry on. My mother, who flew out to Mombasa at the news, was astonished at such foolishness. "I am not returning to America without you," she declared, and my position was not a strong one since I had so little money. We compromised. I would find someone in Kenya to act temporarily as manager, and he, my mother, and I would return to the island with the children for as long as it would take me to teach him the ropes and hand over. This period seemed very long to my mother, who hated island life as much as I loved it, and very short to me and the children. When the time came to leave the island, Digby, age 4, flung himself to the ground and held onto the vegetation, screaming. It was the only life he'd ever known.

We went back to the States for a while, then returned to Astove where I experimented with several more managers, likeminded people who thought island life ideal - in the abstract. Finally Harry Stickley, a radio ham who had been working on Aldabra, asked to come for the low salary I could offer. I found a small cottage to rent in England, got the children into schools and with Harry's help ran the island by radio. Harry seemed fine with the isolation and the Éclat in the ham world his island bulletins gave him; on the other hand the constant stream of complaints and reported confrontations that he passed on about the labourers was worrying.

I decided I had to sort things out in person. At the start of a school holiday I placed the children with various friends, flew to Nairobi, got to Mahé, found a yacht willing to take me as passenger to Astove, wait for me there at least two days, then drop me in the Comoros Islands on its way to South Africa. From the Comoros I could fly back to Nairobi, England and the children.

This complex arrangement worked until we ran into the edge of a Mauritius-centered cyclone which cost us four days of battering under bare poles off the coast of northern Madagascar. After that, I was only able to spend a few hours on Astove listening to both Harry and the labourers - and I still missed the plane connection in the Comoros. Then, once back in England, I got the news that "the men" had burned Harry's house down, not with him in it fortunately; the trouble appeared irreversible and everyone was leaving on the Nordvaer.

I was still wriggling on the hook of "our island home," however, when the government abruptly changed. The new powers that be instituted a policy of get tough with low-income producing expatriates and gave me a year to "invest £10,000 or we cancel your lease." I had already been trying to entice investors, with the aid of the German "island agents" Boehm and Vladi, into some joint enterprise involving tourism or sport fishing but after the coup they got cold feet. "Let's see what happens when things settle down," was the general opinion. All too soon my year ran out.

Meanwhile - there is always a meanwhile, isn't there? - a friend I'd met in East Africa and had even been engaged to when I met Mark wrote me, first, a letter of condolence, and then, gradually, a lot more letters. He was then based in Nepal creating the country's first national parks; his marriage, he told me, had failed. He was separated from his wife; there were four children, the youngest the same age as Ming. Cautiously, in view of our commitments, we arranged to see each other on his next home leave.

We have now been happily married for 25 years, many of them spent in Indonesia, Burma and Bhutan in the course of John's work in nature conservation for the United Nations. Our marriage has weathered the difficulties inherent in all second marriages involving so many people, and the children are all now married themselves with children of their own - we have 14 grandchildren between us, I think mine still look back on their two island homes with affection and pleasure, and each of them has an independent, even entrepreneurial, cast of mind, each with his own business, Rory's is an internet-based travel programme, Ming's a large flower and design company, and Digby is a sculptor and foundry owner in rural Maine. In their way, they lead adventurous lives - but none of them has ever gone so far "out on a limb" as Mark and I did.